A CULTURAL HISTORY OF WORK

Volume 2

A Cultural History of Work (6 vols.)

Winner of the 2020 PROSE Award for Multivolume Reference/Humanities

A Cultural History of Work
General Editors: Deborah Simonton and Anne Montenach

Volume 1
A Cultural History of Work in Antiquity
Edited by Ephraim Lytle

Volume 2
A Cultural History of Work in the Medieval Age
Edited by Valerie L. Garver

Volume 3
A Cultural History of Work in the Early Modern Age
Edited by Bert De Munck and Thomas Max Safley

Volume 4
A Cultural History of Work in the Age of Enlightenment
Edited by Deborah Simonton and Anne Montenach

Volume 5
A Cultural History of Work in the Age of Empire
Edited by Victoria E. Thompson

Volume 6
A Cultural History of Work in the Modern Age
Edited by Daniel J. Walkowitz

A CULTURAL HISTORY OF WORK

IN THE MEDIEVAL AGE

Edited by Valerie L. Garver

BLOOMSBURY ACADEMIC
LONDON • NEW YORK • OXFORD • NEW DELHI • SYDNEY

BLOOMSBURY ACADEMIC
Bloomsbury Publishing Plc
50 Bedford Square, London, WC1B 3DP, UK
1385 Broadway, New York, NY 10018, USA
29 Earlsfort Terrace, Dublin 2, Ireland

BLOOMSBURY and the Diana logo are trademarks of Bloomsbury Publishing Plc

First published in Great Britain 2018
This edition published in Great Britain, 2021

Copyright © Bloomsbury Publishing, 2018

Valerie L. Garver has asserted their right under the Copyright, Designs and Patents Act, 1988, to be identified as Editor of this work.

Cover image © INTERFOTO / Alamy Stock Photo

All rights reserved. No part of this publication may be reproduced or transmitted in any form or by any means, electronic or mechanical, including photocopying, recording, or any information storage or retrieval system, without prior permission in writing from the publishers.

A catalogue record for this book is available from the British Library.

A catalog record for this book is available from the Library of Congress.

ISBN:	HB:	978-1-4742-4492-3
	PB:	978-1-3502-7882-0
	Set:	978-1-4742-4503-6

Series: The Cultural Histories Series

Typeset by Integra Software Services Pvt. Ltd.
Printed and bound in Great Britain

To find out more about our authors and books visit www.bloomsbury.com and sign up for our newsletters.

CONTENTS

LIST OF FIGURES — vi
GENERAL EDITORS' PREFACE — xi
CONTRIBUTORS — xiii

Introduction — 1
Valerie L. Garver

1   The Economy of Work — 13
    James Davis

2   Picturing Work — 31
    Deirdre Jackson

3   Work and Workplaces — 65
    Marie D'Aguanno Ito

4   Workplace Cultures — 85
    Peter Stabel

5   Work, Skill, and Technology — 99
    Valerie L. Garver

6   Work and Mobility — 115
    Nicholas Dean Brodie

7   Work and Society — 131
    Holly J. Grieco

8   The Political Culture of Work — 151
    Robert Braid

9   Work and Leisure — 165
    Jeremy Goldberg and Emma Martin

NOTES — 180
FURTHER READINGS — 211
INDEX — 214

LIST OF FIGURES

INTRODUCTION

I.1   Female healer with orb, early fourteenth century. Miscellanea medica XVIII, MS.544 folio 65ʳ. Wellcome Collection, London.   7

CHAPTER ONE

1.1   Calendar for October, Breviary of Queen Isabella of Castile, c. 1497. British Library, Add. MS 18851, folio 6ᵛ·   16

1.2   Harvest allegory on the "three conditions of women" (virgins, widows, and married wives). *Speculum Viriginum*, c. 1300. Rheinisches Landesmuseum, no. 15326. The Yorck Project.   19

1.3   Eve spinning and Adam delving, wall painting, c. 1300, Holy Trinity Church, Bledlow (Buckinghamshire, England). © Rob Farrow.   20

CHAPTER TWO

2.1   September calendar page. Spinola Hours, c. 1510–20. Bruges and Ghent, Belgium. Los Angeles, The J. Paul Getty Museum, Ludwig MS IX 18, folio 5ᵛ. © The J. Paul Getty Museum, Los Angeles.   32

2.2   Labors of the months. Miscellany, c. 818. Salzburg. Vienna, Österreichische Nationalbibliothek, MS 387, folio 90ᵛ. © Österreichische Nationalbibliothek, Vienna.   33

2.3   Physician with patients. Jean Corbechon, *Le livre des propriétés des choses*, c. 1415. Paris, France. Cambridge, Fitzwilliam Museum, MS 251, folio 53ᵛ. © The Fitzwilliam Museum, Cambridge.   35

2.4   Barber shaving a priest. Pontifical, c. 1435–c. 1440. Milan, or Pavia, Italy. Cambridge, Fitzwilliam Museum, MS 28, folio 10ᵛ. © The Fitzwilliam Museum, Cambridge.   36

2.5   Cistercian monks felling trees. Gregory the Great, *Moralia in Job*, Cîteaux, completed on Christmas Eve, 1111. Dijon, France. Bibliothèque municipale de Dijon, MS 170, folio 59ʳ. © Bibliothèque municipale de Dijon, Dijon.   38

2.6   Shepherds and shepherdesses dancing. Hours of Charles d'Angoulême, 1475–1500. Paris, France. Paris, Bibliothèque nationale de France, MS lat. 1173, folio 20ᵛ. © BnF, Paris.   39

LIST OF FIGURES vii

2.7 Joseph holds the Christ Child while Mary reads. Book of Hours, c. 1460–70. Besançon, France. Cambridge, Fitzwilliam Museum, MS 69, folio 48^r. © The Fitzwilliam Museum, Cambridge. 40

2.8 Lady Reason and Christine de Pizan. Christine de Pizan, *Le livre de la cité des Dames*, translated as *Het Bouc van de Stede der Vrauwen*, 1475. Bruges, Belgium. London, British Library, Add. MS 20698, folio 17r. © The British Library, London. 41

2.9 Butcher in his shop. *Tacuinum sanitatis*, c. 1390–1400. Lombardy. Paris, Bibliothèque nationale de France, MS nouv. acq. lat. 1673, folio 63^v. © BnF, Paris. 42

2.10 Calendar scene attributed to Simon Bening (Flemish, c. 1483–1561). Book of Hours, c. 1550. Bruges, Belgium. Los Angeles, The J. Paul Getty Museum, MS 50 verso. © The J. Paul Getty Museum, Los Angeles. 43

2.11 Monkey schoolmaster with pupils. The Metz Pontifical, c. 1303–16. Metz or Verdun, France. Cambridge, Fitzwilliam Museum, MS 298, folio 76^v. © The Fitzwilliam Museum, Cambridge. 44

2.12 Three orders of society. Gossuin de Metz, *L'image du monde*, c. 1265–70. Cambrai, or Thérouanne/St-Omer, France. London, British Library, Sloane MS 2435, folio 85^r. © The British Library, London. 45

2.13 Labor and Idleness. *Somme le roi (Traite des vertus)*, c. 1295. Paris, France. London, British Library, Add. MS 54180, folio 121^v. © The British Library, London. 47

2.14 The Luttrells feasting. Luttrell Psalter, c. 1340. Lincolnshire, England. London, British Library, Add. MS 42130, folio 208^r. © The British Library, London. 49

2.15 Wild man and his family painted by Jean Bourdichon, c. 1500. Tours, France. Paris, Bibliothèque de l'École Nationale Supériéure des Beaux-Arts, Mn. mas. 90. © Bridgeman Art Library. 51

2.16 Carpenter and his family painted by Jean Bourdichon, c. 1500. Tours, France. Paris, Bibliothèque de l'École Nationale Supériéure des Beaux-Arts, Mn. Mas. 92. Image courtesy of Getty Images. 52

2.17 Creation. Stammheim Missal, probably 1170s. Hildesheim, Germany. Los Angeles, The J. Paul Getty Museum, Getty MS 64, folio 10^v. © The J. Paul Getty Museum, Los Angeles. 54

2.18 Adam and Eve. Boccaccio, translated by Laurent de Premierfait, *Des cas des nobles hommes et femmes*, c. 1415. Paris, France. Los Angeles, The J. Paul Getty Museum, Getty, MS 63, folio 3^r. © The J. Paul Getty Museum, Los Angeles. 55

2.19 Adam and Eve working. Carew-Poyntz Hours, fourteenth century. England. Cambridge, Fitzwilliam Museum, MS 48, folio 15^r. © The Fitzwilliam Museum, Cambridge. 56

2.20	Angel gives tools to Adam and Eve. Carrow Psalter, mid-thirteenth century. East Anglia, England. Baltimore, Walters Art Museum, MS W. 34, folio 22^v. © The Walters Art Museum, Baltimore.	57
2.21	Christine de Pizan. Collected works, c. 1414. Paris, France. London, British Library, Harley MS 4431, folio 4^r. © The British Library, London.	60
2.22	Eadwine. Eadwine Psalter, c. 1160. Christ Church Priory, Canterbury, England. Cambridge, Trinity College, MS R.17.1, folio 283^v. Photo: Universal History Archive. Image courtesy Getty Images.	62
2.23	Richard and Jeanne Montbaston. *Roman de la Rose*, c. 1350. France, Paris. Paris, Bibliothèque nationale de France, MS fr. 25526, folio 77^v. © BnF, Paris.	63

CHAPTER THREE

3.1	Calendar, March, early fifteenth century. France. *Les très riches heures du Duc de Berry*. Wikimedia Commons.	66
3.2	Harvesting, Luttrell Psalter, c. 1340. Lincolnshire, England. London, British Library, Add. MS 42130, folio 172^v.	67
3.3	Shipbuilding. Bayeux Tapestry, eleventh century. Photo: DEA / M. Seemuller. Image courtesy Getty Images.	70
3.4	Baking bread. *Tacuinum sanitatis*, fourteenth century. Photo: Alinari / Alinari Archives, Florence / Alinari. Image courtesy Getty Images.	80
3.5	Butchering. *Tacuinum sanitatis*, fourteenth century. Photo: DeAgostini. Image courtesy Getty Images.	82

CHAPTER FOUR

4.1	Musicians playing at a banquet. The Beaupré Antiphonary, vol. 2, Flemish, 1290. Baltimore, Walters Art Museum, MS W.760, folio H. © The Walters Art Museum, Baltimore.	91
4.2	Cloth Hall, 1200–1304. Ypres. Wikimedia Commons.	94

CHAPTER FIVE

5.1	Two horses draw a harrow guided by a man while another man plants seeds. Glass panel, c. 1450–75. England. © Victoria and Albert Museum, London.	103
5.2	Medieval windmill. Gotland, Sweden. Wikimedia Commons.	105
5.3	St. Hedwig directs the construction of a new convent at Trebnitz, 1353. Silesia, Poland. Los Angeles, The J. Paul Getty Museum, MS Ludwig XI 7, folio 56. © The J. Paul Getty Museum, Los Angeles.	110

LIST OF FIGURES ix

CHAPTER SIX

6.1 Two men threshing a sheaf with flails. Luttrell Psalter, c. 1325–35. London, British Library, Add. MS 42130, folio 74ᵛ. Wikimedia Commons. 126

6.2 Marco Polo sailing from Venice in 1271, fifteenth century. Oxford, Bodleian Libraries, MS Bodley 264, folio 218ʳ. Photo: The Print Collector / Alamy Stock Photo. 128

6.3 Stone cutter's mark on a tower in the medieval Louvre, Paris, France. Wikimedia Commons. 130

CHAPTER SEVEN

7.1 A poor person or pilgrim receiving aid. Refectory of the Old Cathedral of Lleida, Catalonia, Spain, around fourteenth century. Photo: PRISMA ARCHIVO / Alamy Stock Photo. 134

7.2 Saint Louis of Anjou, Bishop of Toulouse serving at the table of the poor. Simone Martini (c. 1284–1344), predella of altarpiece of Saint Louis crowning his brother Robert of Naples. Photo: DeAgostini. Image courtesy Getty Images. 140

7.3 Giving drink to the thirsty, roundel, c. 1430–40. Coventry, England. © Victoria and Albert Museum, London. 144

7.4 Hospital of Innocents, detail from portico decorated with tondos in glazed ceramic. Andrea della Robbia (1435–1525), Piazza della Santissima Annunziata, Florence. Photo: DeAgostini. Image courtesy Getty Images. 147

CHAPTER EIGHT

8.1 Carolingian coins, first half of the ninth century, from the Roermond hoard, discovered in 1968 in gravel from the Meuse River. Archeological collection of Centre Céramique, Maastricht, the Netherlands. Wikimedia Commons. 154

8.2 Construction of the Tower of Babel, c. 1400–10. Regensburg, Germany. Los Angeles, The J. Paul Getty Museum, MS 33, folio 13. © The J. Paul Getty Museum, Los Angeles. 156

8.3 Buying and selling of wares in a silverware shop, fifteenth century. France. Rouen, Bibliothèque municipale, MS 927, folio 145. Image courtesy Getty Images. 161

CHAPTER NINE

9.1 Adam delving and Eve spinning. Hunterian Psalter, c. 1170. England. University of Glasgow Library, Hunter 229 (U.3.2), folio 8ʳ. © University of Glasgow Library, Special Collections. 167

9.2	Aristocratic couple playing chess. Ivory mirror, c. 1320–30. France or Germany. © Victoria and Albert Museum, London.	174
9.3	Labors of the months depicting harvesting in August. English painted roundel, third quarter of fifteenth century. © Victoria and Albert Museum, London.	178

GENERAL EDITORS' PREFACE

Issues around work and the workplace seem to be having a renaissance and are no longer embedded solely in the discourses around Marxism and labor movements. Similarly, new and fresh research has been taking place around guilds, skill, control, and gender issues. *A Cultural History of Work* takes an approach that focuses on culture in order to explore the subtleties of the character and dynamics of work and the people and relationships involved in working and the workplace in a theoretically holistic way to bring together disparate historical traditions and historiographical approaches. The aim and scope of *A Cultural History of Work* is to offer a comprehensive survey of the social and cultural construction of work across six historical periods. This approach that focuses on the *cultural* history of work provides an opportunity to explore the dynamics of work and the people and relationships involved in working and the workplace, helping to rethink boundaries and the issues of work. This is not an "economic" history of work, but a cultural one. Of course, we talk about economics, but the fundamental concept is to explain the ways in which work was situated in and influenced cultural dynamics of the western world. It is a key contribution to the process of rethinking boundaries and issues of work.

A Cultural History of Work draws on "the western world." Contributors approached their chapters with a great deal of freedom, drawing on their specific expertise in national and regional histories, but throughout the thirty-six chapters that make up the series, they have tried to embrace the "West." The series does not intend to "cover" all of western culture, or even all of Europe and North America. Authors instead have aimed at *representing* the broad trends and nuances of the culture of work from antiquity to the present. Thus *A Cultural History of Work* concentrates on the central themes in western work, with some sensitivity to areas we know less about.

This is a work of scholarly reference designed to provide scholars and students with a detailed, nuanced overview. Each contribution has been written as an original chapter presenting an *overview* of a theme in a period, but each also includes a wide range of case material and has a particular thrust or point of view (or points of view) informing the organization of the piece. The series is structured into six time periods—though historians will always quibble about what these periods mean and will blur the edges. That is part of the process of understanding the past. And time does not have the same meaning across regions, much less countries or continents. Each volume covers a long period of time and a broad geography that can and will introduce a range of variables. Each volume uses the same chapter titles so that readers can read on a theme across volumes, or read through a period exploring the range of themes and nuances that each volume presents. There are also overlaps within volumes and across them that enrich the discussion.

The editorial decision to study work rather than labor is suggestive of a broader, more encompassing field of study that lends itself more readily to different periods. For example, in particular it is more appropriate to use *work* for periods such as antiquity and the Middle Ages because labor looks in one sense as an eighteenth- or nineteenth-century concept. English is rather unusual in having two words whose meanings overlap considerably, but are not identical. For example, there is only one word in French, *travail*, like *Arbeit* in German, *arbejde* in Danish/Swedish/Norwegian, *lavoro* in Italian. Some other languages tend to have one primary word also, for example, *trabajo* in Spanish, though there are other usable words. From a definitional point of view we can argue that *labor* means the use of mental or physical capacities/faculties, so it implies suffering and difficulty, whereas *work* has to do with the simple act or fact of doing something/the activity/the action in progress. From the point of view of the political economy, *labor* seems to refer to the Marxist discourse; *work* is more pragmatic and less laden with cultural overtones. So, work describes the parameters of this project while *labor* is one aspect of it, which is more important in the nineteenth and twentieth centuries, and to a lesser extent in the eighteenth. Thus we argue *work* seems more neutral and general and therefore more applicable across six centuries.

Moving from the world of antiquity and into the twenty-first century, the culture of work has shifted considerably as technologies, organization, and locations have changed. Workplace relations have also undergone transformations from small-scale and familial settings to large-scale and potentially less personal environments. And yet, the world of work remains complex with great variations between national cultures, political and economic approaches to managing the fields of work, and especially in the ways that people have negotiated their own spaces and places within them. Work retains many meanings from the simple need to survive to senses of deep satisfaction for the character of the job and the creativity one can achieve. It may be valued for the income or wealth it can generate; conversely, some choose to work less and on their own terms. Part-time, job-sharing, self-employment, and the IT revolution have offered different routes for some people. Workers can, however, remain tied to an employer and though nominally slavery does not exist in the West, there are those, such as sweated immigrant workshops and live-in domestic workers, who may feel that little has changed. *The Cultural History of Work* traces and explores many of these routes and their implications for people and their cultural experience of work.

CONTRIBUTORS

Robert Braid obtained his master's in medieval history from Fordham University, NY, USA, in 1996 and his PhD in medieval economic history from the University of Paris, France, in 2008. He is currently Associate Professor at the Economics Department of the University of Montpellier, France, and works primarily on medieval economic regulation and the history of economic thought.

Nicholas Dean Brodie is a historian and archaeologist based in Tasmania, Australia, whose doctoral research explored vagrancy and poverty in late medieval and early modern England. Since completing his PhD he has published on a broad range of research topics from medieval Europe to early modern Asia to colonial Australia.

James Davis is Senior Lecturer in Medieval History at Queen's University Belfast, Northern Ireland. His research focuses upon the urban, economic, and cultural history of late medieval England, and his publications include *Medieval Market Morality: Life, Law and Ethics in the English Marketplace, 1200–1500* (2012).

Valerie L. Garver is Associate Professor of History at Northern Illinois University, IL, USA. A specialist in Carolingian social and cultural history, she has published on women, childhood, family, and material culture (especially textiles). She is the author of *Women and Aristocratic Culture in the Carolingian World* (2009).

Jeremy Goldberg teaches in the Department of History and the Centre for Medieval Studies at the University of York, England. He is a cultural and social historian of the English Middle Ages. He has published extensively on the issues of women, gender, family, work, and sexuality.

Holly J. Grieco is Associate Professor of Religious Studies at Siena College in New York's Capital Region, USA. Her past research has focused on medieval Franciscan heresy inquisitors in southeastern France and fourteenth-century Franciscan models of sanctity. Currently she is researching medieval Franciscan attitudes toward their own labor.

Marie D'Aguanno Ito is a Scholar in Residence at the Department of History, American University, Washington, DC, USA. She is also a Reader at Dumbarton Oaks and a periodic Lecturer in Medieval History at the University of Maryland, USA. Her research focuses on late medieval Florentine economic history, particularly the grain trade and the market at Orsanmichele. Dr. Ito is also an attorney and has practiced for many years in the field of securities law.

Deirdre Jackson is a Research Associate in the Department of Manuscripts and Printed Books at the Fitzwilliam Museum, Cambridge, UK. After completing her PhD at the

Courtauld Institute of Art in 2002, she worked at the University of Oxford and the British Library. She is author of *Marvellous to Behold: Miracles in Medieval Manuscripts* (2007), *Lion* (2010), and *Medieval Women* (2015).

Emma Martin is Postdoctoral Research Fellow at the Humanities Research Centre, University of York, England, examining the ideas of idleness, work, and leisure in late medieval culture. She completed her BA in English and History and MA in Medieval History at Queen's University Belfast, Northern Ireland.

Peter Stabel is Professor of Medieval History at the Centre for Urban History of the University of Antwerp, Belgium. He has published widely on various themes of the late medieval social history of cities in Europe (textile manufacture, gender, market organization, migration, and so on) and more recently also in the Islamic World.

Introduction

VALERIE L. GARVER

When contemporary popular culture has depicted medieval work—a relatively rare occasion—films, novels, and even television have typically focused on the day-to-day difficulties peasants faced, the dirty conditions in towns and the perils of laboring in the premodern West. In certain respects such scenes reflect the culture of medieval work, and yet they miss the vast majority and most fascinating aspects of the ideas, practices, and expectations of labor between the years 800 and 1450. The period covered by this volume saw many changes in the culture of work. Scholars have modified their views concerning many of these transformations, however, as new evidence has emerged and historians have challenged old paradigms. Much of this recent work on the history of medieval labor has fallen in the area of cultural studies or at least drawn from the approaches of cultural history. Historians, for example, now realize that workplaces manifest cultures of their own, that legal cultures shape and in turn are shaped by cultures of work, and that the development and transmission of labor skills are a form of acculturation. Examination of work in the medieval era offers an opportunity to appreciate the variety and tenacity of the vast majority of medieval people, not merely the ruling and ecclesiastical elite about whom medieval sources provide far more information. Because medieval societies expected nearly every person to work, this volume can serve as a means to learn about the richness of medieval culture writ large through the lens of work.

Examining the concept of work in the medieval era from our modern vantage presents difficulties because modern and medieval people conceived of work in different ways. Some scholars wrote about work, categorizing and explaining it in ways that reflected a predominantly Christian worldview. The Franciscan scholar Bonaventure (1221–74) wrote that work could be either servile, necessary, or pleasurable, and he classified occupations into seven groups: agriculture; cloth fabrication; the working of metal, stone, and wood; the provision of foodstuffs; the mixing of potions and pigments; the work of merchants; and entertainment. His main concern, however, was to explain the importance of observing the Sabbath through cessation of unnecessary work.[1] Such rest from work related to religious practice and not to any conception of leisure or physical health. As Jeremy Goldberg and Emma Martin explain in their chapter, discussing leisure as opposed to work in the Middle Ages may be impossible, for medieval people understood the purposes of work and rest in religious terms and believed work to have been necessitated by the Fall. Rest on the Sabbath was not a form of leisure but rather the duty of all Christians. The word leisure, *leisir*, only came into use in English during the early fourteenth century, when the Middle English noun had more the meaning of a "license" to engage in other activities rather than the modern sense of rest and recreation.

In an agrarian society where the food supply was subject to periods of severe want, working was often a means of survival. Lack of food increased morbidity or susceptibility to death because of disease and physical weakness.[2] One modern response to those on the margins of society is to aid them by providing circumstances, education, or skills to lift them from poverty, but the predominant medieval Christian conception that suffering had redemptive value helped to undergird one conception of the poor—that they were a necessary part of society, there in part to promote the virtues of generosity and empathy. As Holly J. Grieco explains in Chapter Seven, the impoverished served to redeem the sins of the wealthy and to "purify their wealth." The poorest only made up a small portion of society. Those who grew crops and raised livestock comprised the majority of the population for the entirety of the Middle Ages, and agricultural labor was therefore the most common category of work and inarguably crucial to human survival. Yet many grew crops because they had to, either because they owed agricultural dues or labor to lords or because it was the means to feed themselves and their families, not because they chose to do this work above all other occupations.

Of course, some medieval people took up vocations that were highly meaningful to them, particularly those in the religious life. In addition to embracing its emphasis on a life of prayer, many medieval monks and nuns took seriously the admonition in the *Rule of St Benedict*, the most common document to govern religious houses in the medieval era, that: "Idleness is an enemy of the soul. Therefore, the brothers should be occupied according to schedule in either manual labor or holy reading."[3] Whether they focused more on the study of Scripture and the church fathers or on earning their own keep, monks and nuns were to remain engaged in such pursuits during their work days. Cistercians may have taken the idea of manual labor more seriously than other orders; Cluniacs may have focused more on prayer on behalf of their benefactors; and some houses, such as a number of Frankish convents, may have focused substantial labor on the production of manuscripts.[4] Particular religious houses placed an emphasis on certain types of work. Cistercian convents in northern France sometimes grew from informal hospitals, with communities often in proximity to lepers.[5] A number of thirteenth-century Cistercian convents in Liège, for example, found the provision of medical care to lepers and other sick individuals a meaningful expression of their piety.[6] Yet despite variety among monastic communities over time and location, leisure had no part in their workplace cultures.

Another way in which the culture of medieval work contrasts with that of many modern western workplaces is in its lack of emphasis on efficiency. Whereas many modern occupations have embraced time-saving techniques, devices, and technologies, medieval workers did not always adopt a more efficient technology when it came along. As Valerie L. Garver discusses in Chapter Five, even after the development of a plow that could increase agricultural yields substantially and the advancement of windmills, their use did not result in medieval workers ceasing to use older or less efficient (but usually less costly) technologies. Such persistence of older tools and practices may reflect a desire to adhere to traditional ways, insufficient resources, and/or a lack of desire to go to the expense and bother of changing the means of labor, even if it meant giving up recognized gains in efficiency. The adoption of certain technologies in fits and starts in some places but not in others speaks to the difficult conditions under which many worked and the diversity among medieval societies, institutions, and polities.

PROBLEMS, CHALLENGES, AND POSSIBILITIES

What was work in the Middle Ages? On the surface, the answer to this question may seem obvious, but if one thinks of labor as a form of productive activity for gain, the medieval era poses challenges. Much "productive activity" carried out by those in religious orders—monks, nuns, priests, bishops—had the purpose of pleasing God first and foremost. Was prayer a form of work, especially for those living in convents and monasteries where it comprised a principal daily activity that many medieval Christians believed could result in spiritual and/or material gain? Nineteenth-century ideas of labor have shaped scholarly understanding of labor to such a degree that many studies of medieval work have overlooked various forms of labor that were culturally crucial, as Nicholas Dean Brodie points out in Chapter Six, where he emphasizes the movement of information via messengers. Of course, separating the cultural history of work from its economic history is impossible, but expanding the scope of inquiry beyond the making of money allows one to see prominent forms of medieval labor that do not much appear in financial, tax, or trade accounts. For example, in Chapters Two and Three, respectively, Deirdre Jackson and Marie D'Aguanno Ito bring armed combatants, authors, artists, and scribes into the fold of medieval work. Workers had diverse occupations, social status, workplaces, degrees of mobility, access to resources, and levels of skill.

Indeed, medieval work should be writ large. In recent decades, modern people have come to understand contemporary uncompensated housework and childrearing as a kind of work that has a long and complex cultural history. Equally medievalists have begun to take seriously the examination of similar labor in the domestic sphere as a topic worthy of consideration. In Chapter Nine Jeremy Goldberg and Emma Martin outline numerous ways in which medieval sources present the work of medieval mothers and women as "natural" and therefore less "worthy" than male work. Many medieval texts present as ideal a world in which nearly every member of society was working. As James Davis points out in Chapter One, labor was the primary productive force in the medieval era, making workers valuable. Technologies and mechanization would not bring the huge increases in production to the Middle Ages that they did in later centuries; therefore human labor remains central to any understanding of medieval work, underlining the value of cultural history for explicating its social, political, economic, and religious roles.

It is impossible to know what the vast majority of the medieval population thought of work or the cultures surrounding their occupations or the changes to labor conditions that they witnessed in their lifetimes. Most medieval people were illiterate both by medieval and by modern standards, and so only the well educated wrote about work until the twelfth century. Even during the thirteenth to fifteenth centuries, when literacy rates increased, the kind of texts that explicitly discussed work remained limited. Only by the end of the medieval era do documents appear that provide day-to-day examples of how individuals conducted business or went about their work. The Paston letters, for example, are a rich collection of correspondence to, from, and among members of a fifteenth-century English family.[7] One scholar found information within them on agricultural practices in fifteenth-century Norfolk.[8] They contain many references to the business dealings and activities of the men and women of the family, but they reveal rather little about how these individuals conceived of their work.

Archaeological remains have become a key means to learn more about the daily lives of medieval workers, especially in cities where modern construction often results in the discovery of medieval evidence. Among the crafts that leave telltale traces are metal work, textile production, and animal slaughterhouses.[9] Written evidence combined with material culture provides historians opportunities to compare ideal and practice and to make discoveries when archaeological remains supply information not available in written sources. Excavations at Novgorod (Russia) have yielded rich finds because the city has been continuously inhabited for centuries; the location and soil provide excellent conditions for the preservation of artifacts; and archaeological investigation there has been ongoing for decades. Scholars have been able, for instance, to trace developments in local pottery production over long periods, to compare those goods to the range of household objects found in Novgorod and to consider alternate materials because, unlike most other medieval urban sites, wood items sometimes survived at Novgorod, including a twelfth-century ashwood bowl.[10]

Medieval clerics developed theories of work that differed both from modern conceptions and from the lived reality of many individuals in the medieval era. Many of the chapters in this volume note the tripartite division that medieval thinkers often employed to explain society. From as early as the ninth century religious leaders conceived of an orderly world that rested on the contributions of those who worked, those who prayed, and those who fought. Although this volume focuses primarily on those who labored, the chapters here extend a definition of working beyond contemporary conceptions, including those not understood as workers at the time as well as groups who functioned outside this influential model (artisans, craftsmen, traders, artists, physicians). Medieval theorists often failed to account for the many ways in which individual workers supplemented or indeed fully earned their incomes through piece work, casual labor, sale of goods made in the household, and second occupations. During later centuries of the Middle Ages, when towns grew considerably as did specialization of trades, these three orders increasingly failed to account for a variety of labors and new fields of work such as banking.

Banking and finance provide examples of new occupations and conceptions of work that developed during the medieval era. In Frankfurt German kings promoted the city's annual fair, vowed to protect those attending, and provided select immunities from tolls and customs fees. As many other cites did, Frankfurt grew in importance as a trading center from the eleventh into the fourteenth centuries. Through commercial contact with Italy, Germans learned about double-entry bookkeeping and shipping insurance. Soon Italians came to Frankfurt to work in the money trade alongside Jews. Throughout the medieval era across most of Europe, Jews lent money because, unlike Christians and Muslims, their religious beliefs did not condemn usury, and Jews more generally worked in finance because they were prohibited from crafts and trades governed by guilds. In Frankfurt, the Jewish population remained steady despite at least three pogroms against them. This combination of stable royal support, the fair, and a population that understood finance led to the foundation of the first banks between 1402 and 1418 and laid the groundwork for Frankfurt's financial and commercial success in the modern era.[11] Montpellier similarly benefited from contact with nearby Italy, developed early in the medieval era as a trade center, attracted many foreigners because of its university and commerce and therefore had a mixed population of craftsmen, merchants, legal specialists, and nearby agricultural laborers. Although smaller and less technically sophisticated than contemporary Italian and Flemish towns, Montpellier's banking and money-changing industry grew quickly, making the city a financial center, although the devastation of the Black Death there damaged its reputation and activities in that regard.[12]

Discrepancies in the ways historians of one area or period have approached questions of the cultural history of work pose challenges. As Robert Braid points out in Chapter Eight, historians of late medieval England have engaged with the evidence of labor ordinances on a much deeper level than have scholars of continental European history, even when similar evidence is available. Braid notes that the relative lack of change in labor legislation following the Black Death in Castile and France may be one reason that historians have done far less work on the labor ordinances of these European regions. Wider and more penetrating studies of such ordinances across the West promise to underline the variety and responsiveness of late medieval governments to the issue of work.

Some periods are less conducive to the cultural study of work than others. As any reader may note after reading this volume, the study of work in the early medieval era has been more limited than for the last centuries of the Middle Ages. This discrepancy relates to differences in the quantity and types of sources available to historians. Far fewer documents, objects, and manuscripts survive from the early Middle Ages (c. 500–c. 1000) than from the period 1000–1450. Late medievalists simply have more historical materials to study than early medievalists. Yet archaeological excavations provide those studying work from 800 to 1000 with ever more evidence. Studies of textile labor, pottery making, metalworking, and agricultural work have drawn from material culture to increase knowledge about the early medieval culture of work. Artistic and literary depictions offer further insight into issues that more traditional documentary sources ignore, or they corroborate or contrast the evidence of those same written texts. In Chapter Two, Deirdre Jackson, for example, examines calendar images from across the medieval era and Europe as a means to explore details of everyday work life often absent from or little discussed in written sources. Yet sometimes medieval historians simply face gaps in the source base that prevent discussion of certain topics. In Chapter Eight, Robert Braid points out just how little legislation and regulation of work governments instituted prior to the thirteenth century. The growth in this type of information almost certainly relates to broader conditions in Europe. Increased economic activity from the ninth to thirteenth centuries led to more disputes between workers and employers, and the concomitant growth of cities provided more opportunities for these individuals to bring their disputes to political authorities. As a result, governments began increasingly to regulate work.

FAMILY AND GENDER

Family was central to medieval culture, and work was no exception to this defining paradigm. The household was the primary economic unit of the medieval era, where much consumption and production took place. As many chapters in this volume note, family members frequently worked alongside one another or in ways that supported one another's activities and productivity. Men, for example, appear to have engaged more often and more strenuously in agricultural labor; yet because of the vicissitudes of agricultural productivity in this era, every family member had to contribute to the family's need for food. Throughout the period of this volume, most families' primary concern remained putting food on their tables on a consistent basis, for food security was unusual outside the elite.

Women made major contributions to work and production across the Middle Ages, and indeed recent decades have seen many scholars pay far closer attention to the gendered nature of work than previously. Much of this work took place in the domestic sphere. As James Davis mentions, men were far more likely to work a distance from home whereas women tended to work within their own houses or not far from them. Female forms of production in the Middle Ages included ale making, cloth production, dairying, and looking after poultry, all tasks that could take place in or close to the family home. Although one may imagine that these productive tasks gave women a measure of economic and social independence, the reality for most women involved being subject to men, whether a husband, father, or brother, who had guardianship of her and therefore had a right to control the proceeds of her labor. Yet women's access to and direction over some of these forms of labor changed over the course of the medieval era. As Valerie L. Garver explains in Chapter Five, textile work, once practically an entirely female form of production, from the twelfth century onwards came to be dominated by men, especially as cloth production shifted to cities from rural areas, benefited from new technologies, and became acceptable labor for men. Brewing is a prominent example of women's economic and social loss in the face of male encroachment on an increasingly lucrative commodity. Although brewsters dominated the market in ale for centuries in England, by the fifteenth century, they lost out increasingly to male brewers. On the other hand, the Black Death brought such a loss of population that women came more and more to work outside their own households as wage earners.[13]

Marie D'Aguanno Ito, in Chapter Three, notes the many workplaces where women were active and the range of products they helped to produce, including, for example, shoe buckles, fences, bricks, baked goods, and soap. They were also active in various types of work—butchering, selling goods in marketplaces, prostitution, and care of the sick to name a few. Quite a few fields required special training, but even when a woman learned a skilled trade, she often had to take a low status or marginal position within that trade.[14] As Peter Stabel mentions in Chapter Four, women who worked in textile workshops in the later Middle Ages, most often spun, rather than wove, because it was a less-skilled, lower status job.

Women played important roles in medical care even though they could not study medicine at a university. Many medieval medical practitioners, whether male or female, lacked such an education. Most learned "on the job" acquiring skills and knowledge via observation and practice. A text known as the *Trotula* provides a rare example of the transmission of such knowledge, especially in relation to women's health. It was the most popular medieval collection on women's medicine from the late twelfth century on and included information on cosmetics, menstrual problems, gynecological diseases and treatments, contraception, methods for mimicking virginity, pregnancy, and childbirth. Originally composed in Latin, by the fifteenth century, translations in most western European vernacular languages were circulating. An example of the practical knowledge contained in the *Trotula* is the set of instructions for helping women who retain the afterbirth following delivery, a potentially dangerous situation.

> We extract the juice of a leek and mix it with pennyroyal oil or musk oil or juice of borage, and let us give it to drink, and immediately [the afterbirth] will be brought out perhaps because she will vomit and from the effort of vomiting it will come out. Nevertheless, the juice itself has such a power that it is sufficient for expulsion.[15]

One fourteenth-century manuscript of the *Trotula* included an illustration of a female healer with an orb symbolizing her mastery of knowledge concerning women's health (Figure I.1). Providing for women's health care was not solely a female task; men participated in such efforts, but the taboo against men manually examining a woman's vagina meant that women dominated gynecological and obstetric care throughout much of the Middle Ages. Midwives were, however, only one part of a wider community of female medical practitioners.[16]

Children also made up a key component of the medieval workforce. As Marie D'Aguanno Ito notes in Chapter Three, medieval people would have encountered children in many workplaces, often aiding with the work or staying nearby their parents as they labored. Children looked after sheep, helped to mold bricks and even walked on treadmills to operate wooden cranes. Many small children stayed close to their mothers as they worked in the house or nearby. This proximity to work is surely one way that children learned the skills and knowledge needed for certain occupations, but it also

FIGURE I.1 Female healer with orb, early fourteenth century. Miscellanea medica XVIII, MS.544 folio 65ʳ. Wellcome Collection, London.

explains the apparently high number of accidental deaths. Coroners, reports from England reveal some causes: a child struck by his father's axe as he chops wood; one speared by a pitchfork while hiding in a pile of hay; another drowned while fetching water. Some children left their homes at relatively early ages to become apprentices, often agreeing to years of service. Other children worked as servants in the houses of the wealthy and the aristocracy. Both apprentices and young servants appear to have been vulnerable to abuse, particularly girls. The rate of illegitimate births to adolescent female servants was higher than that for most of their peers, further suggesting their vulnerability.[17]

WORK IN THE CITY AND IN THE COUNTRYSIDE

In the growing cities of the central and later Middle Ages, a variety of occupations contributed to the vitality and expansion of urban life, although it is crucial to note that medieval cities were much smaller than modern ones and even many contemporary cities outside Europe. Prior to around 1000, most medieval cities were so small that they were cities mainly in name alone, but starting in the tenth and eleventh centuries, many grew substantially. Some new cities, founded in the eleventh century, were among these, but most major medieval cities existed before 1000. City growth picked up substantially in the twelfth century, and the physical size of cities expanded along with their populations, with the possible exception of those in England. Work shaped the ways cities increased in size. Neighborhoods or boroughs often centered on a particular craft or occupation, such as baking, shoe making, goldsmithing, or drapery. Trades that required access to water, such as fulling and milling, usually occupied areas that gave them access to canals or rivers whereas those lines of work that posed environmental hazards, such as butchers, tanners, dyers, and smiths, often had positions on the outskirts of a city. Trade in agricultural products, manufactured goods, and raw materials often meant these cites stood by rivers, ports, major roads, and bridges.[18] Estimating the population of medieval cities is extremely difficult because medieval sources rarely provide the sort of quantitative data necessary for demographic analysis. Although fraught, scholars have proposed approximate numbers for the pre-plague populations of Ghent (60,000–80,000); Florence (120,000); Milan, Naples, and Venice (all hard to determine but more than 120,000); and largest of all, Paris (50,000–280,000).[19] Marie D'Aguanno Ito, in Chapter Three, explains how medieval cities provided new work opportunities as they grew in size, resulting in increased workplace specialization and new trades.

More medieval people labored in the countryside than in the city. Although it is harder to trace in rural than urban areas, workers began to specialize particularly with the growth in the size of farms in parts of western Europe, especially England, starting in the twelfth century. Raising livestock required significant commitment in this era because the animals were often located in designated areas and therefore required on-site care. Yet scholars have become more cautious in their assessment of the results of this rural specialization, noting that other conditions in the countryside would have mitigated against many laborers' ability to focus on one area of work. These circumstances included uncertain and changing employability, the insecurity of relying on a particular skill for making a living, the concomitant incentive to then own land if possible, and clear resistance by thirteenth-century workers to specializing in one craft or trade.[20] As Peter Stabel points out in Chapter Four, by the thirteenth century the larger farms caused growth in regular employment of servants and workers, who often earned less than occasional workers but had greater job security.

Women contributed to agricultural production, and many tasks related to the raising of crops and animals were not rigidly gendered. Men and women participated in many similar activities as two studies, one of early medieval Francia and the other of late medieval England, show. Both men and women mowed, harvested, and did a variety of field work in addition to raising and tending cattle. A few tasks were gendered. Women generally did not plow fields nor did early medieval men produce cloth. In late medieval England, men dominated butchering and baking, which required capital and skilled training, whereas women often worked in the more unskilled trades such as brewing and tranting, that is, the reselling of purchased goods.[21] Yet, as James Davis notes in Chapter One, most medieval workers engaged in labor outside their usual purview, through casual agricultural work or irregular craft work, such as carding and spinning wool, hemp processing, making baskets, or thatching. Women and men therefore sometimes engaged in atypical labor as needed. In addition, rural workers performed much more than agricultural work.

WORKERS AND SELF-DETERMINATION

Although it is sometimes possible to paint images of medieval laborers in broad strokes or to conduct focused studies of workers in specific locations with sufficient surviving evidence, certain details are lacking in sources. The vast majority of the information available about medieval people who worked for wages or labored under compulsion comes from those who paid them or those who obliged them. Therefore, as one prominent historian in the field put it: "the great mass of evidence concerns things done to workers rather than by them."[22] At times, historical records make clear that workers wanted change in the political agreements and legislation that controlled matters such as wages and work conditions. As Robert Braid notes in Chapter Eight, the Peasants' Revolt of 1381 in England did not bring the workers who participated any more rights than earlier and in fact ignited the anger of aristocrats who wished to teach these laborers their place. Even a study of the anger of peasants involved in revolts from the Jacquerie (1358) in France to the early modern German Peasants' Revolt (1525) necessarily relied not on accounts written by the peasant workers but rather upon chronicles and literary satires. The majority of those involved in these revolts could not write about their emotions or experiences because they were illiterate. Rather others' accounts emphasized the danger and ludicrous nature of peasant anger because the elite saw their ire as irrational.[23] The political culture of work in the Middle Ages favored the elite and the wealthy, not the workers who were typically excluded from political participation.

The existence of guilds provides the clearest indication that workers wanted a say in their conditions, wages, training, and status. These organizations developed across much of Europe during the twelfth and thirteenth centuries, often in response to the expanding economy and opportunities for trade as well as to the competing local authorities among whom many artisans, merchants, and tradesmen had to navigate. Guilds could conduct those negotiations on members' behalf and help provide the best possible conditions for manufacture and sales for their constituents.[24] Many guilds developed systems for providing charity to those within their ranks and sometimes extended charity to outsiders, as Holly J. Grieco explains in Chapter Seven. Some grew into confraternities, charitable organizations that were usually active in cities, although other confraternities arose independently of guilds. Such organizations were one form of cultural identity for workers in this era. As Peter Stabel notes in Chapter Four, however, most medieval laborers worked in rural areas, did not form guilds, and did not earn wages. Rather they carried out the wide variety of work necessary to make their own farms or the lands of their lords productive. Some workers labored outside a guild structure or that of their local village or farming community. Certain casual workers, entertainers, artisans, and merchants were so often on the move that they were detached from such institutional or group identities. As Nicholas Dean Brodie notes in Chapter Six, although it is clear that many medieval workers possessed considerable mobility, offering up evidence for the exact movements of individual workers is only rarely possible.

Perhaps most excluded were slaves and the impoverished. Slavery was common across Europe and the Mediterranean during the early Middle Ages. Among the clerical elite at least, moral arguments against slavery circulated during the ninth century, but more practical matters brought about its demise. As James Davis points out in Chapter One, the coercive actions and organization needed to maintain the practice of slavery caused its disappearance. Already waning by the tenth century, slavery had practically vanished from Europe by the twelfth century, although most former slaves and their descendants ended up in servile positions, owing labor and its fruits to their lords. In Chapter Seven Holly J. Grieco outlines the way clerical writers understood the place of the poor in society as a whole and the ways in which they and other members of society sought the spiritual benefits of providing charity and perceived that helping the poor could promote the common good.

Methodological and source problems hinder the ability of cultural historians to explore medieval work as fully as they can labor in the modern era, but recent studies have engaged in increasingly sophisticated analysis. Gone are the days when historians accepted the regulations of towns, guilds, and governments as reflections of actual practice, but determining the degree to which medieval artisans, merchants, and laborers engaged in "behind-the-door" transactions or broke the rules of labor remains extremely difficult. Only by the fifteenth century does such information start to appear more regularly in the sources, as Valerie L. Garver notes in Chapter Five, with recorded cases of recipe theft and circumvention of or disregard for guild or civic rules. Historians have generally begun to believe that regulations tell us more about the ideals that the leaders and at least some constituents of cities, institutions, and organizations embraced than about day-to-day practices. Informal trading appears to have been a common occurrence in towns and in the countryside where it was much harder to enforce any regulations.[25] As Nicholas Dean Brodie demonstrates in Chapter Six, the intractable nature of most medieval sources in regard to the physical movement of workers has made measuring the mobility of laborers difficult and subject to a degree of uncertainty. Yet historians have employed new methodologies and careful analysis of sources related to other issues that have allowed them to see more movement of the laboring classes than previous scholarship had noted.

Artistic representations provide another avenue into the cultural history of work. The ways in which labor was depicted in medieval art and literature changed over time; yet, as Deirdre Jackson notes in Chapter Two, many conventions governing scenes of workers rested on long traditions, sometimes extending back into antiquity. Where no precedents existed, such as in the case of portraits of illuminators which we lack until the late Middle Ages, new standards developed slowly. Medieval art and literature provide concrete information otherwise unavailable to historians such as depictions of now-lost medieval implements and the ways workers employed them; a window into the humor and playfulness of medieval artists and writers, who at turns parodied human work behaviors, such as in illustrations of animals engaged in human activities; and a visual manifestation of the work ethic so many moralists advocated during the Middle Ages: that men and women needed to work as a result of Adam and Eve's sin.

THE BLACK DEATH AND THE CULTURE OF WORK

This volume notes a number of key turning points in the cultural history of work, but perhaps no event changed the social landscape of the medieval era more than the Black Death (1347–50), a plague epidemic that swept through Europe (as well as the Middle East, North Africa, and Asia) and killed perhaps up to 35 percent of the European population.[26] Earlier European troubles may have exacerbated the effects of plague. The early fourteenth century witnessed an environmental crisis brought on by overcropping, a less favorable climate with a shorter growing season, flooding, and erosion. Crop yields fell, and a severe famine in 1315 followed by a plague in 1316 may have killed as much as 10 percent of the population. These events dealt a particularly devastating blow to cities, the very places where plague spread most easily. Some civic authorities began to restrict immigration. Certain craft guilds started to limit entry to the sons of masters and restricted daughters' ability to inherit their fathers' guild rights.[27]

The changes that resulted from the plague produced literary and artistic expressions of a world turned upside down—perhaps most famously Giovanni Boccaccio's (1313–75) description of the plague and its effects in Florence as well as the specific setting and tales of his *Decameron*. His opening account of the plague emphasized the shattering of social and familial bonds with many fleeing the city, even parents abandoning their children.[28] Yet much of his explanation is literary convention, and many scholars accept that it was, like the Italian Gabriele de' Mussis's (c. 1280–c. 1356) similar description, "an extended meditation on the plague as an expression of divine anger."[29] In fact, social, familial, civic, and economic relationships persisted through the epidemic and beyond. In Bologna during the height of the Black Death, for example, many families stayed in place to help the sick and dying, and neighborhoods, the government, and other institutions and civic groups responded with aid, compassion, and resilience. Such a picture emerges in many other western European cities where notarial documents, wills, histories, and letters survive.[30]

The Black Death did, however, transform many aspects of work. The economy, which had already been slowing prior to the epidemic's onset, saw decreased demand and lower profits at a time when population loss in some areas meant employers had to increase pay to retain workers.[31] Major labor shortages resulted in some areas, which increased wages. In places the cost of labor resulted in social restructuring, with women, for instance, taking up jobs more typically held by men in the past, such as looking after livestock.[32] In response, governments sought to control the supply of labor and to curb the pay workers could receive, even including the meals employers sometimes supplied. As Robert Braid demonstrates in Chapter Eight, however, governments did not respond to the challenges following the Black Death uniformly. Rather, they built upon preexisting structures and practices, with some places, such as in England, employing coercion to keep workers in line and others, including communities in Provence, attempting to attract laborers. In post-plague England, the Black Death accelerated a long-term transformation in the political culture of work. Medieval elites increasingly turning their attention to work and found ways to control it, moving from an early period of indifference to relatively tight regulation by the end of the medieval era. As a result, a new political culture of work emerged which accepted that one of the primary functions of government was to regulate labor. A number of medieval texts raise questions about social changes that accompanied government regulations and the labor supply. Increased spending power from higher wages resulted in the ability of workers to engage in more leisure, that is nonwork activities, and concomitantly caused cultural expressions of concern over that ability to purchase nonwork experiences as Jeremy Goldberg and Emma Martin explain in Chapter Nine.

The Black Death led to a decline in population, but cities continued to attract people, who arrived even as the number of inhabitants of cities dropped. Although some cities tried to keep certain occupations to their traditional quarters, shifts occurred in this period, sometimes for political reasons, at other times for reasons of sanitation or desirable location. Nevertheless some segregation by trade continued to mark urban organization and culture.[33] In addition, although conditions initially became more favorable for female workers shortly after the Black Death, ideological and religious conceptions of women remained relatively static, and women continued to be subordinate to men, to earn lower wages and profits than men, and to work in low-status positions. Their domestic and childcare duties show significant continuity with earlier medieval centuries.[34]

The cultural history of work in the medieval era therefore shows substantial continuity even as changes occurred. Yet charting broad and lasting trends remains difficult because of the length and diversity of the Middle Ages and because of the vagaries of source survival. The chapters in this volume account for variety over time and place, but they cannot provide a comprehensive account. New information from archaeological excavations and untapped written documents will continue to change historical understanding of medieval work. The chapters that follow provide the broad outlines of major developments and continuities with representative examples to demonstrate the vitality and utility of cultural history in exploring work in the Middle Ages. Each emphasizes the creativity, resilience, and vigor of medieval people, a sure counter to any lingering pop culture stereotypes of a dark age.

CHAPTER ONE

The Economy of Work

JAMES DAVIS

The economy of medieval work was about the choices that people made, or had imposed upon them, in earning a living or maintaining a household. At their core, these choices affected their material circumstances and standard of living; for some this was about survival, for others about the accumulation of greater wealth. This chapter will explore the paid and unpaid work that was available to medieval men and women, as well as the time they devoted to work. Without such a foundation, the cultural factors that permeated the organization, perception, and ethics of work cannot be fully understood. The range of experience across Europe and across six hundred years was undoubtedly broad, so the following discussion can only highlight some apparent commonalities without attesting to their applicability in all instances of time and space. Nevertheless, it is clear that labor was the prime productive force in medieval society and this made people into valuable assets for those with work to offer. In medieval Europe, the vast majority worked in the fields, or in gathering other forms of natural resources, and their main unit of production was the small, nuclear household. Yet much of our evidence about medieval work derives from substantial ecclesiastical or seigneurial households, or else from the ruling organizations of the town. Understanding the experience of the ordinary rural worker, male or female, often has to be ascertained through the prism of their employers. To add to this sense of opaqueness, precise figures about wages, prices, and earnings are not easy to come by, with accounts recording wages in an incomplete or localized manner that prevents disaggregation for individuals or time worked.

This chapter focuses on the choices of work that were available, recognizing the environmental, economic, and sociopolitical constraints faced by medieval people in their attempt to make a living. Throughout this period, labor remained the prime means to improve productivity, with technological advances and mechanical aids relatively limited. This meant that an active market in labor developed as the economy grew, but its form shifted in response to factors of demography and crisis. During the twelfth and thirteenth centuries, when the population was growing and wages were low in comparison to prices, employers were prepared to intensify their use of labor in order to boost productivity, through more manuring, weeding, and cropping. After the Black Death, as labor became scarce and wages increased, producers looked for ways to use less labor. They turned more to pastoral husbandry or else leased out parts of demesnes, whereby the proportion of family labor in the economy increased. Thus sheep production grew in England and Spain, while viticulture expanded in Burgundy and along the Moselle.[1] The cost of labor therefore reflected the availability of labor and its demand, both of which could vary chronologically and geographically.

THE CHOICE OF WORK

The choices of medieval tenants and laborers "were not made freely, because they worked within the limits imposed by their social circumstances and technical knowledge, and by the soil, terrain and climate."[2] Across Europe around 1000, some 90 percent of people lived off the produce of land or sea and, wherever we look, there were forms of arable and pastoral agriculture, viticulture, or horticulture. The resources provided by the surrounding natural landscape certainly shaped opportunities for work. Those who lived near woods, forest, fens, rivers, marshland, or the coast may have had an alternative or a way to supplement their income through exploiting the particulars of their environment. This was especially important when the soil was not conducive to more traditional forms of agriculture. For instance, the Breckland of East Anglia (England) lacked the soils for farming but encouraged a multiplicity of working options, from collecting fuel and building materials to catching wildfowl and riverine animals.[3] More upland areas or poorer soils were often used for pasturing sheep or goats, from Castile to northern England. This required less intensive work than cultivating arable regions or the vineyards of the Mediterranean.

The work that was available was also shaped by the type of settlement, whether hamlets, villages, small towns, or cities. As medieval people increasingly gathered in nucleated villages by the tenth and eleventh centuries, integrated and shared working of the land provided more economic efficiency and a balancing of risk. However, it also reinforced the authority of the lords who could more easily raise rents and services upon tenant holdings. The urban population perhaps doubled during the medieval period, providing more nonagricultural work, but it was still less than a fifth of the total workforce—though northern Italy and Flanders contained a substantial share. Nevertheless, the process of urbanization had a broader effect on the types of work and organization of production, not only in the towns themselves but on the surrounding manors and estates. Production for urban markets increased; credit and capital flows developed; and wage differentials stimulated labor migration.

We should not assume that every man in the villages worked in the fields. There were many men who were employed as specialized carpenters, smiths, tailors, bakers, and brewers. Many males may also have engaged in more than one activity, with carpenters and smiths also holding land which they worked part-time. All medieval economies had nonagricultural occupations and a certain level of trade. The extent varied across time and regions, but even outside towns significant pockets of rural industry developed such as pottery, mining, cloth making, and charcoal burning. In the Carolingian period, textile production was a normal by-occupation for peasant wives, while in various parts of eighth- and ninth-century Europe there were workplaces called *gynaecea* where servile women had to undertake obligatory handicraft services.[4] The wide range of occupations and industries available in rural areas by the thirteenth and fourteenth centuries was evident in the tax returns for England, such as the forty different crafts listed in the Wiltshire subsidy of 1332.[5] Some regions had a concentration of particular industries, whether the tin mines of Cornwall and Devon, the lead mines of Derbyshire, Durham, and Northumberland, the metal working of south Germany, or the cloth industries of Flanders and Arras. The development and expansion of such industries stimulated new income streams for workers, as well as boosting local agricultural production and services. Similarly, the growth of towns and market networks across Europe, particularly in the twelfth and thirteenth centuries, provided new opportunities. In response to heightened consumer demand, there were more areas of specialized agriculture that concentrated on cash crops and, in turn, attracted groups of workers. "Fields of crocuses in parts of Tuscany yielded precious saffron. Picardy in northeast France became prosperous from vast fields of woad, planted for blue dyestuff. Plantations of mulberry trees in parts of Greece and Italy supplied the only leaves that silkworms would eat."[6]

Within all these communities, a socioeconomic hierarchy determined who worked for whom. The main employers of a concentration of workers were the big ecclesiastical institutions and wealthy secular lords. Lords controlled much of the land of Europe; while some was leased out to tenants on a range of terms, many would maintain and directly manage a piece of land (demesne) at the core of their rural manors as long as it benefited their coffers. This required workers, whether full-time servants, wage labor, servile labor, or slaves. However, throughout this period, the majority of employment was most likely provided by small-scale holdings and enterprises. Some rural families (free or unfree) may have had thirty acres of land or more, perhaps even akin to the lesser gentry, and were able to produce a significant marketable surplus. Such substantial holdings could not usually be worked by the family alone and thus they would hire a modest amount of wage labor and servants. Next down the scale were smallholders who were only able to produce a very small surplus and relied heavily on family labor. They had only a few acres of land and needed a supplementary trade or wage labor to make a living. Similarly, the landless had to survive primarily through wage labor, but very few enjoyed regular employment. They faced choices of mostly casual and seasonal work, often for their neighbors as much as for a lord.

SEASONAL WORK

Most agricultural work was seasonal and the agrarian rhythm moved from plowing to weeding, mowing, reaping, and threshing. Calendar illustrations reflected these seasonal activities, such as in the early Carolingian *Chronicle of the Months* from the abbey of St. Peter in Salzburg (c. 818). They are also exemplified in the following late medieval lyrics:

Januar	By thys fyre I warme my handys;
Februar	And with my spade I delfe my landys.
Marche	Here I sette my thynge to sprynge;
Aprile	And here I here the fowlis synge.
Maij	I am light as byrde in bowe;
Junij	And I wede my corne wel I-now
Julij	With my sythe my mede I mawe;
Auguste	And here I shere my corne full lowe.
September	With my flayll I erne my brede;
October	And here I saw my whete so rede.
November	At Martynesmasse I kylle my swyne;
December	And at Cristemasse I drynke redde wyne.[7]

January was the month to keep warm, before the hard work from February to May for plowing, planting, and tending to crops. Plowing was tough and it is likely that all the family would be drawn into guiding the plow and directing the oxen. The fields then had to be turned and prepared with manure, while weeding was ongoing. In June and July, the hay was cut and stored, to be followed by the harvest of various grains. In October, pigs were fattened and fields prepared for winter wheat (Figure 1.1). November was for butchering and salting or smoking meat. Other tasks, such as collecting wood, digging drainage, taking care of animals, and general maintenance, continued throughout the year.[8]

The seasons thus determined the work of the household but also the fluctuating demand for waged labor. The above description highlights a northern European arable cycle, but such calendars had their origins in the Mediterranean regions with their greater emphasis on the cycles of the grape harvest between February and April. Similar regional differences in the seasonality of work were seen in areas dominated by pasture. Transhumance was a characteristic of these areas as both people and animals moved

FIGURE 1.1 Calendar for October, Breviary of Queen Isabella of Castile, c. 1497. British Library, Add. MS 18851, folio 6[v].

with the seasons in search of food. The fishing industry was also exemplified by seasonal migration of stocks, requiring an intensive expedition over a few weeks to bring in the catch and share the profits.

The daily work pattern was also shaped by the seasons. The changing hours of daylight naturally varied the length of the working day, with most working from sunrise to sunset. Consequently, it was customary in some regions for a winter day's work to be paid less than for a summer day. Some artisans may have worked by candlelight, but this was frowned upon as both contributing to poor quality and an intention to escape prying oversight. The working day in towns had long been governed by the ringing of the bell that announced the daily rhythm of canonical hours (prime, terce, sext, and none), which determined when the town gates opened and when goods could be sold in the market. But this meant irregular hours depending on the season. French ordinances from the fourteenth century sought to define more clearly when the work day began and ended, as well as when meals could be taken, with the day's divisions marked by bells. An ordinance of the provost of Paris from May 12, 1395 stated: "the working day is fixed from the hour of sunrise until the hour of sunset, with meals to be taken at reasonable times."[9]

Laborers therefore worked long hours, but how efficiently and speedily they worked is difficult to determine. Did the imprecise measurement of time mean that workers were "task-oriented" rather than "time-oriented"?[10] Most did not work on Sundays and by the late twelfth century the church was adamant that the Sabbath was a day for church and not for work—a sentiment that they sought to reinforce in church courts. Only victuallers appear to have been allowed to supply foodstuffs on every day of the week. Poor weather might also drive people home, particularly on frozen days in northern Europe, as well as the main feast days (and vigils) and fairs, which were not timed to accord with agricultural needs. This appears to have been the case for most workers and perhaps 115 days a year were potential nonwork days, though essential agricultural tasks would have continued.[11]

There is some evidence that village communities sought to regulate holidays and the activities of harvest workers, even before the labor legislation of the mid-fourteenth century. Similarly, in towns, craft guilds had long governed matters of working hours and rates of pay in the interests of employers not workers; journeymen were not generally allowed to bargain for their conditions of work. Clocks appear all over Europe from the mid-fourteenth century and become prominent in towns by the middle of the next century. This further regularized the divisions of the working day, particularly for those employed by others.[12]

THE WORKING HOUSEHOLD

The medieval household was the basic economic unit for consumption and production in both town and countryside. Consequently, all members of a household needed to ensure that the household ran effectively and prospered, or else they might be placing their very survival at risk during times of economic uncertainty and vulnerability to harvest failures. Most households were primarily concerned with their consumption needs, produced on a small scale and were heavily reliant on family labor; they had to work within their initial resource base and also the limits of their socioeconomic status. A family in the middle of their life cycle were likely to be at the peak of their production capability compared to those newly married or those reaching old age. The home itself and the surrounding land were often where work was undertaken, surplus produced, income generated, and resources maintained and consumed. It is clear that family labor was predominant in agricultural work, with those working their own holdings effectively self-employed, and thus every able family member had to contribute. This was particularly important for smallholders (perhaps five to ten acres), whose holdings were not sufficient to feed the family and provide a surplus. Finding a balance between resources, labor, and need could be problematic—ultimately the family had to be fed and sheltered—and aspirations to improve their economic and social status or provide for their children were secondary for the majority of those families who simply needed to make a daily living.

It would have been rare for a household to be completely self-sufficient, even where land was the core of their family economy. People frequently supplemented their earnings through irregular agricultural tasks or craftwork. It was often the case that the seasonal nature of agricultural work meant that nonagrarian by-employment was a way of extending labor productivity. Smallholders would thus be readily involved in casual work within their home, such as carding and spinning wool, plaiting baskets, or outside, such as fishing, turf-cutting, salt manufacture, and hemp processing. Few of these tasks required expensive equipment or raw materials and it has been estimated that nonagricultural employment constituted more than 10 percent of rural incomes by 1300.[13] Some developed their skills into a more prominent, even specialized occupation, such as carpentry, smithing, weaving, ceramics, or thatching. Even those with substantial landholdings should not be viewed as entirely self-sufficient, for they had to buy certain commodities such as salt or metalware, obtain cash for rents and taxes, and hire specialist labor. Many thus engaged in some form of by-employment in the locality. This was truly an "economy of makeshifts."

In considering the choices of work available to an individual, attention must be given to gender-specific activity within the medieval economy. Women were substantial contributors to household economies, both in domestic matters and by-employment. However, the contemporary patriarchal consensus was that the husband was superior in his role as head of the family and breadwinner. He dealt with all matters outside the household and it was his duty to provide for and maintain his wife and children. The wife's domain was viewed as the domestic sphere, such as the kitchen and garden, looking after the children and caring for the family, and the evidence does suggest that this expectation was partly reflected in the reality of women's work. The accidents recorded in coroners' rolls indicate that women spent more of their working life around the house and village, while men were more likely to meet their end in fields, forests, mills, and building sites.[14]

This does not mean that the wife was entirely isolated in the domestic sphere of house, garden, and children. Housework meant much more than just cleaning and cooking and childrearing, and there were an array of other work tasks that were considered "women's work." Pastoral work was often delegated to them, such as milking, care of pigs and poultry, making butter, and producing malt. The evidence of court records and labor legislation also highlight the availability of casual labor for married and unmarried women in weeding, hay making, stone picking, gleaning, and washing. Harvest time was a notable time when the urgency of the task meant that the entire household would be drawn into the fields, seemingly working side by side in heavy tasks, as seen in numerous contemporary images (Figure 1.2).

The domestic tasks of wives could also lead to commercial activity and nonagricultural by-employment, most notably spinning, butter making, and ale brewing. Women, married and single, would often travel to the local market to sell their agricultural produce and the products of their labors. Thus hucksters were seen in all weekly markets, carrying baskets in their arms and loudly vending their poultry, butter, eggs, fruit, rushes, thread, and excess grain. Spinning was a very common female task, with the resultant yarn

THE ECONOMY OF WORK 19

FIGURE 1.2 Harvest allegory on the "three conditions of women" (virgins, widows, and married wives). *Speculum Viriginum*, c. 1300. Rheinisches Landesmuseum, no. 15326. The Yorck Project.

sold to weavers, and the distaff became the wife's symbolic identifier. This was a labor-intensive task but profitable for common families because ultimately family labor was relatively cheap. Brewing was also regarded as women's work and wives of varying social status would brew and sell ale as a sideline. This surplus may have been sold as little as once or twice a year for small profit, but women with more capital may have brewed on a more permanent basis, even keeping an alehouse. The most numerous indications of such work are the long lists of women presented in the court rolls, apparently for selling overpriced or unwholesome ale but more likely as a quasi-license for their commercial activity.

Women thus combined a range of economic activities, both paid and unpaid, but there were evident constraints on the choices of work available. John Ball's (c. 1338–81) supposed dictum from the 1381 English revolt stated: "When Adam delved and Eve span, who was then a gentleman?"[15] Although intended to denounce class distinctions, Ball was content enough with a traditional gender division of labor; the men undertook the intensive work of plowing and the women spun wool as an adjunct to their domestic

FIGURE 1.3 Eve spinning and Adam delving, wall painting, c. 1300. Holy Trinity Church, Bledlow (Buckinghamshire, England). © Rob Farrow.

duties (see Figure 1.3). William Langland (c. 1332–87?), too, in *Piers Plowman* in the late fourteenth century, identified spinning, sewing, and care of daughters as women's work while the men plowed and sowed in the fields.[16] The humorous fifteenth-century English *Ballad of a Tyrannical Husband* seemingly suggested that the husband would prefer his wife's duties, but it was part of a trope that implicitly recognized the hard labor of women and the contribution that they made to the household income.[17] The ballad recited how the wife milked the cows and led them to pasture, made butter and cheese, fed the poultry, baked and brewed, carded and spun wool, and beat flax. The husband's jibe is that this is all too easy and she mostly gossips with her neighbors. He is soon rebutted, but, nevertheless, it was a common view that women's work was low skilled, low status, and low paid.

In general, the historical evidence for women's work is difficult to quantify, partly because it was sporadic, but also because women's activities were mostly private and thus escape the documentation of the court rolls. It is difficult to ascertain how much rural women worked outside the household economy. For young, unmarried females, being a servant was a temporary part of the life cycle, but other opportunities in towns were comparatively few. Only in widowhood did women gain a modicum of freedom of choice. It has been argued that "married women could well find that any economic independence was acquired at the expense of physical exhaustion";[18] they were already heavily involved in a myriad of tasks before even considering branching out further. The cash returns from wives' supplementary work might even have afforded women some independence and economic clout within the family unit, but this should not be overemphasized. In particular, this was legally not the case—the husband controlled all the material resources, including the goods brought to a marriage through the dowry and any money she earned through her labor.

The level of integration and interdependence between the work of husband and wife appears to have been higher in the households of craftsmen and journeymen, depending on the nature of the craftwork. For instance, wives of weavers worked at piece rates throughout England, and they often span for their husbands' employers. Urban women were regularly drawn into work beyond the domestic sphere, taking on ancillary trades, such as wives of butchers who might sell cooked meats or make tallow candles. Officially, women were excluded from certain manufacturing crafts and the guilds that ran them, except food and drinks retailing. They may have been permitted to carry on the craft of a deceased husband, and some borough customs defined the length of time they could continue to do so.[19] In a similar manner, some guild regulations recognized that husbands may have taught their wives as well as apprentices the skills of their trade, but others forbade such practices, ostensibly concerned that women did not have the requisite technical knowledge and skills. The weavers of Bristol in 1461 were ordered to distain from allowing wives, daughters, and maids to weave alongside male members of the craft, though an exception was made to wives who already had assisted their husbands for as long as they lived.[20] Indeed, it appears common practice that in many craft workshops, typically part of the home, wives may have overseen apprentices, worked on certain production tasks, bought materials, and sold the finished products. The evidence again demonstrates the adaptability of working women to the economic needs of the household. The wife, from her initial dowry to her labor and by-occupations, was thus vital in maintaining the household economy beyond just the domestic sphere. This was to the mutual benefit of the family and highlighted the interdependent nature of marriage. However, despite common goals, the basic structure of economic and social power in the household remained unaltered. Gender roles were defined according to patriarchal norms, even if they were in reality complementary and overlapping.

The other potential contributors to the working economy were the young. Very young children were, of course, more of a drain on resources than a benefit. Even though they were engaged in gender-defined activities by the age of two or three, it is unlikely that their observation and imitation of adult tasks was particularly productive for the household economy until they were a little older. From about the ages of seven to twelve, children were able to contribute more fully. Again, English medieval coroners' rolls show a gender division, with young girls undertaking household chores or childcare and young boys fishing, gathering food and fuel, or herding small animals such as poultry and sheep. John Wayhe was twelve when he was swineherd in 1348, and we know of him because he was cold one December morning, climbed into a baker's oven to keep warm, and was burned to death.[21] More significantly, such boys could earn a little money by running errands, acting as thatchers' assistants, or binding grain at harvest (at half-wages). Similarly, girls aged seven to twelve contributed by picking fruit and nuts, collecting shellfish, aiding their mothers in fetching water, building fires, cooking, and childcare. In town households, there is evidence that children were used for certain manufacturing processes, perhaps to help work lace or spin. However, in general, children were asked to perform only such work as was suitable for their capacity and it was often seen as part of the child's education, learning the ways of work.

By the ages of thirteen to eighteen, they were working more like adults. Many male adolescents were involved in agricultural work, either at their natal home or as servants to others, though some went into crafts and building as apprentices. Indeed, the life cycle for many young people throughout Europe was traditionally shaped by entry into servanthood in their late teens and early twenties, both in town and in country, in workshops, homes, and fields. They left home just when their working contribution might be expected to become significant. Yet children were rarely expected to contribute to the maintenance of their parents, and there is no real evidence in our period that they sent part of their wages home. The working tasks of women and children may have been vital to many households, but such work was not directly remunerated. This was perhaps most acutely felt either on the death of a spouse or when a son left the household in search of his own land and independence, and thus had to be replaced with hired labor.

Servants undertook a short-term contract with an employer, with an annual stipend tempered by the provision of food, drink, clothing, and accommodation, usually in the employer's house. Indeed, it was this living arrangement that defined a servant. Annual indentures might run from Michaelmas (September 29) or Martinmas (November 11). Servants undoubtedly worked long hours and we should not underestimate the contribution to the working economy by servants of all ages and from a variety of socioeconomic backgrounds. Females appear to have settled into domestic work patterns early, perhaps owing to the need for fuller physical development before males could be involved in certain agrarian work. Overall, servants were a prominent feature of the medieval workforce throughout this period. The late-eighth-century *Life of St. Philaretos* highlights a significant number of servants (*oiketai*) on his Byzantine lands in Paphlagonia.[22] England's *Domesday Book* (1086) suggests a large, mostly hidden servant population who undertook a variety of tasks on demesnes and substantial peasant holdings, while later tax and legal records highlight their ubiquitous presence, such as the poll taxes of England (1377–80) or the *catasto* (tax assessment) of Florence (1427).[23] Servants perhaps made up a quarter of any town's population by the fourteenth century.

The annual contracts for servants became even more attractive to employers after the Black Death, guaranteeing labor at a time of shortage even if the cost had risen.

EMPLOYERS AND WAGE LABOR

Records survived best for the major ecclesiastical and seigneurial institutions, who hired a significant number of skilled and unskilled workers. For example, in the twelfth and thirteenth centuries, farm servants were one of the main labor forces for lords. The *famuli* of England were mostly contracted full-time, but on short terms (usually a year), in return for cash wages and possibly a food allowance, though there were some permanent demesne staff.[24] "The monks of Crowland in the 1290s employed on their Northamptonshire manor of Wellingborough eight ploughmen, two carters, three shepherds, a dairymaid and a cowherd. With the addition of various part-time servants such as a swineherd and tithe collectors for the harvest season, these workers accounted for about half of the labour needed to cultivate the 300-acre demesne."[25] Other workers would be hired and paid for specific tasks, on a daily or piece-rate basis, whether to repair tools, weed, mow, shear, or bring in the harvest.

However, more modest employers also hired servants, apprentices, and casual labor, from more substantial tenants to merchants, artisans, and rectors. In each case this was perhaps just one or two employees on an ad hoc, transient basis, but cumulatively this small-scale activity constituted a high proportion of total employment. Even those contractually employed for a certain task, whether in agriculture, services, or construction, might subcontract and pay further workers. This is seen clearly in the activities of builders, smiths, carpenters, and thatchers, who would have invariably worked day-to-day or on short contracts, with few building projects substantial enough to warrant year-long employment. Wages were often a little higher than for other laboring trades, and they supplied their own equipment and even assistants, but few had landholdings to supplement their main income. We should not draw too firm a line between the employer and the employed; hiring fairs, and even agents, might imply there was a growing distinction, but most work and servant placings were obtained through personal contacts of kinship or neighborhood. The work itself was carried out in intimate proximity, often in the employer's home, who would exert a quasi-parental discipline and morality upon young servants/apprentices. Informal gifts and favors were not uncommon, but this was still a hierarchical, subordinate relationship.

Wage labor was relatively unimportant for agricultural production before the ninth century, but it has been argued that at least a third of the population gained most of their livelihood from wage labor by the end of the thirteenth century.[26] Rural labor was certainly hired for money wages across Europe, but the proportion appears to be higher in England and France than, say, in central, southern, and eastern Europe. French vineyards were dominated by low-paid wage labor.[27] Wage laborers primarily derived from the poorer smallholding and landless class, about whom we know comparatively little since they are sparsely recorded in the documents. We cannot therefore know with certainty what changing proportion of the rural or urban population worked for wages, especially when taking into account the part-time method of engagement. However, it appears that there was a growing dependence on wages among the lower social groups. The poorer elements of medieval society performed much of the waged work and were the people most vulnerable to economic recession, population pressure, or harvest failure. As real wages stagnated or even fell in the late thirteenth century, these wage earners had to work longer to maintain their household's standard of living, but with low demand for their labor this was not always possible. Relatively few worked permanently on employers' agricultural holdings. Instead, they faced seasonal fluctuations in demand, with the harvest time providing a glut of opportunity. Smallholders and the landless, especially, provided a residual pool of labor that could be readily called upon. Such laborers had to leave home during the day to work elsewhere, thus emphasizing the separation of work from household and the duties of husband and wife. However, the search for seasonal laboring work could also mean long absences for poorer husbands and women left to fend for themselves and their children.[28] There was a thin line between a desperate search for work elsewhere and abandonment of their family.

Not all could exercise independent choice in the type or extent of work that they undertook. Beyond the imperatives of sustenance for one's household, there were conditions under which labor was coerced. This pattern of work was embedded in the sociopolitical structures. In the early Middle Ages, slavery was widespread across western Europe and the Mediterranean basin, though this generally consisted of a range of forms of unfreedom (e.g., *servi, ancillae*) rather than extensive "slave plantations."[29] Ultimately, slaves were entirely the property of a lord and under their direction. They were of the lowest status, without legal rights and considered without honor. Ælfric of Eynsham (c. 955–c. 1010), an English Benedictine monk, wrote of a slave plowman: "Yes, the work is hard, because I am not free."[30] Many slaves were used for regular agricultural work, from plowing to herding for men, and as dairymaids for women, and could be bought and sold like livestock. In reality, in areas such as Catalonia, the Mâconnais, and Macedonia, many were occupying land by the tenth century, accumulating goods, using the market, and raising families.[31] The coercive administration involved in keeping slaves was to prove its undoing, more so than the moral concerns circulating. By the eleventh and twelfth centuries, slavery was waning in much of western Europe. However, the numerous freed slaves often ended up as smallholders and in a servile relationship with lords that required heavy obligations, alongside a preexisting dependent tenantry. In many ways, this was more economically burdensome than slavery.

To differing degrees, servile labor emerged as the best means for lords to ensure access to labor for their large demesnes. The rise of the manorial system (or *seigneurie* in French; *Landherrshaft* in German) in ninth- and tenth-century northwestern Europe and Catalonia encouraged the development of serfdom. This obliged unfree peasants to pay rents and provide compulsory labor services (*corvée*) for the lord; the lord implicitly providing protection in return. Lords thus intensified their control over agrarian matters, formally directing the labor of peasants. The uneven development of this system is seen as early as the late eighth century in the Frankish Empire, between the Loire and Rhine rivers, and in northern Italy. The early ninth-century polyptych (land survey) of Saint-Germain-des-Prés, an estate near Paris held by Abbot Irmino (d. 829?), outlined the labor and handiwork services owed by dependent tenants. This included:

> Aclebertus and his wife Frotlindis, an unfree woman (*ancilla*), both dependants of St Germain, have one child named Acleburg … he has to work 4 *aripennos* in the vineyard (of the demesne), pays 3 *modios* wine for grazing tax, one *sestarius* of mustard, 50 osier bundles, 3 chickens, 15 eggs. Handiwork services when and where they are imposed on them.[32]

Similarly, as early as around 1000 in western England, the *Rectitudines singularum personarum* described how a smallholder spent a quarter of his time on the lord's land.[33] Depending on the serf's holding and the coercive assertions of the manorial lord, servile obligations could involve the equivalent of working between one and three days a week on the lord's demesne, as well as extra "boon" days at harvest time. These may have been covered as much by family members as by the head of household. On the bishop of Winchester's manors in the thirteenth century, unfree tenants (villeins) worked as plowmen, laborers, harvesters, carters, cowherds, shepherds, swineherds, and smiths.[34]

It has been noted that the "overall effect of this feudal regime was to alienate the serfs from the fruits of their labour."[35] However, research has revealed the multiplicity of servile arrangements and that burdens varied greatly from onerous to light. A lighter form of serfdom was already evident in twelfth-century France, where the Statute of Lorris provided a model contract of money rents and less onerous labor services, which enabled the king to attract people into new villages.[36] In twelfth-century Tuscany, landlords often commuted services into rents of money or in kind, though still insisted on oaths of loyalty. Similarly, the *praktikon* (1219) of Lampsakos in Asia Minor stated that tenants owed forty-eight days of labor services each year, but these were mostly commuted to a cash payment.[37] The reality was that many labor services were commuted into money rents when population pressure and economic trends meant that work was cheap to buy. Labor services were not always easy to administer and enforce, with many lost owing to sickness, feast days, and absenteeism, while their customary nature could impose restrictions on their use, including debate over the exact hours stipulated by the obligation or the food allowance that workers were due. Evidence from Wisbech in mid-fourteenth-century Cambridgeshire (England) indicates that the productivity of labor services was much lower than that of hired workers and that demesne managers were aware of this discrepancy.[38] It was simply not worth the coercive effort to enforce labor services when a simple money payment might then allow the employment of a more productive wage-laborer. Commutation thus provided flexibility for lords at a time of increasing commercialization and a more favorable labor market.

Lords would hire laborers to undertake tasks that were seemingly covered by labor services, and low wages sustained demesne farming. However, it is noticeable that many lords kept boon works for harvest time, when the intensity of labor needs was paramount. The market ultimately determined the balance between those who controlled the land and those who were expected to work on it. This was equally the case for free peasants, who remained a sizeable group from northern Italy to England and rarely owed labor services for their holdings. Yet they remained in thrall to the vagaries of the market. Many peasants were smallholders, such as the cottars in Domesday England or the *paroikoi* around the Mediterranean, with no agricultural surplus and thus requiring other ways to supplement their incomes. Some were also subject to different forms of coercion upon their labor. For instance, through a combination of money and grain rents, many tenants in northern Italy, Flanders, and Byzantium were, in effect, piece-rate laborers or sharecroppers who kept half of the fruits of their labor.[39]

Payment for wage labor was not only in cash, but also included forms of food allowance, clothing, accommodation, and other in-kind options. "On the Bec manor of Combe in 1307–8, some workers got a quarter [of grain] every ten weeks, the hog-herd received his livery only every 12 weeks, a cowherd-harrower a livery every 14 weeks, and a dairymaid hers every 16 weeks in winter only."[40] Harvest workers would be partially reimbursed through a communal meal. How these payments in kind equated to cash wages would differ according to the broader economic conditions affecting prices and thus the purchasing power of money. Allowances of food provided some protection against inflation, but some lords responded by reducing grain liveries. Although wages apparently increased incrementally from the ninth to thirteenth centuries, real wages appear to have gone in the opposite direction as grain prices rose more substantially. In England, "mowing an acre of meadow, for example, cost 5d in the 1340s, between 6d and 7d in the 20 years after the first plague, and 7½d in the 1370s and 1380s."[41]

URBAN WORK

The proportion of urban work gradually increased across the medieval period, but agricultural work was always predominant. It is estimated that 10 percent of the population lived in towns by the eleventh century and engaged in manufacture, trade, and services. Manufacturing occupied perhaps 50 percent of any medieval urban population, with others engaged in trade, services, transport, and building. There is also evidence that a significant number retained interest in farming the surrounding fields. The *Livre des métiers* listed the regulations of 101 trades in Paris in the 1260s, identifying this division of specific tasks but also who could practice these occupations and the terms of apprenticeship.[42] The 1292 Paris taille—a hearth tax—provides 172 different occupations.[43] Registers of freemen reveal some 60–70 occupations in early-fourteenth-century Norwich and 100 in York.[44] Larger towns may have thus had some 60–200 different occupations. It was here that people would find luxury goods produced by, say, an armorer or bell-founder, as well as the wealthy merchants who dealt in international trade; they worked alongside the more common artisan and petty traders that were also present in small towns. However, it must be remembered that many more townspeople were engaged in unskilled work, such as carrying water, waste, and building materials. These workers had no expectation of steady employment and would gather every day at designated places, such as a cross, waiting to be hired for the day. Others, particularly women, could sell the goods produced by others by acting as petty retailers, but the rate of return on such activity was pitiful if they failed to sell all their wares.

Archaeological evidence also highlights the range of activities in medieval towns: food-processing was the most common, but we see glimpses of woodworking, metalware, tanners, jewellers, weavers, shoe makers, and pottery. Indeed, pottery was one industry that relocated from the countryside into towns by the tenth and eleventh centuries, as the scale of production benefited from a close agglomeration of workers. The success of towns was predicated on such a concentration of artisans, which allowed both competition and cooperation. Specialization of work, such as with butchers, skinners, tallowers, tanners, and cordwainers in processing cattle, or carders, spinners, weavers, dyers, fullers, and tailors in the cloth industry, facilitated the efficiency and quality of production. As the political economist Adam Smith (1723–90) argued, division of labor made producers more able in their particular task and thus they took less time in their work.[45] Even in the countryside, aspects of the clothing and building trades became the domain of specialists. However, one has to question the extent to which medieval nomenclature in legal records might hide an individual's multiplicity of occupational activities. As in the countryside, those in the towns would not always have been defined by one type of work, particularly those that dabbled in the food and drink trades. Even these ranged from the more high-status vintners, taverners, and spicers to the petty hucksters with baskets of fruit, eggs, and vegetables. It is difficult to know exactly how medieval workers divided their time between their primary tasks, supplementary activities, and domestic duties.

As in the country, there was thus a social and economic hierarchy. A basic outline can be given. At the bottom were very poor families struggling to subsist and reliant on casual labor and petty retailing, and who faced regular periods of unemployment at times when the labor supply was abundant. They lacked economic and political rights within the town, and could not organize, and this shaped their working experience. Training and capital would exclude individuals from certain trades, particularly metal working or the trade in well-finished cloth or leather. Entry into these trades was guarded by the system of apprenticeships and guilds, otherwise individuals were working with small quantities of raw materials and relatively basic tools. Journeymen, often with their own families, worked for other craftsmen in return for wages. Above them were the craftsmen and substantial tradesmen who held their own workshop or market stall and who also comprised the main membership of guilds. At the top of the socioeconomic scale were the mercantile and professional households. Mostly, craftsmen and traders worked out of their own houses and thus within their households, and they were able to organize their own time. Even journeymen, who did not have the capital to set up an independent business, would often undertake the actual work in their own house with their own tools, even though the materials would be supplied by the master craftsman—what was known as the "putting-out system," effectively selling their labor to others—but the urban household remained the principal locus of production and unit of labor organization.

CHANGING PATTERNS OF WORK

Working options were influenced as much by the general demographic and political conditions as by the socioeconomic status of individuals and their position in the life cycle. Economic strategies in times of high population, surplus labor, low wages, and land scarcity were very different to conditions of low population, labor scarcity, high wages, and land surplus. In the former situation, living standards were low and many families might struggle to subsist and find adequate land or work. In the latter, the opposite was the case, though high mortality did affect the survival of their children.

As the European population grew during the twelfth and thirteenth centuries, the number of smallholders and landless grew. The repercussion was a substantial pool of wage labor that provided flexibility not only for seigneurial agriculture, but also for more substantial peasant producers and the independent artisanal workshops. Flexibility for employers meant low earnings and poor conditions of employment for workers, with a low point perhaps reached in the 1270s. This was an era of underemployment and sticky wages; the conditions and opportunities for work were shaped as much by economic fluctuations as by institutional forms. The huge demographic decline and continued stagnation after the Black Death of 1347–50 invariably meant that the rewards for work quickly increased by at least a third, whether in cash or in kind, and significantly more by the end of the fifteenth century. The purchasing power of a day's labor had perhaps doubled by this time. This was also the case for piece rates as much as wages. In England, this coincided with a growth in the rural cloth industry that better rewarded workers but remained cheaper and more flexible for employers beyond the restrictions of urban guilds. Indeed, one interesting by-product of a severe labor shortage was that "the gap between skilled and unskilled workers narrowed," thus making the boundary between them more permeable as skilled tasks lost an element of their status.[46] Employers were well aware of the difficulty of finding workers and frequently expressed annoyance at the assertions of their previously more pliant employees. Consequently, there were adjustments in the economy to meet this shift in the labor market. Agricultural land went out of use and more was invested in sheep flocks and cattle, which did not require as much working time to manage. This did, however, mean that there were more full-time shepherds and cowherds.

In the aftermath of the Black Death, those seeking work were prepared to negotiate more favorable contracts, often working by the day or task for higher wages, and to move to another place if their demands were ignored. This stimulated reactive legislation across Europe but did not alter the fundamental fact that the supply of labor was relatively scarce.[47] There was a concept of the just wage in medieval Europe and beyond, just like the just price, but both were ultimately linked to market forces. Governments were usually unsuccessful in the long run in trying to fix wages and only attempted it in the wake of crises. Labor legislation in England, France, Aragon, and Catalonia followed the Black Death and tried to peg wages to pre-plague levels and induce compulsory labor for all those able-bodied. Pedro IV (r. 1336–87) promulgated an ordinance for Catalonia in the immediate aftermath of the Black Death in 1349, and followed it up with further legislation in Aragon a year later. Castile followed this trend in 1351, requiring all to work. The French king issued the Grand Ordinance in 1351, highlighting in particular the shortage of vineyard workers, setting winter wages at a lower level than summer wages, and also attempting to control food price inflation. However, this crisis had produced long-term conditions for rising wages and depressed agricultural prices that were difficult for governments to counter. Employers were desperate for labor and often offered inducements through payments in kind or by tacitly allowing less work for the same pay, which effectively undercut the legal prohibitions. In 1350, Roger Swynflete, keeper of the abbot of Selby's manor of Stallingborough, tempted the plowman John Skit away from a contract with Sir John d'Argentene by offering a range of payments in kind.[48] English evidence from the enforcement of the Statute of Laborers after 1351 reveals workers preferred short-term contracts and the freedom to travel, often in groups, from employer to employer in search of the best wages and added benefits.[49] They refused to work under the same conditions as before the plague.

The repercussions of this new economic environment thus meant that there was a greater choice of available work for those who wanted it. Indeed, the demand for labor meant that those whose opportunities had been limited were now encouraged into the workforce more consistently to fill vacancies. This included women, children, and the elderly. With the combination of labor shortages and sectoral growth in certain manufacturing trades, it was a powerful enticement for women to enter the workforce as independent economic agents, generating benefits for their household incomes and individual spending power. It does appear that after the Black Death, women were more often employed in extra-household tasks. In York between 1350 and 1450, women were able to find better employment and wages, though such gains were apparently short-lived. Women certainly earned higher wages then before the plague, but this still constituted some 70 percent of men's wages.[50] They also remained at a great disadvantage in a patriarchal society, excluded from political office and guild positions. It was difficult for women to gain full trading privileges. Consequently, their extra work was still the same as traditional "women's work," such as weeding, harvesting, hay making, and dairying. The tasks of brewing, spinning, and weaving were also more abundant, but again this did not represent a move away from what was regarded as the traditional female sphere. Women were treated as a reserve pool of labor, available when male labor dried up and to be paid lower wages for the same task. They certainly had more chance for regular employment in low-skilled work, particularly unmarried younger women, but the extent to which these opportunities extended to more skilled or heavy tasks is disputed.[51]

In general, whether annual earnings, and thus standards of living, increased by the same level as real wages after 1370 is difficult to determine. Craftsmen's wages appear to have generally risen, from England to Germany, though this was not evident everywhere and in France artisanal demand and thus payment remained stagnant.[52] Well-paid work still remained seasonal and opportunities varied year to year, while some workers preferred to spend their extra income in the alehouse rather than work the same hours as previously, even though more were on offer.[53] This aroused the ire of medieval moralists, such as John Gower (c. 1330–1408) and William Langland, who upbraided the lazy, greedy laborer. However, this contemporary view has to be tempered by the evidence for a growing demand for better clothes, food, and ale from the lower echelons, all of which had to be paid for. Households were also able to tap into the increasing demand for other by-employments, which employed more members of the household. However, such work was intermittent even in the post-Black Death era. "Full six-day weeks were by no means the norm and many building workers were hired by the same employer for three days one week and five other weeks."[54] Most workers still sought the backup of a small amount of land or even a cottage and commons access, which allowed supplementary means for making a living.

CONCLUSION

The vicissitudes of economic circumstances ultimately affected the availability and profit of most work. Those dependent on paid work could find their livelihoods threatened when employment opportunities were limited or real wages fell. This could happen transiently after poor harvests and more fully as population increased. The pattern and experience of work thus change as economic circumstances shifted, signalled by urbanization, commercialization, demographic fluctuations, and environmental or climate change. The medieval economy was very much based on the household unit, with few industries that gathered workers in large numbers. Work was often piecemeal, irregular, and uncertain, with a significant proportion of the population engaged in a portfolio of ways to make a living. Their livelihoods were dependent upon economic factors beyond their control, including the weather and disease, and the changing circumstances of their wealthier neighbors who might cut their number of employees at times of difficulty. For much of this period, the economy of work was very much a household affair but also an economy of makeshifts and multiplicity, with the development of specialization and protoindustrialization a slow, uneven process.

CHAPTER TWO

Picturing Work

DEIRDRE JACKSON

Illuminated manuscripts form an immensely rich literary and artistic heritage. Both texts and images preserved in these precious artifacts are vital to our understanding of how people in the Middle Ages conceived of work in general and accomplished specific tasks. Images, such as the calendar scene shown in Figure 2.1, not only inform us about technologies and methods of working, but also evoke medieval landscapes and seasonal rhythms of life.

Information about medieval labor can, of course, be gleaned from other forms of visual art, including stained glass windows, monumental sculptures, and paintings on walls and panels. Nevertheless, paintings in manuscripts, which survive in far greater numbers and better condition than artworks in other media, are the richest single source of pictorial evidence that has been preserved. This chapter, which approaches images as critical evidence of the ways people in the Middle Ages thought about and engaged in work, examines three key issues: the concept of the ideal society, philosophical and theological ideas relating to the origins of work, and gendered divisions of labor.

Most people associate medieval work with agriculture and this is a valid assumption. In the United Kingdom today, agriculture employs an estimated 2 percent of the workforce and contributes less than 0.1 percent to the national income, but in the Middle Ages, agricultural products exceeded all other exports, and agricultural labor provided at least three-quarters of England's income.[1] The dominance of agriculture in the premodern economy throughout Europe is reflected in illustrated calendars, featuring the twelve signs of the zodiac, typically paired with images of peasants performing a range of seasonal tasks, from pruning vines to slaughtering pigs. Preserved in thousands of liturgical and devotional books, from modest volumes to the famous *Très riches heures*, depictions of the "labors of the months," especially late examples, are among the most widely reproduced, and consequently, familiar, medieval images devoted to the theme of work.

THE LABORS OF THE MONTHS

Two Anglo-Saxon manuscripts, the Julius Hymnal and Tiberius Miscellany, preserve the earliest surviving medieval calendars incorporating tableau-style scenes of workers in landscape settings.[2] These illustrative cycles, dating, respectively, from the early eleventh century and the second quarter of the eleventh century, show groups of men digging and sowing, cutting wood, bringing in the harvest, and completing other tasks relevant to the given months. In both manuscripts, the December calendar pages are illustrated

FIGURE 2.1 September calendar page. Spinola Hours, c. 1510–20. Bruges and Ghent, Belgium. Los Angeles, The J. Paul Getty Museum, Ludwig MS IX 18, folio 5ᵛ. © The J. Paul Getty Museum, Los Angeles.

PICTURING WORK 33

with threshing scenes. Details, including a man with a tally stick who records the amount of grain threshed, are thought by some scholars to reflect actual Anglo-Saxon farming customs.³ However, women, regardless of their industry, are absent from these scenes.

With their groups of energetic workers, these exceptional Anglo-Saxon images stand outside the broad tradition of medieval calendar illustration, which is characterized by the use of twelve separate figures to represent the twelve months, a convention rooted in late antiquity. Made in Salzburg around 818, the manuscript shown in Figure 2.2, which includes works on calendrical calculations and astronomy, is the

FIGURE 2.2 Labors of the months. Miscellany, c. 818. Salzburg. Vienna, Österreichische Nationalbibliothek, MS 387, folio 90ᵛ. © Österreichische Nationalbibliothek, Vienna.

earliest extant volume to include a solitary male figure, one for each month, engaged in an appropriate activity, from warming himself at a fire (January) to butchering a pig (December).[4]

From the twelfth century onwards, across western Europe, calendars decorated with similar male figures, one allotted to each page, were produced in vast numbers. The figures were typically set within a small roundel or frame, providing little, if any, sense of place. Gradually, as more space was devoted to the labors of the months, particularly in lavish books of hours, illuminators began to depict women working alongside men and to provide more descriptive settings. Far from declining, the art of illustrating calendars was reinvigorated in the sixteenth century as the Middle Ages drew to a close. In northern Europe, painters, including the Flemish master Simon Bening (c. 1483–1561), depicted workers in increasingly naturalistic ways, often devoting two facing pages to each month and creating complex compositions replete with details inspired by daily life. In some late medieval calendar scenes, which reflect economic realities, townspeople, including butchers and market traders, are represented among the workforce. Paintings by Pieter Bruegel the Elder (1525–69), including his famous *Harvesters* (1565), a monumental reinvention of a medieval calendar scene, attest to the vitality of a pictorial tradition dating back 800 years.

DEPICTIONS OF WORKERS

Although the majority of people throughout Europe were employed in agrarian jobs, countless other types of workers, spanning all social classes, from rulers and high-ranking ecclesiastics to tradespeople and artisans, are represented in medieval manuscripts. Resplendent in their academic robes, masters are shown, for example, disseminating knowledge in a cycle of images from an early-fifteenth-century Parisian copy of Jean Corbechon's *Le livre des propriétés des choses* (*On the Properties of Things*), a French translation of Bartholomaeus Anglicus' popular encyclopedia, *De proprietatibus rerum*. As shown in Figure 2.3, in the miniature introducing the fifth book, concerning the body, a physician, holding a urine flask, makes a diagnosis and prepares to treat his patients, including a man with a wounded chest and a woman with a heavily bandaged arm. Evidently, the illuminator was attuned to the text, which describes a range of ailments requiring medical intervention.

An opulent, Italian pontifical made for Francesco Pizolpasso, bishop of Pavia (1427–35) and archbishop of Milan (1435–43), includes over one hundred initials showing bishops conducting liturgical ceremonies. Among these scenes, reflecting the power and pomp of the clergy, is an image of a barber performing a less elevated but equally essential task. As depicted in Figure 2.4, wielding a straight razor and wearing a short white apron on which to wipe it, he prepares a priest for the Mass, to the apparent fascination of an acolyte. In addition to secular ecclesiastics, nuns and monks engaged in the work of God (*opus Dei*) are well represented in medieval manuscripts. In the *Rule of St. Benedict* (c. 530–40), the most influential monastic rule in western Europe, the spiritual duties undertaken by monks and nuns are compared to tools (*instrumenta*) and the monastery itself is likened to a workshop (*officina*). Besides the devotional labors expected of every monk and nun, priors and prioresses, sacristans and cellarers are also shown performing specific jobs assigned to them. For example, in an initial from a copy of Aldobrandinus of Siena's, *Régime du corps*,

FIGURE 2.3 Physician with patients. Jean Corbechon, *Le livre des propriétés des choses*, c. 1415. Paris, France. Cambridge, Fitzwilliam Museum, MS 251, folio 53ᵛ. © The Fitzwilliam Museum, Cambridge.

made in northern France, around 1265–70, a monk in charge of provisions is shown fetching wine from the cellar, tasting it first to ensure that it is fit to serve.[5]

MONASTIC CONCEPTIONS OF WORK

Early Christian monks placed a high value on physical labor, but as monastic communities, endowed with land, grew wealthy, fewer monks worked with their own hands. Achieving a balance between the active and the contemplative life was the objective of reformers such as the Carolingian monk Benedict of Aniane (747–821), whose work ethic was

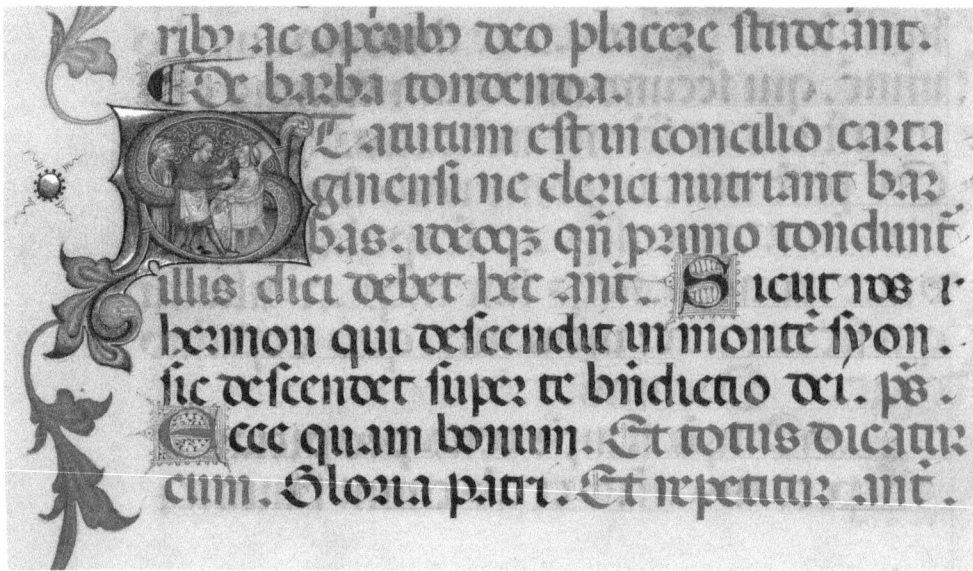

FIGURE 2.4 Barber shaving a priest. Pontifical, c. 1435– c. 1440. Milan or Pavia, Italy. Cambridge, Fitzwilliam Museum, MS 28, folio 10ᵛ. © The Fitzwilliam Museum, Cambridge.

unsurpassed. Combining physical labor with spiritual exercises, he would recite the psalms as he plowed, and although he prayed without ceasing and devoted himself to writing, he also undertook menial tasks, including working in the kitchen and polishing shoes.[6] Another great reformer, the Cistercian Bernard of Clairvaux (1091–1153), likewise stressed the importance of manual labor. Writing to his cousin Robert of Châtillon, who had left the monastic community at Clairvaux in favor of a less ascetic lifestyle at the Benedictine monastery of Cluny, he chided:

> Rise up, gird yourself, stop being lazy, show strength, do something with your hands, work in some way, and you will find you need to eat only to satisfy your hunger, not to tempt your appetite ... Laziness makes you fastidious, work makes you hungry, and it is wonderful to find how work will bring back the taste to that which idleness has rendered insipid. Vegetables, beans, roots, bread, and water are poor fare to a lazy man, but they seem very good to someone who works hard.[7]

The decorated initial reproduced in Figure 2.5, which shows Cistercian monks felling trees in order to clear land on which to build, embodies the early ideals of the Order, founded in 1098 by a group of monks led by Robert Molesme.

INTERPRETING IMAGES

Medieval illustrations of laborers are not, of course, straightforward reflections of historical realities. Children are very rarely shown working, for instance, although it was normal for medieval children to perform set tasks, and many worked full-time as soon as they were physically able. In addition to acknowledging gaps in the visual record, it is important to recognize that paintings are governed by artistic conventions. Among the most common types of manuscripts that have survived are Books of Hours, devotional books that were often lavishly illuminated. It was standard for illuminators to include in the sequence of miniatures illustrating the Hours of the Virgin a depiction of the Annunciation to the Shepherds, showing a group of male peasants in a pastoral landscape, watching over their flocks. In France, in the late fifteenth century a change occurred; women began to be incorporated in compositions of this type. It would be a mistake to interpret the proliferation of shepherdesses in these scenes as proof of a burgeoning female workforce schooled in livestock management. Rather, the inclusion of women is a reflection of changing artistic styles and tastes.[8] Placing women alongside men transformed the conventional imagery and added a romantic charge to the happy occasion. In a full-page miniature from the Hours of Charles d'Angoulême, reproduced in Figure 2.6, the shepherds and shepherdesses join hands and dance to the consternation of their sheep, whose quizzical expressions betray their surprise.

An image of the Nativity from another French Book of Hours, shown in Figure 2.7, likewise departs from the standard iconography because it depicts Joseph, rather than Mary, holding the Christ child. By the late fifteenth century, when it was painted, ideas about Joseph's character and relationship to Mary had undergone a paradigm shift. In both the visual arts and medieval drama, particularly in German Nativity plays, he was assigned greater prominence. No longer an isolated, elderly foster father, distanced from his son, he was shown performing childcare duties, including cooking baby food, rocking the cradle, supervising at bath time, and drying diapers.[9] In the plays, especially, he is often treated as a figure of fun, an inept bumbler incapable of completing the simplest task, but, over time, his maternal duties were interpreted more positively as a demonstration of love for his wife and child.[10] As Joseph gained respect as a virtuous family man, he came to be regarded as the patron saint of fathers, a role he fulfills to this day, alongside his role as patron saint of manual workers, especially carpenters. Images like the one shown in Figure 2.7, reflecting constructions of masculinity, also shed light on the work of parenting.[11]

In order to interpret images in manuscripts it is crucial to understand both the social circumstances in which they were conceived and the textual contexts in which they appear. Taken at face value, the image reproduced in Figure 2.8 shows a noblewoman supervising her female gardener. But the illustration, from a Middle Dutch copy of *Le livre de la cité des Dames* (*Book of the City of Ladies*), a polemical book, written as a vindication of women by Christine de Pizan (c. 1364–1431), is more complex than it first appears. It is actually an allegorical illustration, showing Christine and a female personification of Reason clearing the Field of Letters of misogynist opinion in preparation for building the utopian "City of Ladies." Reason, wearing a conical headdress, hoists up her gown to avoid getting it sullied, while Christine, the protofeminist, whose dress mirrors the garment worn by Reason, digs with the "spade of her intelligence." This manuscript is the only extant copy of the Middle Dutch version of Christine's *Book of the City of Ladies*, and the very first translation of the text into any language. Completed around the same time as the manuscript (c. 1475), the translation, *Het Bouc van de Stede der Vrauwen*, predates the first English version by about fifty years.[12]

Illuminators copied motifs from completed manuscripts, model books, and other visual sources, and they invariably worked from preparatory sketches and written instructions rather than live models. Some most likely had little knowledge of the texts that they were called upon to illustrate, while others could understand the contents. Regardless of their degrees of literacy, illuminators exercised freedom of interpretation, and depictions of

FIGURE 2.5 Cistercian monks felling trees. Gregory the Great, *Moralia in Job*, Cîteaux, completed on Christmas Eve, 1111. Dijon, France. Bibliothèque municipale de Dijon, MS 170, folio 59ʳ. © Bibliothèque municipale de Dijon, Dijon.

workers were often shaped by personal observations. For example, illuminators typically portrayed styles of dress according to fashions worn by their contemporaries. Dressed in a simple gray tunic, the butcher depicted in Figure 2.9, an illustration from an Italian health handbook (*Tacuinum sanitatis*), is easily distinguished from his customer, who clutches a pair of gloves and wears an elegant blue robe, ornamented with fur. Whether monastic habits, royal robes, or ragged breeches, garments were the most obvious signs of social rank in a hierarchical society. Since relatively few medieval garments have survived, paintings in manuscripts are an unrivalled source of information about the kinds of clothing worn by workers, which varied from period to period and region to region.

PICTURING WORK 39

FIGURE 2.6 Shepherds and shepherdesses dancing. Hours of Charles d'Angoulême, 1475–1500. Paris, France. Paris, Bibliothèque nationale de France, MS lat. 1173, folio 20ᵛ. © BnF, Paris.

Because illuminators also based agricultural implements and other tools on items in use in their own day, images of workers—even legendary, historical, or biblical figures—are grounded in the real world. Given the sparse survival of artifacts, there are, in fact, tools

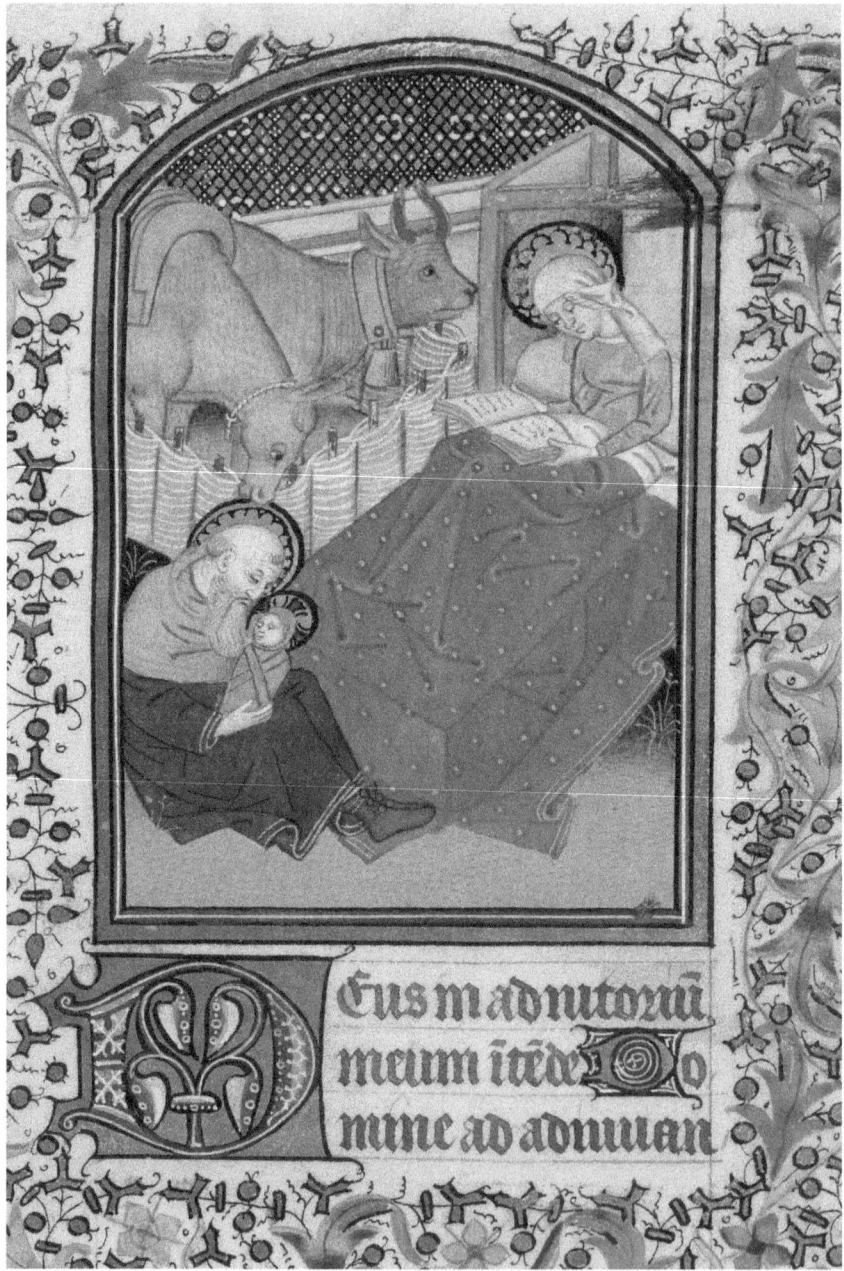

FIGURE 2.7 Joseph holds the Christ Child while Mary reads. Book of Hours, c. 1460–70. Besançon, France. Cambridge, Fitzwilliam Museum, MS 69, folio 48ʳ. © The Fitzwilliam Museum, Cambridge.

and working methods that we would not know existed if we relied on archaeological evidence alone.[13] And even when we are fortunate enough to have tools uncovered by archaeologists, the objects in isolation do not tell the full story of their use. Paintings in

PICTURING WORK 41

FIGURE 2.8 Lady Reason and Christine de Pizan. Christine de Pizan, *Le livre de la cité des Dames*, translated as *Het Bouc van de Stede der Vrauwen*, 1475. Bruges, Belgium. London, British Library, Add. MS 20698, folio 17ʳ. © The British Library, London.

manuscripts, which show people in action, provide unparalleled insights into the world of work, augmenting and often surpassing information derived from both the archaeological record and written sources. The calendar scene attributed to Simon Bening, which is shown in Figure 2.10, not only records the size and shape of a medieval billhook, the traditional cutting tool used for trimming trees to clear away dead branches, but also shows the implement in use.

Far more effectively than any other source, pictures in manuscripts preserve information on methods and techniques of working, showing us, for example, the appearance of a spinning wheel, turned by the touch of a finger on the spokes rather than a pedal. Many workers are pictured in border decorations or *bas-de-page* scenes unrelated to texts. This rich and often comic body of evidence, which includes hundreds of pictures of animals lampooning human activities, such as Figure 2.11, offers unparalleled insights into medieval ways of working and modes of thought.[14]

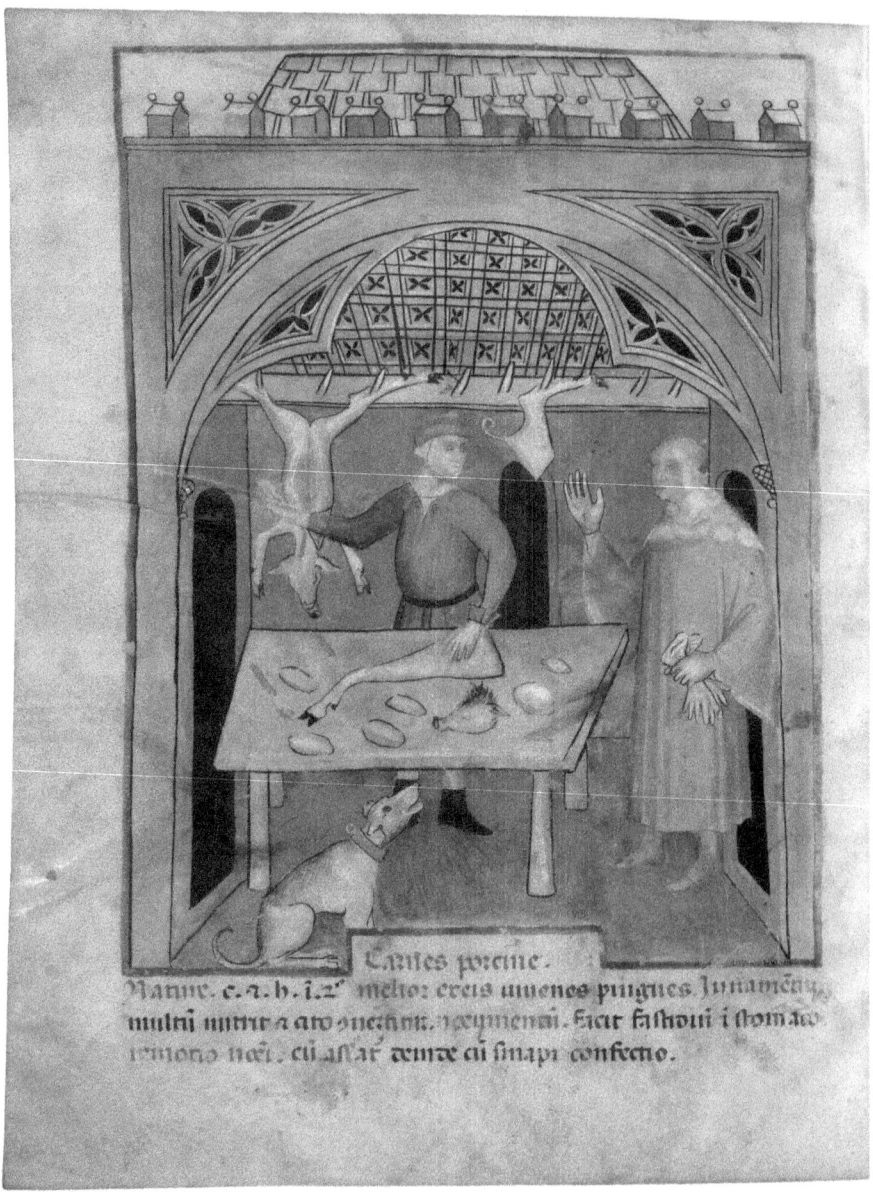

FIGURE 2.9 Butcher in his shop. *Tacuinum sanitatis*, c. 1390–1400. Lombardy. Paris, Bibliothèque nationale de France, MS nouv. acq. lat. 1673, folio 63ᵛ. © BnF, Paris.

THE THREE ORDERS

Medieval philosophers and writers conceived of society in various ways. No single model prevailed.[15] By the late twelfth century, however, one of the dominant ideas was that medieval society consisted of three orders or "estates." One of the earliest known references to this concept in western literature is found in the work of the ninth-century

FIGURE 2.10 Calendar scene attributed to Simon Bening (Flemish, c. 1483–1561). Book of Hours, c. 1550. Bruges, Belgium. Los Angeles, The J. Paul Getty Museum, MS 50 verso. © The J. Paul Getty Museum, Los Angeles.

Anglo-Saxon king Alfred the Great (871–99). In his Anglo-Saxon translation of Boethius' *Consolation of Philosophy*, he glossed a passage on temporal power, adding that for a king to govern successfully he should have "a well-populated land ... [comprising] men of prayer, men of war, [and] men of labor."[16] Writing around 1025, Gerard, bishop of Cambrai, divided society in a similar way, stating: "from the beginning, mankind has been divided into three parts ... men of prayer, farmers and men of war."[17]

The idea of a society composed of *sapientes, militares,* and *vulgares* was also known to classical antiquity. Plato's *Republic*, which describes an ideal city, was not available to western European thinkers in the Middle Ages. However, a summary of it was inserted at the beginning of Plato's *Timaeus*, a work that had been translated from Greek into Latin by the fourth-century philosopher Calcidius, who wrote an extensive commentary on it. Because the *Timaeus* was the only Platonic dialogue continuously available to western scholars from classical antiquity to the renaissance, its influence was wide-reaching.[18] In his version of the *Timaeus*, Calcidius emphasized the hierarchical nature of the tripartite model, with those who pray occupying the highest level, knights the middle tier, and common men (*vulgares*), the lowest position.

An historiated initial illustrating the concept of the three orders occurs in a copy of a popular encyclopedia in French, entitled *L'image du monde* (*The Image of the World*), composed by the priest Gossuin de Metz around 1245. Gossuin's encyclopedia, which survives in approximately seventy manuscripts, covers a range of subjects, including cosmology, the seven liberal arts, theology, astronomy, and natural history.[19] The initial, shown in Figure 2.12, introduces the sixth chapter, which is devoted to the three orders, as outlined in the rubric, which reads: "Of the three types of men which the philosophers set in the world." Shown in the large initial C (for clergy), the opening word of the chapter, are a priest, a knight, and a laborer. The text emphasizes both the importance of the clergy and the power wielded by the knights in France, and these figures do, indeed,

FIGURE 2.11 Monkey schoolmaster with pupils. The Metz Pontifical, c. 1303–16. Metz or Verdun, France. Cambridge, Fitzwilliam Museum, MS 298, folio 76v. © The Fitzwilliam Museum, Cambridge.

dominate the composition. Standing on the knight's right, a position of privilege, the priest gestures with authority as he addresses his companion who is encased in armor. Although the knight's helmet restricts his vision and presumably muffles the lecture, his raised hand suggests that he is actively engaged in the conversation.

As explained by Gossuin de Metz, the chief duty of the knight is to protect members of the other orders, an obligation symbolized by his large, orange shield. Significantly, the knight is not shown with a sword—his shield alone indicates that he is the defender of the realm. The laborer, on the knight's left, is not included in the discussion, although he listens from the periphery, like a shy guest at an exclusive party. Nevertheless, as articulated in the text, his contribution to society is equally vital. By his work in the fields, symbolized by his spade, he supplies members of the higher orders with necessary provisions.

The tripartite model continued to influence political thought throughout the medieval period and was further disseminated by William Caxton's English translation of Gossuin de Metz's *L'image du monde*. Published in Westminster in 1481, Caxton's translation, entitled *The Mirrour of the World*, was the first illustrated book to be printed in England.[20] A division between intellectual and physical work is inherent in this political schema, as articulated by the Dominican Robert Kilwardby, archbishop of Canterbury (1272–8), who wrote: "Physical activity is more suited to insignificant and common people, the peace of meditation and study to the noble elite; in this way, everyone has an occupation fitting his station in life."[21]

The theory of the three orders is undeniably hierarchical, but it is also collaborative. According to this model, members of each order have specific obligations associated with

FIGURE 2.12 Three orders of society. Gossuin de Metz, *L'image du monde*, c. 1265–70. Cambrai or Thérouanne/St-Omer, France. London, British Library, Sloane MS 2435, folio 85ʳ. © The British Library, London.

their professions; as they fulfill these, a harmonious society can be achieved. Each member of society must perform his or her duty, and negligence leads to ruin. In his seminal article on ideological representations of peasant labor, Jonathan J. G. Alexander called attention to several images depicting the negative consequences of idleness.[22] Among Alexander's earliest examples is an image of a shepherd with his flock from the Aberdeen bestiary, a beautifully illustrated English manuscript, made around 1200 (Aberdeen, Aberdeen University Library, MS 24, folio 16ᵛ). Overcome with fatigue, the shepherd falls asleep, leaving his charges in jeopardy, a situation exploited by an opportunistic wolf that is undeterred by the snarling guard dog. In a Parisian miniature (Figure 2.13) painted approximately one hundred years later to illustrate a deluxe copy of the *Somme le roi* (*Survey for the King*), most likely made for Philip IV (1268–1314) king of France, the virtue of labor, represented by an energetic sower, is contrasted with the vice of sloth, typified by an idle plowman who cradles his head in his hands, as if overwhelmed by his task. Despite Alexander's assertion to the contrary, the plowman is not shown sleeping. Rather, he stares listlessly to one side, as if overwhelmed by depression, rather than fatigue.

THE VICE OF SLOTH

In its original iteration, the vice of sloth (*paresse*) was equated with failure to perform spiritual duties, a lack of motivation on the part of monks and nuns who neglected singing the Psalms, for instance, or clerics who skipped their devotions or avoided services. Though some might have willfully avoided these responsibilities, for others the problem was not so much one of laziness, as of doubt and despair, feelings closely related to melancholy. In the late medieval period, when slothfulness was more broadly defined, the term was applied to anyone who shunned practical work. For the English Dominican John Bromyard (d. c. 1352), idlers who contributed nothing to the economy, were worthy of eternal damnation. In his *Summa praedicantium*, he stated:

> God has ordained three classes of men ... And all the aforesaid who maintain their status are of the family of God. The Devil, however, finds a certain class, namely the slothful, who belong to no Order. They neither labour with the rustics, nor travel about with the merchants, nor fight with the knights, nor pray and chant with the clergy. Therefore, they shall go with their own Abbot, of whose Order they are, namely, the Devil, where no order exists, but horror eternal.[23]

To describe the vice of sloth, Bromyard resorted to several metaphors, including an unused plow.[24] The analogy may have been suggested by Proverbs 20:4, which reads: "because of the cold the sluggard would not plough he shall beg therefore in the summer, and it shall not be given him." It is probable that the connection between the vice of sloth and this tool also inspired the depiction of the listless plowman in the image from the *Somme le roi*, reproduced in Figure 2.13.

THE VIRTUE OF LABOR

Medieval Christians generally equated industry with virtue, an idea articulated in hundreds of moralizing works. Few are as engaging as Ælfric of Eynsham's *Colloquy on the Occupations*, written by the Benedictine master in the 990s as a Latin teaching aid for his male pupils—novice monks, and possibly boys from affluent families, who were being educated at the abbey of Cerne Abbas in Dorset. The *Colloquy* consists of a dialogue between a master (the role played by Ælfric) and various laborers and craftsmen (adult roles played by his young pupils). Ælfric must have devised this exercise to appeal to his charges, which suggests that children took as much pleasure in imitating adults in Anglo-Saxon times as they do today. Each pupil/worker describes his job, emphasizing the great effort he expends, from the plowman who prepares his lord's fields to the merchant who risks his life crossing the seas to buy foreign treasures. The discussion ends with a debate over which occupation is superior, with primacy given to the religious life by a counsellor who advises each worker to "pursue his trade diligently," stating, "whoever you are, whether priest or monk or peasant or soldier, exercise yourself in this, and be what you are; because it is a great disgrace and shame for a man not to want to be what he is, and what he has to be."[25] Ælfric's *Colloquy* reminds us that in his day, as in late antiquity, occupations remained central to the formation of personal identity and served as markers of social status. People continued to be defined by their jobs throughout the Middle Ages. Workers were expected to perform to the best of their abilities, whatever their calling, in order to make a vital contribution to the common good.

FIGURE 2.13 Labor and Idleness. *Somme le roi (Traite des vertus)*, c. 1295. Paris, France. London, British Library, Add. MS 54180, folio 121ᵛ. © The British Library, London.

A society composed of different members who know their place and complete their allotted tasks without dozing or dissenting is presented in a sequence of *bas-de-page* scenes in a justifiably famous Psalter, made around 1340 for the landowner Sir Geoffrey Luttrell, lord of the manor at Irnham in Lincolnshire. In one image, which emphasizes Luttrell's role as knight of the realm, he is shown mounted on his steed, receiving his helmet and lance from his wife Agnes Sutton, and his shield from his daughter-in-law Beatrice Le Scrope (London, British Library, Add. MS 42130, folio 202ᵛ). All three are outfitted in clothing emblazoned with their heraldic arms, garments that celebrate their family ties and aristocratic standing. An inscription written directly above the image, "Dominus Galfridus louterell me fieri fecit" (The Lord Geoffrey Luttrell caused me to be made), further identifies Luttrell as the proud commissioner of the book. Although patrons are often portrayed in medieval devotional books, comparable inscriptions are exceedingly rare, and, in fact, "no other owner of an elaborate illuminated manuscript of the period had himself portrayed in this way."[26]

This idealized portrait of lordship is best understood in the context of a unique *bas-de-page* cycle of images of men and women working on Luttrell's estates. Some are engaged in agricultural tasks, such as the plowman, while others, including cooks and servants, carry out domestic duties. Overseeing their efforts is Geoffrey Luttrell, portrayed at the center of the banqueting scene (Figure 2.14) as a benevolent patriarch dining with members of his household, including two Dominican friars, at hand to offer their counsel.[27] Men who pray, men who fight, and men who work are juxtaposed in this image, which evokes the tripartite model. As Geoffrey Luttrell fulfills his knightly and administrative duties, his dependents, laborers and spiritual advisors perform their assigned tasks. These images contain naturalistic depictions of tools deployed by workers, and are valuable sources of information on medieval dress, but they cannot, of course, be interpreted uncritically. The connection between occupation and social status is firmly expressed in the images of the Luttrell Psalter, which uphold the status quo.

Based on an inequitable distribution of resources, the feudal system, which limited social mobility and justified extreme imbalances of power, did not go unchallenged.[28] The English Peasants' Revolt of 1381 is but one expression of dissatisfaction by workers, but it is notable for its size and because it was the first time that peasants and tradesmen, rather than members of the aristocracy, led a rebellion against the English state. Thousands of insurgents gathered in London to air their grievances before the young king Richard II.[29] From Essex, Kent, and London the rebellion spread elsewhere, including Cambridge where it resulted in the burning of the ancient charters of the university by the mayor and townspeople who resented the royal privileges enjoyed by the academic elite.[30] In the fifteenth century, religious reformers were also critical of the unequal distribution of wealth and power, deeming the oppression of the workers by the rulers and clergy to be the antithesis of the egalitarian ideals advocated by Christ.[31]

THE FOUR ESTATES

The idea that it is possible to exist on the fringes of society and lead a self-sufficient life with a minimum of effort is not a product of the 1960s. The captivating miniature by Jean Bourdichon shown in Figure 2.15, one of a series of four, painted around 1500, depicts a wild man, standing at the entrance to his cave, which is conveniently located beside a bubbling spring.[32] Seated nearby on the grass is his attractive, blond wife who suckles their contented infant. Like the other paintings in the series, this one survives as a

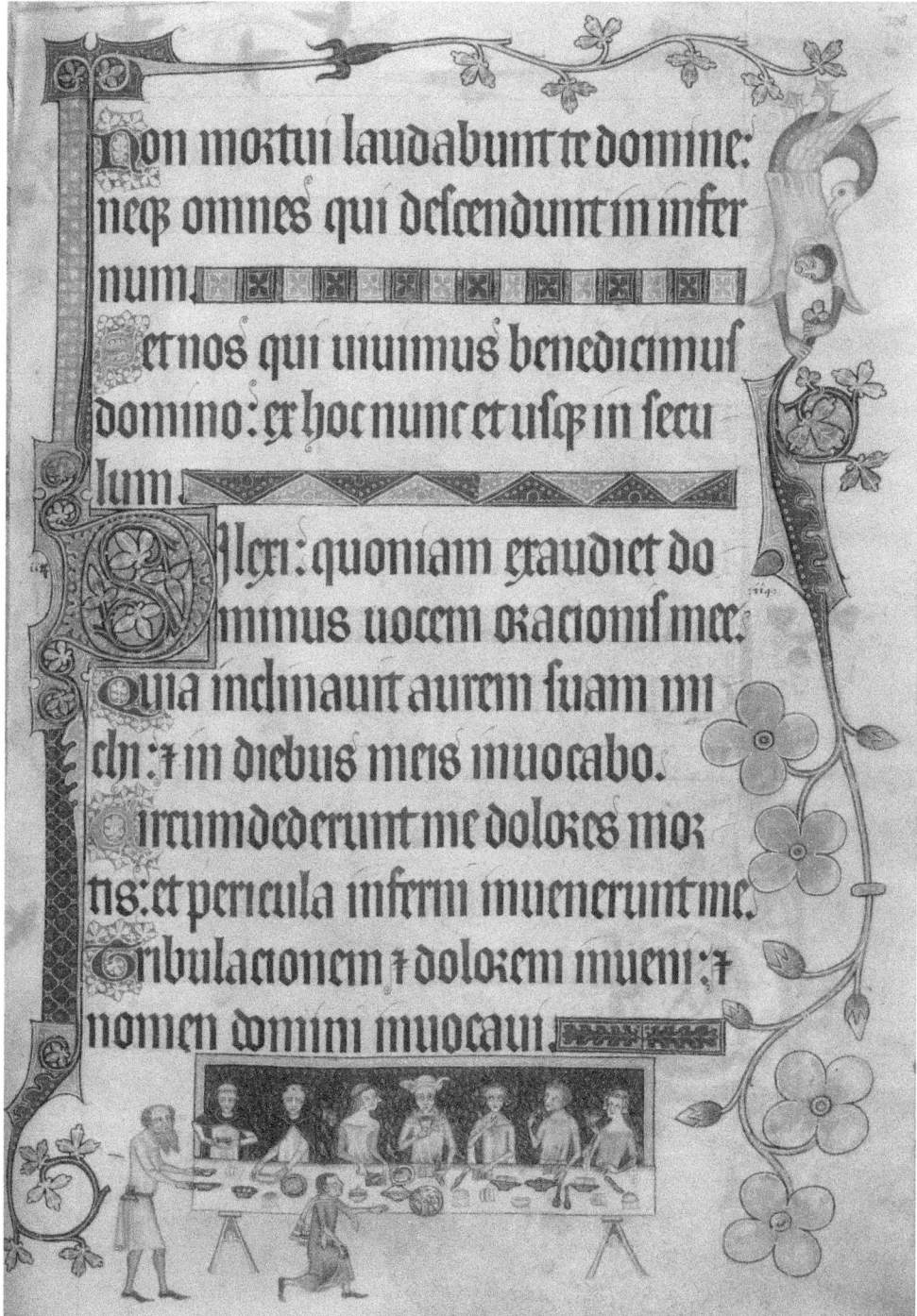

FIGURE 2.14 The Luttrells feasting. Luttrell Psalter, c. 1340. Lincolnshire, England. London, British Library, Add. MS 42130, folio 208ʳ. © The British Library, London.

detached leaf that is blank on the reverse; it was either cut from a manuscript or intended from the start to be displayed as an independent work of art. Research has revealed that the miniatures were inspired by a sequence of anonymous ballads concerning the "four estates of society": *état de sauvage, la pauvreté, le travail*, and *la noblesse*.[33]

The ballad of the wild estate (*état de sauvage*), expresses the wild man's personal philosophy. In the fifth stanza, he proclaims:

> I live according to what Nature has taught me—
> Free from worry, always joyously.
> For mighty castles, grand palaces I do not care.
> In a hollow tree I make my home.
> I do not delight in fancy food
> Or in strong drink.
> I live upon fresh fruit alone,
> And so I have, thank God, enough.[34]

As shown in the miniature, he has turned his back on the lofty fortresses rising up in the distance, a stance that accentuates his rejection of social norms. "Prince," he declares in the final stanza, "what good is it to live so proudly / And to plunder just to lead a pompous life, / When at the moment of one's death / A shroud alone will be enough." For the wild man, an independent life, uncluttered by possessions, is superior to any other.

A more moderate viewpoint is expressed in the ballad of the working life, which served as the basis of an image of a carpenter planing a board in his workshop, which is filled with a wide array of tools. As shown in Figure 2.16, intricate carvings, including the linenfold patterns on the bench in the foreground, advertise his skill. Like the wild man, the carpenter has accepted his lot in life. Although he must work to support himself, his wife helps him by spinning, which augments the family's income. Even his young son, who gathers the wood shavings that have fallen onto the floor, is cheerfully occupied. Having seen men ruined by poverty and riches alike, the carpenter asserts, "there is none better than the middle way."[35] Although the ballad mentions spinning—the labor undertaken by the worker's wife—it does not disclose his occupation. Instead, it presents a generic picture of the worker as "everyman," stating simply that he is "happy in his trade." It is probably no coincidence that for this positive portrayal of working life, Bourdichon chose to depict a carpenter, the trade practiced by Jesus' father, Joseph.[36] Late medieval images of the Holy Family often show Joseph in his woodworking shop as Mary attends to her needlework or spinning, and the infant Jesus plays nearby.

BIBLICAL PARADIGMS

More than any other single source, the Bible shaped medieval conceptions of work, but the message articulated was ambivalent. The labor undertaken by God in order to create the cosmos, the earth, and all living things is described in the first chapter of Genesis. No one could accuse God of procrastination; having completed his work in six days, He rested on the seventh—as represented in the Stammheim Missal (Figure 2.17). God's boundless creativity and exceptional work ethic served as positive models for medieval Christians. Another positive allusion to work occurs in Genesis 2:15, which explains that after God

FIGURE 2.15 Wild man and his family painted by Jean Bourdichon, c. 1500. Tours, France. Paris, Bibliothèque de l'École Nationale Supériéure des Beaux-Arts, Mn. mas 90. © Bridgeman Art Library.

FIGURE 2.16 Carpenter and his family painted by Jean Bourdichon, c. 1500. Tours, France. Paris, Bibliothèque de l'École Nationale Superiéure des Beaux-Arts, Mn. mas 92. Image courtesy of Getty Images.

had made Adam, he placed him in Eden, described as a "Paradise of Pleasure" (*paradiso voluptatis*), "to dress it and keep it." A negative paradigm was, however, presented in the story of Adam and Eve's temptation by the serpent and disobedience, which led to their exile from Eden and consigned them to work.[37]

As recounted in Genesis 3:16–19, because they had sinned by eating the forbidden fruit, Adam was condemned to a life of perpetual labor and Eve to a life of pain and subordination. To the woman God said: "I will greatly increase your hardship and your pregnancies: in pain you shall bring forth children, and you shall be under the control of your husband, and he shall rule over you." And to Adam he said:

> cursed is the ground that you shall work: in toil you shall eat of it all the days of your life. Thorns and thistles it shall bring forth for you, and you shall eat the crops of the earth. By the sweat of your face you shall eat bread until you return to the ground from which you were taken.[38]

Both the Fall and its aftermath are depicted in a stunning frontispiece (Figure 2.18) attributed to the Boucicaut Master, one of the leading Parisian illuminators of the first decades of the fifteenth century. Saturated with color, the large miniature is found in a deluxe copy of Laurent de Premierfait's *Des cas des nobles hommes et femmes*, a French translation of Giovanni Boccaccio's *De casibus virorum illustrium* (*Concerning the Fates of Illustrious Men and Women*), which opens with the story of Adam and Eve. Rendered in cotton candy pink, a hexagonal wall separates the verdant Garden of Eden, where the couple succumbs to temptation, from the harsh world into which they are driven by an angel. At the top left, Adam, bent over his hoe, tills the dry ground, and at the top right, Eve tends her flock and spins. As shown on the lower right, as they approach Boccaccio, to tell him their story, their stooped figures, gnarled features, and unsteady steps betray long, hard lives of unremitting labor.

As noted above, in the biblical narrative, Adam is assigned a specific task, but no particular job, other than bearing children, is allocated to Eve. Nevertheless, as early as the fifth century, Eve is shown spinning while Adam digs, and the motif became standard by the twelfth century.[39] That both of them must work as punishment for their sins is emphasized in the caption of a *bas-de-page* scene in the Carew-Poyntz Hours, shown in Figure 2.19, which was made in England around 1350–60. Written in Anglo-Norman French, the caption reads: "Coment Adam et Eve conquistrent leur viure par travayle de corps" (How Adam and Eve gained their living by physical work).

How Adam acquired his spade is not explained in the Old Testament. However, in some medieval images, including Figure 2.20, a full-page painting in the Carrow Psalter, made in East Anglia around 1250, an angel, swooping down from heaven, gives Adam and Eve their respective implements.[40] Miniatures showing the angel distributing these tools to Adam and Eve date back to the twelfth century.[41] It is possible, however, that a textual source, rather than a pictorial model, inspired the image in the Carrow Psalter. A thirteenth-century Middle English paraphrase of Genesis, for example, describes how an angel was sent by God to help the distraught couple to cope with the cruel realities of their new lives and to assure them that Paradise would one day be restored.[42]

Eve, the first woman to become adept at multitasking, is frequently shown caring for her children as she spins, and sometimes she also tends a pot of food, bubbling on the hearth.[43] There is a clear distinction between the domestic sphere in which she works and the larger world in which Adam toils, unconstrained by the bounds of the household. Images of this type not only reflect medieval ideas about gendered divisions of labor, but

FIGURE 2.17 Creation. Stammheim Missal, probably 1170s. Hildesheim, Germany. Los Angeles, The J. Paul Getty Museum, Getty MS 64, folio 10^v. © The J. Paul Getty Museum, Los Angeles.

PICTURING WORK 55

FIGURE 2.18 Adam and Eve. Boccaccio, translated by Laurent de Premierfait, *Des cas des nobles hommes et femmes*, c. 1415. Paris, France. Los Angeles, The J. Paul Getty Museum, Getty, MS 63, folio 3ʳ. © The J. Paul Getty Museum, Los Angeles.

also served to reinforce such distinctions for their original viewers. Confronted by images of Adam and Eve working, medieval men and women would have understood that their own lives were conditioned by the Fall and its consequences.

GENDERED DIVISIONS OF LABOR

In a patriarchal society, divisions of labor based on gender were the norm. Although some women performed jobs traditionally assigned to men, the reverse was rare. One of the main obstacles that prevented women from making a greater contribution to the medieval economy was the idea that women's work differed from men's in fundamental ways. Though some women were surely capable of guiding a plow or swinging an axe, they were generally denied these opportunities. According to his biographer, Odo of Cluny, when the saintly Count Gerald of Aurillac (c. 855–c. 909) happened to see a woman plowing, he demanded to know why. When she confided that her husband was ill and that she had no one else to help her, he gave her enough money to hire a laborer so that she could "cease from doing the work of a man" (*opus virile*). After recounting this anecdote, Odo adds approvingly: "Nature flees from everything artificial ... and its author, God, abhors what is unnatural."[44]

That jobs were socially determined is suggested by the fact that a task like sowing was rarely relegated to women although it was less demanding than other agricultural chores, such as weeding and shearing sheep, which they were permitted to do. The sower of the crop—the disseminator of seed—was, invariably, male. Conversely, the task of spinning, almost never undertaken by men, was a job that women of every social class were taught to perform, and one that came to define them.[45] Among the "womanly accomplishments" that he expected

FIGURE 2.19 Adam and Eve working. Carew-Poyntz Hours, fourteenth century. England. Cambridge, Fitzwilliam Museum, MS 48, folio 15ʳ. © The Fitzwilliam Museum, Cambridge.

his daughters to master, Charlemagne (c. 742–814) listed learning to spin and weave wool.[46] More than any other job, apart from childcare, spinning was viewed as women's work, and the distaff, more than any other tool, was viewed as a symbol of femininity. Few women were exempt from this activity. According to a late medieval source from Strasbourg, even a

FIGURE 2.20 Angel gives tools to Adam and Eve. Carrow Psalter, mid-thirteenth century. East Anglia, England. Baltimore, Walters Art Museum, MS W. 34, folio 22ᵛ. © The Walters Art Museum, Baltimore.

woman with no hands and only one foot acquired the skill. Exploiting her disability, the man who discovered her charged onlookers a penny each to watch her work.[47]

Women who devoted themselves to embroidery or spinning viewed the Virgin Mary as a role model because it was believed that she had been taught to weave at the Temple in Jerusalem where she had been educated as a young girl. Theologians contrasted the virtuous work of Mary with the punitive labor imposed on Eve. In medieval art, innumerable women are depicted with distaffs, rods on which flax or wool was wound before being spun with the attached drop spindles. In the Luttrell Psalter, for example, a distaff is shown tucked under the arm of a woman feeding chickens, reminding us that women and girls frequently did their spinning while performing other chores.[48] Various manuscripts contain images of women brandishing distaffs with which they attempt to chase foxes away from their prized ducks, chickens, or geese.[49] Some depict disgruntled women beating men with their distaffs.[50] Images of women triumphing over men are not, of course, advertisements for female emancipation, but serve instead as satirical comments on the discourse of power between the sexes.

Although spinning continued to be one of the main tasks relegated to women throughout the Middle Ages, by the mid-eleventh century, as the production of textiles grew more commercialized, the locus of manufacture shifted from rural homes to urban workshops. Around the same time, men, working as dyers, weavers, and fullers, began to infiltrate the cloth industry. These changes were concurrent with the development of a market economy based on widespread trade and more streamlined patterns of production, with merchants overseeing the entire process from procuring the raw materials to selling the fabrics. Although women continued to spin and make cloth on a domestic scale, as the trade became more profit-oriented, female weavers were increasingly marginalized.[51]

Professional occupations, including jobs within the church, academe, and the law, were reserved for people with an education, which was the prerogative of the male elite. Neither women nor men from the lower ranks of society would have had access to learning, and literacy was not widespread. While class largely determined whether or not a person learned to read, gender also played a part. Girls were excluded from the grammar, cathedral, and collegiate church schools where boys received instruction, and women were barred from attending universities. Many women, both lay and religious, were educated in convents, and most royal and aristocratic women would have received some instruction from tutors. However, the fact that men controlled access to formal education prevented the majority of women from participating fully in intellectual culture and from pursuing careers related to the production of knowledge.

Christine de Pizan, one of the first women to earn her living as a writer, was an exception. A prolific and versatile author, Christine experimented with different genres. Her literary output encompasses poems, biographies, conduct books, mythological, military, and political treatises, and prose allegories, including her famous *Book of the City of Ladies*, rebutting misogynistic rhetoric. Secular, female authors were almost nonexistent in her lifetime, a fact stressed by Christine who characterized her works as "new things deriving from a woman's perspective."[52] Christine acknowledged that women who wanted to realize their intellectual potential in a society that privileged men had to move beyond the traditional roles of wife and mother. In effect, they had to undergo a metaphorical transformation and adopt a male gender themselves, as Christine herself had done when she was suddenly widowed at age twenty-four in 1389.[53]

In a deluxe copy of her collected works (London, British Library, Harley MS 4431), an anthology of thirty texts, embellished with 130 miniatures, she is depicted at her desk, making notes in a bound volume, while her little dog waits patiently at her feet. Reproduced in Figure 2.21, the image, which functions as a pictorial verification of her authorship of the text, reflects artistic conventions, rather than actual practices. Texts were normally written on unbound sheets of parchment, but medieval authors, translators, and compilers, as well as scribes, are frequently shown writing in bound volumes. Furthermore, although authors are generally portrayed working in isolation, making manuscripts was a collaborative process. Authors often dictated texts to scribes rather than wielded a pen themselves. Idealized images of writers at work, including Christine de Pizan, "are about authorial possession of the text rather than its production and are emblematic in intent rather than literal."[54]

Other miniatures in the same manuscript that reinforce Christine's learning and authority show her presenting copies of her works to her royal patrons. Unlike so many images of authors, which are retrospective "portraits," these ones were painted in Christine's own lifetime. More importantly, we can be sure that she sanctioned them because in the prologue to the volume, which she presented to Isabeau of Bavaria, queen of France, in 1414, she states that her ideas shaped both the *histoires* (images) and *escriptures* (texts). Christine possibly wrote some passages or annotations in her own hand, but professional artists and scribes, working under her guidance, completed the bulk of the work.

THE PRODUCTION OF MANUSCRIPTS

Both men and women, secular and religious, were involved in making manuscripts. The thousands of volumes that survive in libraries worldwide bear witness to this productive medieval workforce. Copying lengthy texts onto parchment with a quill and ink required concentration, stamina, and dedication, and a single text could take several years to complete. A scribal note (colophon) inserted in a Bible produced at the abbey of Bonne-Espérance in Hainault (Brussels, Bibliothèque royale de Belgique, MS II.2524) states that the text was copied by a monk named Heinrich who started the task on August 26, 1132 and finished the job in July 1135, almost three years later. As Heinrich explains, he could have finished earlier, but he "took breaks during time of fog."[55] Evidently, he was working outdoors, almost certainly in the cloister. Adverse weather conditions not only thwarted scribes. While writing one of his books, apparently in his own hand, the English chronicler and Benedictine monk Orderic Vitalis (1075–1142) was so numbed by the winter cold that he decided to postpone the task until the return of spring.[56]

The physical demands of copying texts is alluded to in an inscription inserted at the end of a large, lavishly decorated Bible made in Paris in the mid-thirteenth century (Cambridge, Fitzwilliam Museum, MS 1, folio 478ʳ). Written in Latin verse, it reads: "Pen, stay silent; I give praise to you, O Christ; may the dismal task be over; the work and the book are completed."[57] For some authors of religious works, including the sixth-century Roman statesman and writer Cassiodorus, copying sacred texts was not a dismal task but the equivalent of battling the forces of evil. Describing his efforts he wrote:

> What happy application, what praiseworthy industry, to preach unto people by means of the hand, to untie the tongue by means of the fingers, to bring quiet salvation to mortals and to fight the Devil's insidious wiles with pen and ink! For every word of the Lord written by the scribe is a wound inflicted on Satan. And so, though seated in one spot, the scribe traverses diverse lands through the dissemination of what he has written.[58]

FIGURE 2.21 Christine de Pizan. Collected works, c. 1414. Paris, France. London, British Library, Harley MS 4431, folio 4ʳ. © The British Library, London.

Given the arduous nature of their craft, it is not surprising that some scribes requested a reward when they completed a job, or expressed relief. A fourteenth-century French copy of Hrabanus Maurus' *De universo* (Leiden, Leiden University Special Collections, MS VLF 5, folio 172ᵛ), ends with a colophon, reading: "This work is written; master, give me a drink; May the right hand of the scribe be free from the oppressiveness of the pain." Although it may be tempting to view this as a personal plea, the phrases are standard formulas repeated with minor variations in other manuscripts. For example, elsewhere we find written, "May the head of the scribe be free from the oppressiveness of the pain," and "The entire [work] is finished, give me a drink of wine."[59]

Though less common, scribal notes of a genuinely personal nature, stressing the difficulties experienced by the copyist, are found in some volumes. While surveying over two hundred manuscripts copied by Italian nuns in the fifteenth and sixteenth centuries, Melissa Moreton discovered, in addition to generic expressions of conventional piety and humility, several personalized colophons. At the end of a copy of Bridget of Sweden's *Revelations* and other devotional writings, the Florentine nun Sister Cleofe (Ginevra di Lorenzo Lenzi), based at the convent of Santa Brigida del Paradiso, left an inscription, dated April 26, 1495, stating that she wrote the work "with much effort and much discomfort, most of it by lamp light."[60] At least seventeen manuscripts copied by her have been preserved, including another written by lamplight at night "with much effort and discomfort," making her the second most prolific scribe at her convent.[61]

Each letter inscribed on parchment bears witness to the scribe's talent and labor, an idea eloquently conveyed by the famous portrait of the Benedictine monk and scribe Eadwine, inserted in a monumental Psalter produced at Christ Church, Canterbury, around 1160 (Cambridge, Trinity College, MS. R.17.1), one of the most ambitious English manuscripts ever made. As shown in Figure 2.22, in the full-page image on folio 283^v, he is seated at a lectern, quill and penknife in hand. An inscription, written around the perimeter of the image, supplies his name. It comprises a dialogue between Eadwine and his work, in which he asks "the letter" to vouch for his skill and to ensure that he will be remembered by posterity. Translated it reads: "I am the chief of scribes, and neither my praise nor fame shall die; shout out, oh my letter, who I may be." The letter replies: "By its fame your script proclaims you, Eadwine, whom the painted figure represents, alive through the ages, whose genius the beauty of this book demonstrates. Receive, O God, the book and its donor as an acceptable gift."[62]

The layout of the Psalter is particularly complex because the volume contains seven different texts simultaneously on each page (the three main Latin versions of the Psalms, an interlinear Latin gloss, an Old English translation, an Anglo-Norman French translation, and a marginal Latin commentary). Several scribes were responsible for completing the manuscript, but only Eadwine's contribution was acknowledged in this way. In this remarkable "portrait," which is possibly a posthumous tribute to Eadwine created by his fellow monks, the craftsman's work literally testifies to his skill.[63]

Images of medieval authors can be found in countless copies of their works, and scribal portraits bear witness to specific copyists. Far fewer in number are images showing medieval illuminators plying their craft, or, for that matter, artists of any description, apart from allegorical, legendary, and biblical figures. It is unlikely that the scarcity of depictions of contemporary illuminators is a result of the arbitrary destruction of evidence. How, then, can we explain it? Was the work of the illuminator, a mechanical craft, perceived to be inferior to the intellectual work of authors and scribes? Ongoing research into the changing status of illuminators over the centuries across Europe is offering fresh insights into the question. Praise showered on individual masters by their collaborators, peers, and patrons, as well as the high demand for their work, suggests that the issue is not one of social status alone. A reasonable conclusion is that depictions of medieval illuminators are rare because images of this type, including self-portraits, were not based on a long-standing tradition. Portraits of authors and scribes had a venerable pedigree because they followed classical and early Christian antecedents, but similar conventions of portraiture did not exist for illuminators.⁶⁴ Most unusually, the Oxford-based scribe and illuminator William de Brailes included his "portrait" in at least three images, which he painted in the mid-thirteenth century. Significantly, in all three, William presents himself as a penitent and pious clerk rather than an artist.

FIGURE 2.22 Eadwine. Eadwine Psalter, c. 1160. Christ Church Priory, Canterbury, England. Cambridge, Trinity College, MS R.17.1, folio 283ᵛ. Photo: Universal History Archive. Image courtesy Getty Images.

PICTURING WORK

FIGURE 2.23 Richard and Jeanne Montbaston. *Roman de la Rose*, c. 1350. Paris, France. Paris, Bibliothèque nationale de France, MS fr. 25526, folio 77ᵛ. © BnF, Paris.

Though relatively small in number, images of actual illuminators at work have been much reproduced and discussed by modern scholars. Among them is the twelfth-century image of Hildebertus cursing a mouse that has invaded his workshop, the mid-fourteenth century *bas-de-page* scene of the husband and wife team Jeanne and Richard Montbaston depicted at matching desks (Figure 2.23), and the assured self-portrait of Simon Bening, seated at his easel, clutching a pair of spectacles, painted in 1558 when he was seventy-five years old.[65] These images of illuminators evoke a craft that is much more amply attested by surviving paintings on parchment. Without the industry of illuminators, we would be lacking a fundamental source of knowledge of medieval life and culture, including innumerable facets of the world of work.

CHAPTER THREE

Work and Workplaces

MARIE D'AGUANNO ITO

Work and workplaces in the medieval world were as varied as life itself. Whether rural self-contained communities, such as monasteries or manors, or locations as sophisticated as late medieval cities, the types of work and their venues reflected the multifold aspects of society at the time. Work was often driven by basic needs and values, including food, clothing, housing, worship, and defense. Work typically reflected some degree of human interdependence. While a few people dwelled alone in remote locations, most lived in some form of community and relied on the efforts and products of others. Labor, whether agricultural, industrial, commercial, or artisan, skilled or unskilled, supported the welfare and lifestyle of those in the community, wealthy and poor. Like today, work was part of daily medieval life, generally with breaks for the Sabbath and holy days. While men formed the core of the work environment, women, and not infrequently children, joined men in their labors.

This chapter will examine different types of work across social levels within medieval Europe, pointing to the relatively complex and integrated economy of the time. It will consider agricultural labor; entrepreneurship within monasteries; the war industry; commodities transport and sales; market fairs and trading networks; the labor involved in building medieval cities; and the efforts of running businesses, markets, and manufacturing operations within the cities, among some examples. Work affected almost all: peasants; lay, monastic, and ecclesiastical aristocrats; those at sea; and those in urban areas across northern and southern Europe and across the Mediterranean. Many of the medieval innovations and work processes extended to the early modern and modern era, such as credit finance, crop rotation, spinning, and cotton cloth production. Let us observe these and other examples of medieval work and workplaces.

ESTATE LIFE AND EARLY MEDIEVAL AGRICULTURE

Much of the work during the medieval period was agricultural or related to food production. Manors, which were typically large royal, ecclesiastical, monastic, or aristocratic estates, provided the basis for peasant work, village life, worship, and lordship by those in control of the lands.[1] The work performed often reflected one's socioeconomic status. At the top, elite warriors, generally from an aristocratic or royal heritage, focused on combat and political leadership. They tended to possess the larger blocks of land, providing for agriculture and village life. Many monastic houses, also often part of royal or aristocratic lines, focused on prayer and book production while similarly operating large estates. In addition, ecclesiastical leaders, such as bishops, who held both spiritual and temporal powers, controlled church wealth and lands.

Powerful landholders placed their estates into productive use, requiring a labor supply. Workers, often poor and in need of housing and protection, were generally tied to the land juridically and economically. Whether free or unfree, they performed much of the agricultural labor. Peasants typically owed a set number of days' work per week and rendered a significant portion of their produce to their overlords for consumption or to sell at markets. Some held independent status and worked their own small lands (allods) or hired themselves as farm labor, but the majority worked and lived within the estate system.

Agricultural workers performed various duties. Large segments of land were designated for crop cultivation, animal husbandry, pastures, or forest, which served for hunting and for grazing pigs. Workers accordingly plowed lands, grew and harvested crops, raised livestock, shepherded animals, or worked in other areas of food or commodity production. Skilled and unskilled workers also built and maintained physical structures on the estate. These included the manor house, peasant dwellings, churches, protective walls, barns, mills, furnaces for bread making, smithing quarters for making weapons, gates, utensils, cooking vessels, tools, and implements, and other buildings associated with production, storage, or village life. The various types of agricultural and artisan work supported an interdependent, if relatively self-contained, community and economy within the manor, while instances allowed for external trade (see Figure 3.1).

An archetype of manorial production is found in the *Capitulare de villis*, a Carolingian prototype for estate management dating to around 800. Typical labor described included "sowing or ploughing, harvesting, haymaking," and wine production. Workers tilled fields using oxen, cows, and horses. Stewards oversaw cultivation and were afforded grain at daily meals. They supervised peasants raising chickens and geese and tending fish ponds,

FIGURE 3.1 Calendar, March, early fifteenth century. France. *Les très riches heures du Duc de Berry*. Wikimedia Commons.

vegetable gardens, pigsties, sheepfolds, and goat pens. Workers gathered hay, herbs, and fruit from cultivated trees. The extensive manufactured products included smoked and salted meat, sausage, lard, wine, vinegar, and, per the document, "mustard, cheese, butter, malt, beer, mead, honey, wax and flour."[2] Women operated workshops supplied with linen, wool, soap, and oil, among other items. Officials attended markets to sell excess commodities. The *Capitulare de villis* reveals several other estate occupations, including foresters, stablemen, cellarers, toll collectors, millers, and fishermen. Forests and fields were loci for falconers, fowlers, and hunters. Houses were to have guarded watchfires. Officials administered justice. Workers produced household objects, including beds, mattresses, pillows, linen, tablecloths, seat covers, and soap. Artisans included shoe makers, carpenters, bakers, net weavers, and shield makers.

Outside of Carolingian territories, such as in Anglo-Saxon England, workers similarly engaged in agriculture, and they manufactured a wide assortment of goods. As on the continent, craftsmen on estates, monasteries, and in towns also produced luxury items, including ornamented brooches, elaborate vestments, and vessels made with ivory, silver, bronze, and luminous stones. Merchants in nearby towns traded commodities and high-end products locally and between the isles and the continent. Anglo-Saxon missionaries and pilgrims also presented often expensive gifts to lay, ecclesiastical, and monastic leaders across Europe.[3]

Estate inventories or polyptychs from the ninth and tenth centuries provide a closer slice of life, documenting landholdings, the workforce, services owed and performed, and in-kind and monetary payments on vast abbatial, aristocratic, and royal estates (see Figure 3.2). The Carolingian abbey of Wissembourg, north of Strasbourg, for example, held twenty-five separate manors.[4] Each had extensive acreage that included farmsteads, meadows, vineyards, mills, rivers, and other properties. Workers produced wheat, rye, oats, straw, cows, pigs, poultry, and eggs. They tended vines, gathered and pressed grapes, prepared vessels, and made wine. Some made bread, beer, and bricks. On some of Wissembourg's manors, workers owed three days' labor per week; others owed one day; and still others owed fixed terms per year. Certain workers were free and others were unfree. Women made cloth, shoe buckles, and fences for the manor.

FIGURE 3.2 Harvesting, Luttrell Psalter, c. 1340. Lincolnshire, England. London, British Library, Add. Manuscript 42130, folio, The British Library, London.

The monastery of Bobbio, in what is now the Emilia-Romagna area of Italy, exemplifies another productive estate.[5] By 883, Bobbio controlled 123 local and distant properties.[6] Laborers worked on the monastery's central estate nine weeks per year and sowed arable land rendering annually 260 measures of grain, 150 amphorae of wine, and 600 cartloads of hay. Some workers fattened pigs in the woods. Others gathered salt from the manor's four mines. In a nearby valley, workers produced wine, hay, honey, beeswax, and sheep. On Bobbio's manor at Montelungo, peasants served two days per week, sowing land, making wine, raising animals, fattening pigs in groves large enough for 1,000, and producing up to 60 pounds of cheese.[7] Bobbio held outlying estates, including those at Piacenza and Pavia, which ran pilgrimage inns.

Wissembourg and Bobbio represent vast holdings. Bobbio's holdings were so large that, according to a polyptych of 862, its lands and workers could produce 1,873 measures of grain, 1,074 amphorae of wine, 1,494 carts of hay, and 2,890 fattened pigs. It also held 590 farmsteads where workers rendered 2,820 measures of grain, 10 pounds of silver, 889 chickens, 2,885 measures of oil, and 174 pounds of cheese. In 883, according to a second inventory, Bobbio's estates maintained sufficient acreage and labor to produce 2,011 measures of grain, 1,228 amphorae of wine, and 1,500 carts of hay. Its woods could sustain 4,190 pigs.[8] Work performance was not uniform. In 1117, for example, the abbot of Marmoutier complained about the "negligence, the uselessness ... and the idleness of those who serve" on the abbey's estate.[9] He altered his labor arrangements as a result. The manorial records nevertheless provide evidence of types and locations of agricultural work through the early medieval period. Many agricultural practices endured through the preindustrial age, but noteworthy changes affected later medieval work, particularly following the Black Death. Population declines dwindled labor forces. Worker compensation increased and shifted from in-kind to monetary wages in certain locations. Labor conditions generally improved; occupational change became flexible. Diminishing large-estate systems enabled laborers to become tenant farmers on rented properties, while some fields converted to pasture. Certain tenants and peasants overtook lands ignored or abandoned by distant estate holders.[10]

REGIONAL VARIATIONS AND EARLY AGRICULTURAL ADVANCES

Agricultural labor adapted to and varied with geographical and ecological localities and shared history, whether Roman or Germanic. The ancient Mediterranean Roman practice of growing olives for food and lighting, grapes for wine, and wheat and some cereals for bread continued into the medieval period. In northern Europe, early Germanic peoples and their medieval successors consumed more meat and dairy than Mediterranean Romans. They cultivated, in addition to wheat, grains such as rye, barley, and oats, which were suited to northern soils. Northern Europe ushered dairy into the general diet, including milk, cheese, and butter. Workers brewed ale from grains while producing beer from hops harvested in the region.[11] Northern and southern customs spread across Europe and blended over time, adapting to the needs and resources of particular regions. In the fourteenth century, for example, rye, barley, and other grains were commonly sold to the Florentine populace along with varieties of wheat.[12]

Mountainous regions had their own culture. Those in the hills of the fourteenth-century southern French village of Montaillou, for example, adapted work to the terrain. Peasants cultivated one or more small plots of land, growing wheat and oats, turnips, and hemp. They also raised livestock and sheep. Workers relied on oxen, donkeys, and mules for transportation and commodity carriage rather than carts and more expensive horses. Men performed the heavy agricultural labor of plowing and harvesting, and they hunted and fished. Women tended kitchen gardens, weeded, and tied crops, and they cooked and made bread, among various tasks. Children tended sheep.[13] The environment appears to have been more localized and enclosed within a village than a coastal town or city might have been.

Agriculturalists and manufacturers similarly adapted their practices based on natural resources and connections with other places. Tuscans produced saffron from local crocuses, while merchants travelling to the eastern Mediterranean also imported saffron and other spices. Workers in Picardy grew woad, a plant used for blue cloth dyes. Woad in turn was exported to distant markets. Mulberry trees attracted silk worms; Lucca in Tuscany became a notable silk production area. England and Spain developed large-scale sheep industries, important for wool and meat production. Workers fished at ponds, rivers, coastal areas, and in the open sea, using lines, nets, and weirs.[14] Advances in agriculture altered work and production. Where the relatively arid fields of Mediterranean climates were suited to a light scratch plow, northern medieval farmers engaged heavy plows better suited to thick soils. Northerners typically tilled long, open fields because oxen-drawn plows could not turn easily.[15] Horses, adapted with a collar and horse shoes, could be used and were more efficient, but they were expensive; thus oxen remained a plowing staple.[16] Workers enhanced production by using a three-field crop rotation system, rather than the earlier Roman two-field practice; moreover, they valued manure for fertilization. Workers also engaged in milling for food and commodity production. Carolingian estates maintained grain mills.[17] By the millennium, workers milled in both rural and urban areas. The diverse renderings included malt, oil, mustard, paper, and cloth fulling via watermills, with the addition of windmills over time.[18] Waste was avoided. A fourteenth-century Florentine miller ground grain and sold flour, but also sold leftover wall scrapings and flour containing millstone particles.[19]

EARLY COASTAL AREAS: SHIPBUILDING, TRADE, AND INVASIONS

Early medieval work life was not limited to manors. Those living in coastal areas engaged in fishing, shipbuilding, trading, and work that supported town life. Early northern European towns, often fortified areas known as "burhs," frequently became commercial centers. Trade was local but also extended across Europe, even to Byzantine Constantinople, across the North Sea and Baltic Sea, and between England and the continent. Anglo-Saxons traded with Frisia (the Netherlands), the Rhineland, Pavia, and Mediterranean territories, as silver from the German Harz Mountains brought new currency into commerce.[20] Scandinavia held annual fairs for the exchange of goods. The region hosted scattered rural and town markets, some tied to pagan sites and, with Christianity, to churches and feast days. In Norway, furs and skins were traded for fabric, salt, and leather. Gotland permitted Sunday marketing of cheese, butter, poultry, fish, and meat.[21] In Holland, workers engaged in land reclamation as early as the eleventh century, turning swamps into productive land. While not focused on grains, locals raised animals and produced dairy.[22]

In coastal regions, shipbuilding was a significant industry. Vikings constructed long, shallow-bottomed vessels, which could navigate open seas and rivers, as they plundered but also engaged in trade and settled in various locations.[23] Normans built ships that carried men, horses, and equipment to England in 1066 as part of their conquest (see Figure 3.3).[24] Pisans, Genoese, and Venetians employed galleys, which were used for trade and war. Venice developed extensive shipbuilding and storage enterprises at its Arsenal and other locations, operated on a public–private basis.[25]

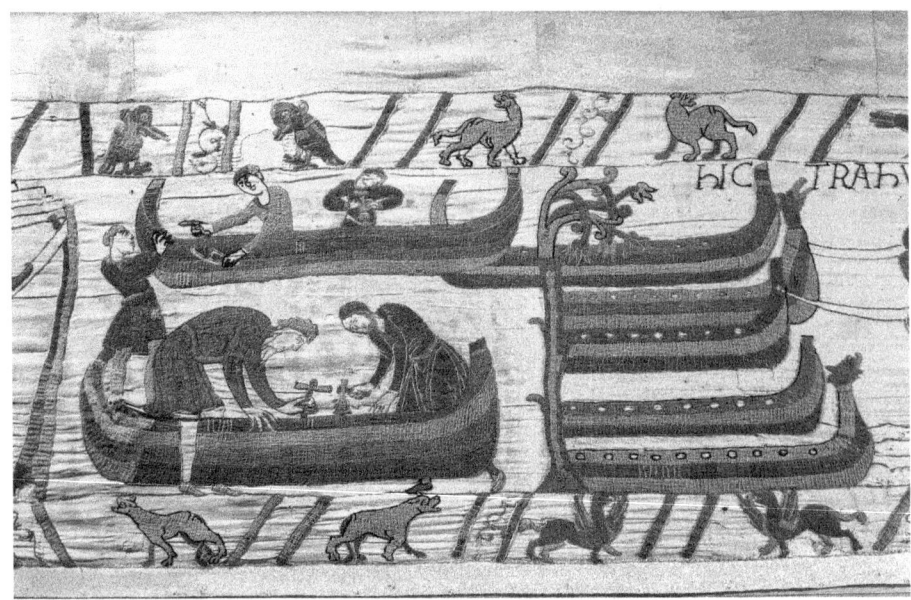

FIGURE 3.3 Shipbuilding. Bayeux Tapestry, eleventh century. England. Photo: DEA / M. Seemuller. Image courtesy Getty Images.

INDUSTRY OF WAR: PREPARATION IN NORMANDY AND THE SIEGE ENGINE IN ENGLAND

War was its own industry. Horses, and their breeding and care, remained vital for elite combat, along with the stirrup, saddle, pommel, and horseshoes. Medieval warriors spent time practicing maneuvers using horses in preparation for combat. A tenth- or eleventh-century Norman warrior would have practiced daily, defending his territory, riding at least ten miles and back, and training his specially bred war horse, the *destrier*.[26] Castle building, maintenance, and guarding supported the defensive culture of the time.[27]

Preparation for war engendered the manufacture of weaponry and protective gear. Smiths crafted swords, lances, axes, and shields and later more advanced weaponry such as crossbows. Production often started at the highest levels. In thirteenth-century England, for example, King John ordered a constable to provide his crossbow maker at Windsor "glue, sinews and horn" for production.[28] Outerwear included metal helmets often with nose plates, chain mail (outer coverings of interlocking metal links), and, by the late medieval period, full metal armor. Weapons, protective coverings, and horses were vital for elite warriors, and they were emblematic of a noble and royal lifestyle for much of the medieval period. At the other end, bows and arrows remained useful for infantry and trained peasantry.[29]

Preparation for war could be elaborate. In twelfth- and thirteenth-century England, the construction and use of siege engines and other artillery, a key part of medieval warfare, involved teams of skilled artisans and resources such as timber, iron, ropes, and hides.[30] Carpenters, often resident in the royal household, were commissioned by crown officials in London, who coordinated logistics with local counterparts. Writs and royal and ecclesiastical funds enabled the engagement of personnel, tools, wagons, horses, and drivers to move materials to construction and storage locations. Work sites included royal fortresses and forests, such as Windsor and the Forest of Dean, which also provided storage facilities. Sheriffs, constables, and other local and royal officials oversaw and protected the construction work and the supply and storage units. Each phase of the project was closely documented, with redundant bookkeeping to ensure accuracy and honesty.

Europe's war industry, plus commerce, expanded to the eastern Mediterranean with the Crusades from the late eleventh century. Noble and royal warriors were joined by a league of Italian traders who established commercial zones in conquered areas. Even after the fall of Acre in 1291, western merchants remained active throughout the Mediterranean and beyond. The Florentine trader Francesco Pegolotti's fourteenth-century commercial guide, the *Pratica della mercatura*, reveals the wide geographic and product reach of northern Italian merchants. Trading extended to numerous cities and regions, including Constantinople, Cyprus, Acre, Alexandria, Tunisia, Palermo, Naples, Barcelona, Pisa, Genoa, Marseilles, Bruges, Paris, London, and other locations around the Mediterranean and northern Europe. Commodities included cloth, grain, wine, oil, cheese, nuts, spices, sugar, salt, wax, and dozens of commercial goods, which were in turn generally traded at markets and fairs, both local and international.[31]

By the late medieval period, war reflected a changing society. Mercenaries, troops paid to fight, increasingly replaced once elite feudal warriors. Where feudal bonds, particularly in northern Europe, typically required forty days of military service to one's overlord, new mercenary-involved war engagements, free of such time constraints, started to extend over longer periods. In this vein, realms were beginning to use state-supported standing armies rather than retainers of the king or a lord. Mercenary service fostered social mobility for the ambitious and talented. New industries accompanied these changes. Cannons and gunpowder transformed war and created new work opportunities and production locations. Workers turned their efforts to making metal suits of armor rather than of interlocking chain mail. The longbow was effectively manufactured and used. War was becoming more of a structured enterprise.[32]

ENGLISH MONASTIC ENTERPRISE: WOOL SALES, FINANCE, AND MANUSCRIPT PRODUCTION

While focused on prayer, many monasteries also became entrepreneurial centers. Peasant labor engaged in agricultural and commodity production, often for commercial sale. Thirteenth- and fourteenth-century English monasteries raised sheep and sold forward contracts to Italian merchants, who essentially purchased wool up to twenty years in advance of delivery.[33] The Italian monetary advances to the monks benefited monastic operations and guaranteed a pool of buyers. The merchants benefited from known prices and a steady wool supply, which was shipped to northern Italian cities and manufactured into wool cloth, for reexport to a myriad of locations.

Monasteries were also important for manuscript production, particularly the copying of ancient Roman and Greek texts, Scripture, and early Christian works, as well as philosophical, theological, and other writings. Manuscripts were produced in stages. Workers first cleaned sheep, cow, or calf skin, soaking it in lime for days before stretching it on a large frame with ropes and tightening implements. They cleared the skin follicles and stitched holes where possible. When taut, the skins were cut into large sheets, then folded in half or in quarters to form pages or "folios." The folded sheets were stacked and stitched down the middle to create sections or "quires" (like modern book sections). Several quires, secured between boards, perhaps covered with leather, formed the book or codex.³⁴

Skilled monks, working up to six hours daily in a dedicated room or *scriptorium*, copied text onto the skin using carbon-based ink, while others added decorations or illuminations, the latter depicting images using bright colors and even gold leaf. Colors were derived from stone, insects, plants, metals, and other sources, and were affixed with egg, honey, or natural gums. Ink and colors were added carefully so that they remained on the parchment and did not "bleed." Some monks wrote notes or "glosses" in the margins. Some added scenes illustrative of the text, while others drew comical images having little to do with the text. Major manuscripts, such as certain Scriptural or liturgical texts, often bore special ornamentations, as well as gold and precious or semi-precious stones on their covers.³⁵

LAY MANUSCRIPT AND DOCUMENT PRODUCTION IN THE LATER MIDDLE AGES

By the later Middle Ages, lay people also produced commissioned manuscripts. The Limbourg brothers, for example, rendered the magnificent *Les très riches heures du Duc de Berry*. Unlike monastic productions, often in rural settings, Paris was the center for French commercial texts into the early fifteenth century. The area of Notre Dame became the hub for labor on parchment, script, illuminations, bindings, and other features. By the late fourteenth century, some lay manuscript producers worked for the king or court directly.³⁶

Written texts extended beyond manuscripts, to royal, imperial, ecclesiastical, or papal documents, which were executed by scribal experts. Such documents were issued for executive, legislative, or judicial purposes, for land grants, business transactions, or other reasons. Royal bureaucracies from the twelfth century onwards employed teams of professionals who produced reams of written documents and records. In addition, particularly in northern Italian cities, notaries became central to the documentation of business dealings, property transfers, legislative records, and other private and public transactions.

THE COMMERCIAL REVOLUTION—GROWTH OF WORK AND WORKPLACES AFTER THE MILLENNIUM

After the millennium and the waves of external attacks and internal political fragmentation that followed the decline of the Carolingian Empire, Europe experienced new commercial growth, the blossoming of cities, and increasing economic integration. Local and regional fairs proliferated in northern Europe often supplementing permanent markets. The fairs, some of which grew to international importance, generated foreign commerce, new work opportunities, and new products. Marketplaces, particularly in Italy, began to expand as cities grew. Western Europe started to benefit from an array of commodities that arrived with traders who ventured to the eastern Mediterranean during the Crusades. The rise of economic activity, particularly in the Mediterranean region, became so vigorous that the movement has been termed a "commercial revolution."³⁷

With advancements in ship design and sailing, as well as overland transport from the thirteenth century, trading networks expanded on several fronts. The earlier east–west nexus stretched firmly across northern Europe, covering England, Scandinavia, the

Netherlands, German lands, and the Baltic eastward. The north–south axis expanded between northern Europe and Mediterranean territories, including Spain and Italy. Cross-Mediterranean trade blossomed between the Levant and the West.

Commodity transport was an important source of employment. Many cities emerged as commercial and transportation hubs. Dordrecht in Holland, an important crossroad for east–west trade, handled wine, wood, salt, and grain. A 1274 Haarlem excise charter cited production of beer and textiles, but also saddles and ships.[38] In the 1270s, German Hanseatic towns, a confederation including Lübeck, Hamburg, and Bremen, among others, conducted east–west trade with northern realms, including Norway, bringing "flax, cloth, corn, flour, malt, ale, wine" and biscuits, copper, and silver in exchange for butter, salmon, and other fish and fish oil, furs, and wood.[39] Hanseatic traders even transported Scandinavian herring and cod to Holland.[40]

Over time, Hanseatic traders established connections with several northern cities, including Amsterdam, Antwerp, Bruges, London, and Rouen, as well as the southern cities of Barcelona, Lisbon, Marseilles, and Naples, among others.[41] German operations could be extensive. In late medieval Bergen (Norway), for example, Hanse representatives maintained an area with twenty-eight "yards," where about two to three hundred merchants lived and based their operations. During summers, the Hanse property hosted up to 2,000 adult and young males, including sailors, who worked in international commerce, shipping, and local business.[42]

COMMERCIAL FAIRS OF NORTHERN EUROPE: EXAMPLES OF ENGLAND AND CHAMPAGNE

In northern Europe, fairs, as opposed to permanent markets, became important venues for enterprise. As centralized trading posts, fairs lowered transaction costs. They were flexible and generally had low administrative costs, requiring an open area, tables, and canopies. Aside from dealer inventories, fairs required relatively little capital compared to permanent markets.[43] But, as with permanent markets, accessible roads or rivers, safety for travelling merchants and merchandise, seigneurial or civic tax relief, and contract enforcement were important for their success.

English fairs originated around saints' feast days, when merchants sold wool, grain, and local goods to parishioners.[44] From the late twelfth into the fourteenth centuries, England maintained important fairs at Stamford during Lent, St. Ives at Easter, Boston in July, Winchester in September, Northampton in November, and Bury St. Edmunds in December.[45] In addition, 2,300 smaller fairs dotted the English countryside.[46] The large fairs were under the control of the crown or manorial rulers, whether secular or ecclesiastical, and they were frequented by foreign traders, including those from Scandinavia, Flanders, Lucca, and Rouen.[47]

Fair venues varied. St. Ives' merchants sold ale, oats, and fish from rented boats, while booths and other spaces housed spicers, provisioners, stone cutters, iron and gold smiths, butchers, bread sellers, cloth cutters, and tailors, among others. Cloth and wool were among the larger commodities traded at the fairs; yet they also saw traffic in significant quantities of wine, metals, spices, livestock, and pelts, among other products. Merchandise and guilds were grouped by product, which also aided regulators' inspections.[48]

Strong regulations applied. Cooks, bakers, and metalworkers at the fairs of St. Ives and St. Giles used open flames; thus they were set apart, especially because central structures contained wood or cloth. St. Ives' fair houses were required to have pits of water. Animals and livestock vendors at St. Giles were similarly separated from the main booths. Butchers held licenses and were located near water to dump waste. Winchester prohibited its merchants from placing debris in the streets.[49]

Royal, aristocratic, monastic, and ecclesiastical leadership also participated in and oversaw English fairs. Monastic houses attended the fairs, which provided a ready market for their wool. By charter, the bishop's staff required Winchester bakers, fishmongers, and butchers, to sell "wholesome, useful and sufficient victuals." The king's peace prevailed at fair venues. Armed constables provided security. Market rules governed trading to impose order, product quality, and uniform weights and measures and to prevent price manipulation and fraud. Merchant courts administered civil and criminal justice, enforced peace, upheld regulations, and handled contract enforcement and transactional issues.[50]

Foreign merchants were active at English fairs, as was typical of larger venues in northern Europe. Flemish traders sold spices, furs, and wax to the English crown at Bury St. Edmunds. Spanish traders sold wax, spices, leather, and fruit at Southampton and Sandwich while providing dye, soap, and oil to Southampton and Bristol. Dealers from Hamburg, Lubeck, and other Hanse cities transported "wax, furs, honey, timber, potash, iron, canvas and rope" to both England and Bruges.[51] The Flemish maintained tight control over their English operations. They travelled by convoy, and, in order to monopolize high-quality cloth sales, they restricted outsiders, small traders, brokers, and artisans. The Flemish brought inspectors and guild officials from Douai and Ypres to serve as commercial judges. They also inspected the cloth and wool and guarded against fraudulent labels claiming a higher quality or Flemish origin. Flanders maintained its own court in England for merchant complaints.[52]

At times, foreign merchants prevailed over local traders, particularly in England. Luccan and Florentine dealers bought English wool at the markets and engaged in finance.[53] Henry II and Richard II benefited traders from St. Omer and Cologne. Thirteenth-century woad dealers from Picardy were favored over London merchants.[54] Although royal cloth purchases were important to domestic textile producers, 50 to 65 percent of royal acquisitions were from Douai (Flanders) rather than from local merchants.[55] The same was true in major cities, such as London. From the mid-thirteenth century, Italians importing fine cloth, jewels, and wine to England, became royal bankers and collected papal tithes, thereby gaining significant access to London markets, where they established a residence. Likewise, Germans maintained fortified warehouses in London, known as the Steelyard. In 1319, Venetians, demonstrating their might, shipped 10,000 pounds of sugar and 1,000 pounds of candy to London alone.[56]

From the twelfth until the mid-thirteenth century, the fairs of Champagne, near Paris, became the largest and best known of the medieval fairs. Organized by the counts of Champagne, they consisted of six markets operating in rotation: Lagny, from January 2; Bar-sur-Aube during Lent; Provins in May; Troyes in late June; Provins in September; and Troyes again in early November. Each fair lasted about six weeks.[57] The typical cycle involved setting up for eight days; cloth sales for ten days; leather (cordovan) sales for the next eleven; sales of items by weight, such as spices, and transaction settlements during the next nineteen days; and post-fair execution of financial documents over four days. According to R. D. Face, the fairs represented the "western hub of an expanding, truly international commerce" that "dominated the commercial and banking relations between the north and south of Europe in the late twelfth century and throughout the thirteenth."[58] Champagne's unique success also lay in the counts' vigorous protection of merchant travel to and from the fairs. Like England, the Champagne fairs attracted foreign merchants, including those from Italy, Germany, Flanders, Spain, French royal territories, and the Brabant.[59] Many arrived with their wares via caravan, others by sea and land.[60] Italians sold spices and bought French and Flemish cloth. Merchants, grouped by trade, bought and sold wood, woollen cloth, gold works, hides, and livestock, among other commodities. As in England, Champagne provided administration, oversight of weights and measures, notaries, guards, a court to provide justice and handle transactional issues, and a system for the enforcement of court decisions.[61]

Partnerships were common at Champagne, as at English and other fairs. In a typical arrangement, one partner travelled to the fair, while the other maintained business at home. Distant merchants also similarly used agents and brokers. Italians employed professional couriers, who took a loyalty oath to the merchants and travelled to the fairs in advance of the merchandise caravans. They obtained "news, business reports and credit instruments," which they reported upon return. In addition, distant merchants hired contract shippers, who drove the caravans.[62] Advance work for the fairs thus involved multiple operations and was essential for the success of the travelling merchants. Credit was an important feature of the Champagne fairs, with lasting effects on early modern finance. As with the English fairs, many goods were sold on a book-entry basis, creating important business for financiers such as the Florentine *Cambio*. Financiers exchanged currencies and negotiated promissory notes as part of the payment process. Rather than hauling large volumes of coin, which was both expensive and risky, Italians employed letters of credit, allowing sales made in one location to be paid in another. Italian firms expanded this hallmark of the Champagne fairs to their operations in various parts of Europe, making credit a standard trading convention.[63]

In addition to England and Champagne, other localities held fairs regularly. Holland operated both retail and wholesale fairs, important for the dairy business. The Akersloot fair issued 5,500 cheeses and 23 tons of butter. Edam shipped 82,200 cheeses in the fifteenth century; Hoorn exported 1,928 tons of butter. At Gouda, 2,000 horses were traded per year by the early sixteenth century.[64] In the 1380s, fairs near Mt. Genèvre transported 7,000 sheep across the Alps annually. Lombard fairs traded livestock and horses from the Swiss provinces, local areas, and the Veneto. Lanciano (Abruzzi) featured livestock and sheep. Merchants there also traded saffron, metal ware, cloth, leather, and Venetian luxury items. In Sicily, the Randazzo fair hosted cattle, but also linen and fustian cloth.[65]

THE GROWTH OF CITIES: CONSTRUCTION, TRADE, AND MARKETS—NEW WORK OPPORTUNITIES

From at least the twelfth century, economic growth brought movements of people from the fields into cities where growing infrastructure and industries provided work for the skilled and unskilled alike. City life opened opportunities for entrepreneurs and artisans, who operated workshops and retail outlets, often as families. New urban prosperity through increased trade promoted the growth of a merchant class. Merchants and artisans not only produced essential goods of life, such as bread, clothing, and building materials, but many began manufacturing and consuming luxury goods on a widespread basis, in earlier times reserved only for the political and ecclesiastical elite.[66] City life was stratified. Although aristocratic elites often governed early cities, successful traders, often operating internationally, began to control economic resources and political positions, forming a new urban aristocracy. Middling merchants supported the domestic life and economy. Many who came to the city from the fields, particularly in northern Italy, exchanged one harsh environment for another as they labored in often difficult and grimy phases of production. Unskilled workers generally served as day laborers, moving from site to site, without benefits, and were only paid for work performed.[67]

As cities grew, so did the need for the design and construction of infrastructure, employing both skilled and unskilled labor. New walls replaced or expanded original Roman walls. Cathedrals and churches were redesigned and enlarged from their late antique or early medieval foundations. The construction of government and guild halls accommodated new urban civic and commercial leadership. Market squares and surrounding buildings, with shops and taverns, grew as centers for commerce, social activities, and news. Cities increasingly paved once-muddy urban roads and improved routes between trading hubs. Family housing mushroomed, whether urban palaces or more modest dwellings.

Cities also engendered new levels of intellectual enterprise and supporting infrastructure. Universities, for example, with their own signature buildings and communities, proliferated across Europe. The new universities brought construction opportunities for architects and laborers alike. As they grew, universities created new classes of scholars and professionals, who were often itinerant in the course of their pursuits. Universities opened intellectual engagement and work in fields such as philosophy, theology, law, and medicine.

The growth of cities in short presented new types of work and workplaces. Major building projects required architects, supervisors, accountants, treasurers and financiers, suppliers, and skilled and unskilled construction crews. Cathedrals and civic and guild structures alone used large volumes of brick, stone, wood, glass, and metals, among other features. Builders coordinated with brick makers, quarries, artisans, and laborers.[68] Skilled and unskilled labor built and ornamented the new structures.

Suppliers provided an important labor force in the building effort. Brick makers operated across Europe. By the thirteenth century, Holland had significant operations. Brickmaking proliferated in cities such as Bruges and Hull (England), in Baltic areas and northern Italy. Workers near Niedenburg produced 5,000 bricks per firing, while French kilns rendered 20,000. Certain sixteenth-century Florentine kilns operating every three weeks could produce 272,000 bricks per year. Florentine brick makers worked as independent businesses, using rented kilns. Kiln masters could earn a good living. One Florentine made a hefty seventy florins per year. Brick molders earned four lire for 1,000 bricks, producing several thousand per day. Day laborers made significantly less. In Florence, men, women, and children worked as brick molders. In seventeenth-century Holland, women joined men as transporters. Carriers often ran their own businesses.[69]

Laborers also worked in quarries for construction materials, while gathering sand and gravel from river beds. Normandy, Tournai, and other parts of northern Europe used limestone for churches, baptismal fonts, and monuments, among other structures. Marble adorned the cathedrals at Orvieto, Siena, Pisa, and Florence. Workers transported stone by river to remote locations, as at St. Victor of Xanten in northern Germany. In some instances, monasteries even controlled the quarries used for their massive construction undertakings.[70]

Stone-carving and architectural labor flourished. Northern Italian stone cutters often operated independently under contract, buying from quarries and fashioning it in their workshops. Artisans produced ornamented capitals, doors, window frames, and other decorative and structural features for important buildings. Iron, on the other hand, was part of a multistage manufacturing process. Pisans and Florentines, for example, obtained ore from the island of Elba and transported it to the distant Apennine Mountains for smelting at water mills. Iron manufacturers then sold the product to smiths in a variety of locations.[71]

FLORENCE: A SOUTHERN EUROPEAN CITY

Cities also engendered permanent markets, which contrasted with fairs in their stability, use of public civic space, monuments, and often elaborate infrastructure.[72] They were supplemented by shops, workshops, and other commercial venues. The markets hosted a wide variety of occupations in most large European cities, including London, Paris, Milan, Venice, and large German Hanse cities. Florence in Italy and Bruges in Flanders provide good examples of southern and northern European urban marketplaces.

Florence had three large marketplaces and numerous smaller ones. The Mercato Vecchio ("Old Market"), active from at least the eleventh century, was situated at the old Roman forum, now the Piazza della Repubblica. In the late medieval period, merchants sold various foods and merchandise.[73] The fourteenth-century poet Antonio Pucci bragged that the market "feeds the whole world."[74] The populace could buy varieties of vegetables, fruit, poultry, eggs, dairy, spices, meats, and mustard. Vendors sold other products as well, such as glassware, wool and linen cloth, hose, hats, and iron products, among a long list of merchandise.

The Mercato Vecchio was a mirror of Florentine society and its working world. Wealthy commodities merchants and financiers had a substantial presence and were involved in the market's oversight together with the civic government. More so, the market reflected the work of the middling and lower commercial groups. It provided opportunities for enterprising merchants and families, both men and women, to sell their inventories of goods. Women were active, and according to guild statutes operated under relatively equal terms with their male counterparts, who were usually spouses or family members. Dealers in meat, groceries, and provisions, often small or family businesses, managed established tables and worked under the weight of professional rules. The market also evidenced many roving marginal vendors who sold produce from carts and baskets. Traders could be rough. As Pucci claimed: "female costers of all sorts ... quarrel[ed] all day long over two dried chestnuts, swearing badly and calling one another whores."[75]

Merchants of the Mercato Vecchio were vital to the Florentine populace. In the late medieval period, the city imported annually 55,000 *cogna* of wine, and for butchering, 4,000 cattle, 60,000 sheep, 20,000 goats, and 30,000 pigs. One July alone, grocers delivered 400 cartloads of melons daily.[76] The Mercato Vecchio was generally larger than other European urban markets, but it shared core features with central markets of other European cities.

In addition to the Mercato Vecchio, Florence had markets dedicated to finance, at the Mercato Nuovo ("New Market"), and grain at the piazza of Orsanmichele. The *Cambio*, a guild of the leading Florentine financiers, was present at the major domestic and foreign markets and established its own space for monetary exchange and banking at the Mercato Nuovo. The centralized grain market at Orsanmichele hosted large wheat dealers and medium-to-small grain traders who worked daily except for the Sabbath and holidays. Large merchants imported much of the wheat and grain from southern Italy and Sicily, supplying Florence and many cities around the Mediterranean and Adriatic.

At its peak in the early fourteenth century, Orsanmichele merchants sold from open barrels (*moggia*) four types of wheat and twelve classes of grain and legumes, including millet, rye, vetches, fava beans, and sorghum.[77] The transaction volume was large. About 1.2 million bushels (*staia*) were sold annually, sufficient to feed a population of 100,000 one bushel per person per month.⁷⁸ In addition to merchants, the city and market employed several grain officials for transaction oversight, supply issues, product quality inspections, governance of weights and measures, and other essential functions.

Independent businesses supported the market, including grain transporters, millers, and bakers, some of whom were women. Carriers earned about ten shillings (*soldi*) per *moggio* (twenty-four bushels). Communal flour mills operated along the Arno River and could process over 200,000 bushels (*staia*) annually.⁷⁹ But Florentine enterprise extended beyond large markets. Smaller venues were located near the Rubaconte Bridge and in the Oltrarno.⁸⁰ Chronicles and guild statutes mention numerous retail shops (*apothece*), workshops (*botteghe*), and stalls in various neighborhoods around the city.

Like the piazzas, small outlets sold foodstuffs and consumer items. Manuscript illustrations, such as the northern Italian *Tacuinum sanitatis* (a healthy living guide), depict sales of specialty goods, including fish, bread, meat, and pastas. Individual vendors also hawked commodities around the town and outside the city walls, although statutes attempted to restrict such activity. In short, Florence epitomized medieval Italian commerce and industry. Its economic output was significant. During the 1330s, 200 workshops produced 70,000–80,000 lengths of wool cloth, worth over 1.2 million florins. There were also 146 bakeries, 80 financial tables, 80 judges, 600 notaries, 60 physicians and surgeons, 100 medicinal and spice shops, and 300 shoe boutiques.⁸¹

BRUGES: A NORTHERN EUROPEAN CITY

In northern Europe, Bruges became an important commercial center. The city was surrounded by a moat and walls made of four million bricks. By 1300, its walls supported seven windmills, with four water mills on internal waterways. By the fourteenth century, workers paved the city's streets. By 1331, Bruges had a major brickyard in Ramskapelle, transporting bricks via canal. Its buildings of limestone, wood, iron, and stone were crafted by carpenters, plumbers, blacksmiths, and much unskilled labor.⁸²

Bruges held a market fair in May, but its commercial environment was better represented through permanent structures. The city constructed stone sales halls, merchant outposts (hostels), and financier venues. Bruges' central market was the Grote Markt, a dedicated area with a complex of commercial buildings which included a landmark tower called the Belfort. Merchants sold a variety of goods from various market halls, including wool, cloth, grain, fish, meat, and imported figs and raisins. Specialty markets proliferated. The Spice Hall offered spices and dyestuffs. The Glovemakers' Hall contained shops, with money-changing tables nearby. The Waterhall allowed goods to be unloaded through a unique indoor system and provided second-floor storage. Boterhuis merchants sold cheese, milk, and butter from eighty stalls, near the egg market. By the late thirteenth century, large wooden cranes, operated by children on treadmills, lifted bulk goods like wine and beer. Like Florence and other cities, Bruges had numerous inns and taverns, which enhanced local business and tax revenue. The city's administrative system supported commerce. Bruges' notaries, like their Florentine counterparts, executed records and contracts, and a court system rendered justice.⁸³

Occupations in late medieval Bruges included a variety of trades. Merchants accounted for 20 percent of the labor force; construction, 13.65 percent; textile and tool producers, over 12 percent each; with food and general manufacturing workers constituting over 10 percent each. Luxury goods production made up almost 8 percent of the workforce, while money changing, transport, and security accounted for over 2 percent. Military, agriculture, and education were marginal employers.[84] Despite labor integration, social segregation prevailed: the wealthy tended to live on major roads, while the poor dwelled on back streets. Some also worked separately. For example, "fullers, dyers, leather workers and brewers" labored near water, such as rivers and canals.[85]

By the fourteenth century, Italians in Bruges dominated money changing, which also grew into banking services. In Florence, mendicant orders, churches, and charities sponsored preaching and alms-giving around the city, while Bruges' religious orders were situated near taverns, bathhouses, and centers of illicit activity. Even charity was insufficient at times, and some impoverished women worked as prostitutes, as they did in London and other cities. But Bruges also generated great individual wealth. The notable English wool trader William de la Pole, for example, rented space in Bruges from 1339 to 1340, where he stored and sold over 2,400 sacks of wool.[86]

Bruges, like other markets, hosted foreign traders. The English had operations with weigh houses and a dedicated street and square. Merchants travelled from Scotland, Ireland, Spain, and Portugal and several northern Italian cities. Immigrants also made up the part of the labor supply, with 26 percent working as tailors, leather artisans, and harness and stocking makers. Almost 19 percent of immigrants worked in textiles, and over 13 percent served as gold and silver smiths and artists (miniature and panel painters). About 12 percent worked in construction.[87]

TEXTILES: EXAMPLE OF COTTON CLOTH MANUFACTURING

In many cities, textiles comprised important industries. Flanders was long reputed for its cloth output. Manufacturing also extended to northern Italy, where urban workers engaged in wool, silk, and cotton cloth production. Cotton provides one example. Cotton was grown in regions as far east as India and China, in Islamic territories, and along the eastern Mediterranean, including areas near Jerusalem, Jaffa, Damascus, and Tyre. During the Crusades, Venetian, Pisan, Genoese, and other Mediterranean traders maintained warehouses in eastern ports and exported cotton westward.[88]

By the twelfth century, Genoese merchants imported cotton by sea from Alexandria, Antioch, and Sicily. Venetians also transported cotton from Calabria and Apulia (southern Italy). From Venice, traders moved cotton inland via the Po River to Lombardy, and by water or land to Bologna, Perugia, and Tuscan cities. Sicilian cotton made its way to Marseilles, and eventually as far north as Champagne and Flanders. Cotton not only became cloth, but also "candle wicks, gloves and bonnets." An intricate long-distance network developed for cotton transportation and for cloth manufacture and sale. By the mid-fifteenth century, Genoa imported almost 11,000 tons of Turkish cotton for re-export to Lombardy, England, Flanders, and other locations.[89]

Several stages of labor were involved in cotton cloth production. Workers separated seed from fiber, beat fibers, and removed debris. They raked the fibers between pegged boards, spun fibers into threads, and wove thread into cloth. They bleached and dyed the thread or cloth. When woven, they washed, stretched, and dried the cloth. Finally, workers sheared the cloth and pressed it with wooden blocks. Spinning was the most time-consuming aspect. The advent of the spinning wheel, rather than the distaff and spindle, revolutionized workers' output of thread and permitted standardized thicknesses and specifications. The cotton cloth industry has been viewed as an early form of mass production that changed the standard of living. It introduced new clothing, such as undergarments; robes for professional groups, such as lawyers, judges, doctors, and monks; household materials, including mattress stuffing, pillows, tablecloths, and towels; and decorative arts, such as tapestries and embroideries. Cotton was also used for sailcloths and paper production.[90]

The process was similar for wool cloth manufacture. Wool dying was strenuous and dirty work, conducted by both skilled and unskilled labor. Bruges had a dedicated area for dyers, the *Verversdijk*.[91] Both men and women in Europe worked as combers and beaters, and both were master weavers. In Bruges, women also served as seamstresses and traders.[92] In Florence, women typically worked as spinners, typically domestically, earning piecemeal and often minimal wages.[93] Florence at times prohibited women from spinning on public roads, public benches, or while selling herbs, bread, or other consumables (see Figure 3.4).[94]

FIGURE 3.4 Baking bread. *Tacuinum sanitatis*, fourteenth century. Photo: Alinari / Alinari Archives, Florence / Alinari. Image courtesy Getty Images.

Like weaving, many trades required specialized training. Apprenticeships provided a practical way for young people to learn a craft. The occupations varied, including bakers, barbers, stone, wood and iron workers, butchers, grain dealers, goldsmiths, painters, and shoe makers, among others. A father typically contracted sons, and sometimes daughters or other family members, to work with a master for a specified time, and may have paid for upkeep.[95] While not a luxury, apprenticeship contracts appeared to be available to those who had disposable income. Others undertook less formal training, practiced within families from youth, such as shepherding, transporting commodities, or hawking foods locally.

WOMEN IN COMMERCE

Beyond textile manufacturing, women were an integral part of the commercial life of late medieval Europe. Women appeared in markets as sellers and consumers. They hauled and hawked their wares inside and outside of the city, in shops, in transient stalls, or along roadsides. They were members of guilds, and they were the subject of urban commercial legislation. They worked together with their husbands, or they sold their goods alone. Women tended to operate in the world of everyday necessities, foodstuffs, and food production, making ale and cloth. Women typically did not operate in the higher circles of finance or international trade, nor did they usually participate openly in the political life of cities; yet women were not hidden behind closed doors. They had a clear public presence, working with their male counterparts in businesses that were fundamental to the needs of their households and communities.[96]

Florentine provisioners' guild statutes demonstrate a range of occupations that women practiced together with men. These included dealers in oil, cheese, salt, drinking and bottle ware, plates, and various foodstuffs. They sold meats, fish, lard, cheese, eggs, legumes, figs, nuts, fruits, and vegetables, as well as soap, candles, and household merchandise.[97] Women worked with men as butchers—buying, selling, and processing cows, pigs, buffalo, goats, sheep, and other animals and products (see Figure 3.5).[98] In nearby Prato, women owned businesses or worked as bakers, moneylenders, kiln operators, and sellers of kitchen goods, leather ware, and corsets.[99]

Many of the female occupations of Florence had direct parallels in Germany and Paris, among other cities. In Germany, workshops typically were joined to the household; thus women could perform both domestic and artisanal labor. Women also held external positions. In Nuremberg's fourteenth-century Holy Ghost Hospital (*Heilig Geist Spital*) women acquired food and provisions for the kitchen and bedrooms. They admitted patients and inventoried their possessions. They supervised maids and cooks and were engaged in beer and bread distribution. Similarly, Frankfurt, Stuttgart, Nuremberg, Constance, and other German cities deputized midwives as sworn officials, and the government compensated them if the patient was unable to do so.[100] In 1292 Paris, women served like men as tanners and furriers, metalworkers, food provisioners, retailers, servants, carters, wood and construction workers, wool, silk and linen workers, innkeepers, and candle makers.[101] The proportion of service between men and women may have differed, but both genders were vital to urban labor.

For certain occupations, governments regulated women and men equally. The Munich city code of 1340 provided, "A woman who stands at the public market and who buys and sells has all the rights that her husband does."[102] In Florence, male and female carters, city oven operators, millers, and bread makers all faced the same licensing and operating

FIGURE 3.5 Butchering. *Tacuinum sanitatis*, fourteenth century. Photo: DeAgostini. Image courtesy Getty Images.

requirements.[103] Male and female millers and bakers alike needed to display a sign of the Florentine lily for bread sales.[104] Similarly, small-scale male and female provisioners were held to equal standards for sales within city limits and along roadsides, and for hoarding goods and selling outside of established market hours.[105]

Women also ran domestic businesses. In fourteenth-century England, female ale brewers were ubiquitous. They brewed from home, often supplementing their spouses' income. Women purchased the barley, oats, and malt for brewing. They soaked the ingredients and brewed the mixture in vats. Brewsters worked in cities and on manors. They sold the ale locally in the streets and from houses, as it did not transport well over long distances. Ale was central to the daily diet. Water was often unhealthy and wine was expensive, thus ale was consumed at all three meals. Even children drank some. Ale became a relatively large business. Assuming an average daily consumption of a quart, the cumulative production output would have been seventeen million barrels per year. Individual brewsters were generally in the middle socioeconomic ranks. The industry was flexible, and some women were able to continue working after their husbands died. After 1350, however, beer began to compete with ale, as hops gained popularity. Beer was also more easily transported and had a longer shelf life. By the late fifteenth century, as beer became popular in England, males overtook the brewing industry, professionalized it, and drove women out.[106] Men similarly dominated the German beer trade in Denmark, and German women lost many economic and business freedoms after the medieval period, when men replaced them in these occupations.[107]

CONCLUSION

Medieval work was as diverse as life of the time. Work was part of an interconnected commercial environment throughout Europe. Labor took place in fields, cities, at sea, for war, in workshops, at homes, at marketplaces, and at a host of other locations. Work encompassed virtually all societal levels, and many occupations included women and at times children. Medieval work, whether agricultural or urban, built a complex and increasingly sophisticated society and economy. Whether through markets and finance, or through milling, construction, or brick making, medieval labor and trading produced many techniques, business practices, and innovations that sustained life and carried into early modern and modern times.

CHAPTER FOUR

Workplace Cultures

PETER STABEL

A cloth manufacturer from around 1150 in Ypres, already by that time one of the leading cloth-manufacturing cities of medieval Flanders, would have had great difficulty recognizing his work environment two centuries later in the same city. Not that the importance of the industry, nor even the technological skills he required, would have changed a lot. The most important technological changes had already been introduced before his own generation of textile workers. The broad horizontal loom, which necessitated complex labor relations, came to characterize urban cloth manufacture most likely by around 1100.[1] Certainly, the range of woollens produced would have differed slightly across those two centuries. In the 1350s the output of Flemish cloth workers had become significantly smaller and was aimed at manufacturing only the most expensive luxury fabrics. Although they aimed at producing large quantities of cloth in different price ranges, the twelfth-century cloth manufacturers had already been producing expensive scarlets dyed in the most exclusive colors like their late medieval colleagues. Even the division of labor had reached extremely high levels by around 1150. More than fifty manufacturing stages were required to produce a piece of fine woollen cloth, and many of these were executed by specialist craftsmen, both men and women.[2]

But despite these great continuities, a lot had changed. Instead of a makeshift townscape of wooden market infrastructures, the cities had built impressive cloth halls, sometimes, like in Ypres itself, cathedral-like buildings where cloth manufacturers brought their woollens for inspection and where these were sold mostly to foreign merchants coming from the Hanseatic territories along the Baltic, Italy, and the Iberian Peninsula.[3] In the 1350s textile workers were organized in powerful craft guilds, many of which succeeded in acquiring direct access to political power in the city councils.[4] But most importantly, many craftsmen had also gained access to key roles in the complex manufacturing networks that structured the production of cloth. It was no longer mercantile elites who controlled manufacture directly, but instead the most successful artisans organized the successive production stages.[5] Even the urban soundscape had changed. Instead of one bell defining the work hours, a multitude of market and labor bells announced not only the beginning and the end of the working day but also the hours for lunch breaks and for marketing cloth and labour.[6] From a highly informal labor market that was dominated by a tiny minority of wealthy entrepreneurs, where rules and regulations were limited, serving above all the interests of the dominant mercantile elites in providing flexibility and a steady supply of labor, labor markets had become much more regulated. Institutional arrangements had been adapted to deal with new economic circumstances. Perhaps, above all, two fundamental things were quite different in the 1350s as opposed to the 1150s.

Foremost the social identity of the workers and their attitudes toward work had altered dramatically. The realities of the workshop had shifted along with them. Work had become synonymous for civic virtue, and those ideas reached out not only to the leading groups in urban society, but also to the majority of guild-organized craftsmen and retailers.[7] Perhaps this change was expressed most clearly in how the textile trades were described in the charters of Mechelen, another cloth city in the Low Countries. In the first part of the thirteenth century, cloth weavers and fullers were not allowed to participate in the organization of manufacturing. They had no access to entrepreneurship, which was reserved to the mercantile elites of the city. These merchants were organized in a merchant guild in order to defend their privileges abroad and monopolize political power at home. In the charters of the cloth trade, craftsmen were even described as belonging to the despicable trades (*fallacis officiis*). Shortly before 1300, however, the craftsmen gained access to the wool trade, first by organizing themselves in formal craft guilds of their own and then by being allowed to become entrepreneurs (and enter the merchant guild, albeit with the financial penalty of a higher entrance fee). After guild revolutions took place around 1300, a watershed occurred when guilds gained access to political power and merchants lost their interest in organizing cloth manufacture. From despicable trades, the key workers in the Mechelen textile trades became cornerstones of urban society.[8]

Secondly, the influence of new urban middle classes on city politics and the organization of society and the economy had grown. Through a process of compromise and sometimes bloody conflict a new deal was struck with the traditional landowning and mercantile elites.[9] The changed political economy was felt in each and every workshop. Craft guilds and their members started to appropriate a discourse of the common good in society and packed it with their own value system of solidarity, brotherhood, and workmanship. This discourse had roots, of course, in earlier developments. In the course of the twelfth century the urban mercantile elites had emancipated themselves from their feudal surroundings by creating communes, an urban body politic that was based on shared values and interests.[10] Although theoretically designed to incorporate all citizens, it had never become all-inclusive. But by appropriating the idea of common good, craft guilds did not create an inclusive value system either.[11] Even if the economic success of the guilds boosted the level of political influence of the urban middle classes, not everyone was able to participate in these developments.[12] There were also losers in urban society.

Guild ideology was by no means geared toward creating an egalitarian society, not even among guild members themselves. If declining inequality rates from the fourteenth century onwards seem to imply a more even distribution of economic opportunity and economic gain (the redistributive effects of the Black Death were crucial in this process), not everyone was able to benefit from the opportunities. Within the craft guilds subcontracting flourished, giving entrepreneurial initiative to a select group of wealthy guild masters and reducing the other masters to mere employees.[13] From then on, formal hierarchies defined workshop cultures. There were many thresholds for achieving mastership, and even more informal ones for becoming established entrepreneurs embedded in social networks and with easy access to capital. As a result, success ratios for already-established guild families were significantly higher, making the task for newcomers much more difficult. Many guild members therefore remained wage-earners as journeymen or dependent masters in the service of a group of successful guildsmen.[14] Women also lost economic agency in the process, and even the relatively advantageous circumstances for workers after the demographic collapse in the fourteenth century did not allow them to profit from better job opportunities or wages in the guild economy.[15] Unskilled workers were outside the guild system regardless and found it increasingly hard to achieve social promotion. Finally, city dwellers constituted only a minority of those who made their living from labor. The majority of the population, even in the most densely urbanized regions of medieval Europe, lived in the countryside and continued to till the earth.

WORK CULTURES IN THE COUNTRYSIDE

For most medieval Europeans farms, fields, and pastures remained the main places of work. In general, most of Europe was characterized by an unstable and changing relationship between two basic types of rural work. On the one hand, peasants worked on farms. Labor relations were organized within the context of the household, in most parts of Europe a nuclear household. There were gender-specific roles: weaving textiles and brewing were originally among the tasks of women; hard physical labor on the field, such as plowing and even harvesting, was usually entrusted to the male members of the household. But, in general, family members shared labor, and wage labor by outsiders was kept as limited as possible. On the other hand, there was work on the estates of the landlords (demesne farming), whoever they were, and on larger independent farms. Here work could no longer be provided by the household alone. Labor varied in these often different organizational constructs, from bound labor on manorial estates, where serfs were obliged to carry out labor services for their lords usually in exchange for access to their own land, to free wage labor, often seasonal but sometimes also permanent, leading to more stable relations between employer and employee.[16]

This duality of work in the countryside did not mean, however, that it was an unchangeable world, nor that it lacked common features that connected both types of work environments. Custom was important in deciding workplace cultures; physical boundaries had to be set, often with the involvement of the community in highly ritualized procedures, or the community had to agree to collective agricultural practices, such as crop rotation or access to the all-important commons.[17] But power relations aggravated by the increasing Malthusian tension between population growth and food supply in the thirteenth century and the demographic cataclysm of the fourteenth century also changed workers' lives.[18] The same holds true for the power of nascent and developing markets, concentrated throughout most of Europe in cities and small market towns. All these elements changed the conditions under which people worked and the ways they thought about work. Regional diversity was perhaps even stronger for rural work than for urban work despite the immense disparities of urban ratios across Europe. In some regions, barely 5 to 10 percent lived in towns, while in others urban ratios reached 25 to 40 percent. Whereas craft guilds or guild-like institutions were present in one way or another in most European cities of some importance, more recent research into rural society has demonstrated enormous differences across Europe, not only in the organization of agriculture or the quality of the land but foremost in the different power relations that determined access to land and labor, the so-called social property relations. As a result, labor practices differed strongly from one region to another.

This diversity had old roots. As more recent scholarship about the large (post-)Carolingian rural estate has shown, the relationship between labor and land and the impact of the coercive power of landowning elites differed dramatically between the Carolingian heartlands in northwest Europe and Mediterranean Europe with its Roman inheritance (let alone the more peripheral regions of Anglo-Saxon England, Scandinavia, and central Europe), leading to fundamental differences in the nature of rural work.[19] In the ensuing feudal society of the tenth and eleventh centuries, so-called tenurial land gradually lost importance in some regions, certainly in what had been the Carolingian heartland, while it remained as or even more important in other regions, most notably in early Norman England of the eleventh and twelfth centuries. The nature of those relations was not stable either. Social homogenization seems to have characterized the emerging feudal society; the social categories of slaves and free were gradually transformed into a more generally unfree and bound labor force. Yet this homogenization did not result in similar patterns across Europe. In some regions serfdom remained important until the end of the Middle Ages and sometimes even beyond (England, Catalonia), and in others serfdom became even more important in the late Middle Ages (eastern Europe). But in most regions of western Europe where demesne farming was the norm, serfdom and the fixed relations between work on tenurial and manorial land gradually dissipated. Monetization of labor relations in the countryside, especially after 1100, strengthened this process.

Work identities were primarily constituted by access to land, but access to land changed over time. As a rule, prior to 1000, landowning elites started to usurp royal authority and political authority fragmented. Europe became characterized by cellular power structures.[20] This process often led to different kinds of labor relations, levels of commercialization and monetization, sensitivities about the juridical status of peasants, and so on. No wonder that this patchwork of different systems also led to a patchwork of ways in which workplaces were organized, of who was involved in them and who could profit from easier access to land and property. The fact that peasants wanted to guarantee the continuity of their holdings is a key element for explaining the relationship between the users of the land and their labor. In most of western Europe tenurial land constituted the most dynamic part of the rural economy. It was land in theory owned by large landowners, but in practice fully owned by peasants in exchange for increasingly monetized rents. On the one hand, inflation eroded these rents and land became more affordable. But on the other hand, peasants were also threatened by demographic growth and the permanent risk, in regions of egalitarian inheritance practices, that their holdings would be split up into tiny plots. High levels of indebtedness among peasants resulted. With each generation, they had to rearrange properties in order to keep them sustainable. Sometimes hierarchical relations developed between tiny peasant smallholdings and larger farms, which had gradually grown from manorial land or from clustered peasant plots. As the lord's income eroded because of fixed monetary rents in many places, various waves of feudal reaction led to changing power relations and increasing duties on peasant income outside regular land rents.[21] Moreover, in some specific regions, commercialization pushed the rural economy toward specialization in order to meet the demand for food, fuel, building materials, and raw materials in growing cities, particularly Paris and London, and of course the dense urban regions of northern Italy and the Low Countries.[22]

Hence extreme variety according to place and time characterized the workplace of most peasants. But they had one element in common. Whether bound by manorial arrangements (serfs) or, in practice, legally free (peasants), wage labor in the countryside seems to have been rare before the thirteenth century and despite increasing urban demand and the introduction of more productive agricultural techniques, room for specialization was limited.[23] The need to feed an ever-increasing population led to the dominant cultivation of cereals. This meant that, as a rule, peasants tended not to be specialists. In particular regions, of course, cattle and dairy farming, sheep, woodland, and vineyards were predominant; yet most peasants had plots of land dedicated to mixed farming. Most work took place on one's own farm (or in some regions on the lord's manor) and the basic unit of work was defined by the family, even in this period mainly the nuclear family, in which the available labor was pooled. Wage labor was, as a rule, limited on these small peasant holdings.[24]

The basic unit of work was, of course, different on large farms. Thanks to the spread of leaseholding from the thirteenth century and the rise of urban investors, the scale of agriculture changed dramatically in some regions. This required labor drawn from outside peasant households. Long-term contracts with servants, both male and female, constituted the backbone of agricultural work on large farms. Servants often lived on the farm and became integral members of farmers' households. Their wages were often substantially lower than those of irregular workers, but in exchange they were provided room and board and a certain degree of employment security. Because real wages tended to decline in the period of medieval growth and were irregular at best in periods of crisis, job security was no small asset.[25] But the small workforce active in long-term contracts was usually not sufficient to deal with the seasonal peak periods of the agricultural year. Besides the permanent household, a floating labor force was also occasionally put to work. Most workers were probably peasants who had their own smallholdings in the vicinity and combined work on their own holdings with wage labor on large farms. This was possible because the countryside was characterized by chronic hidden unemployment. Because of the seasonal nature of agriculture and the changing relations between land and population, a lot of the available labor was underused, a phenomenon that became more acute as population pressure built up and the average size of holdings declined. As land became ever more scarce, extra input of labor became available to increase land productivity, but at the cost of declining labor productivity. The relations between small peasants and large farmers were not entirely monetized, although irregular pay undoubtedly constituted a welcome addition to the income of smallholders. Relations of dependence were involved as well, as poor peasants often lacked the capital to invest in expensive agricultural tools and draft animals, mostly horses.[26] Some cattle for manure and dairy was often all they could manage, and therefore they relied on large farms for these services.[27] When protoindustrial development came into play, at least from the late Middle Ages onwards, the supply of raw materials and the control of financial and commercial networks proved another element in the hierarchical relations between large farmers and poor peasants.[28]

But specialist laborers were also involved. The uncertainties of weather conditions in the relatively short harvest period and the labor-intensive harvesting procedures in grain- and wine-growing regions meant aristocratic landowners and later large leasehold farms needed to attract extra laborers in peak periods. Work cultures were entirely different for these seasonal specialists. In contrast to peasants they were often very mobile, travelling beyond the boundaries of their usual locale (their own village or cluster of villages).[29] Habitually they took on the form of established gangs, including both men and women. The phenomenon seems even to be growing in the late Middle Ages, when labor became scarcer. Travelling gangs of specialist laborers often used their bargaining power to negotiate higher wages than other rural groups, who were often prepared to undercut normal wages in exchange for more permanent employment or relations of dependence. As such these groups probably developed a working culture of their own and a proper identity. They were, however, not alone in doing so. In fact, the countryside boasted a lot of other specialist trades.

Besides agricultural work, many other activities took place in the countryside. Every village had its share of nonagricultural trades.[30] Blacksmiths, millers, soldiers, even specialist trades such as moneylenders, and, of course, clergymen abounded. Although sources do not allow scholars to trace their activities, they are duly recorded in charters and accounts. In some regions, these activities even outnumbered agricultural ones. In mining settlements hundreds of workers, skilled and unskilled, clustered around one central activity, leading to often complex entrepreneurial relationships and a proper working identity of miners, linked to transfer of skill and knowledge.[31] In the period of the bipartite estates in the post-Carolingian era, manufacture of textiles on large estates was sometimes concentrated in workshops, so-called *gynaecea*, employing above all unfree women.[32] As a rule a lot of activities in the countryside, agricultural or not, were gendered just as they were in cities. Women tended to be active in brewing and textile production.[33] Yet this gendered identity was not always stable. As protoindustrial textile manufacture developed in the countryside in the late Middle Ages, the weaving of linen or woollen fabrics was usually entrusted to male members of the household, while spinning was exclusively female.[34] In general, nonagrarian activities became increasingly important as commercialization took off, and in many regions an equilibrium had to be found between work in industry (mainly as miners and protoindustrial textile manufacture), in shipbuilding and fishing in coastal regions and in land or river transport. The spread of protoindustrial activity, and the added income it generated for households, even lowered the threshold for splitting up peasant holdings, leading to tiny farms that barely allowed the household's survival. But as a rule, these developments did not seem to have altered workers' identities that much. The household itself, and the reservoir of labor contained within it, remained the core of the labor system. It was also the starting point for all kinds of collective action, from the organization of common land to legal actions against an oppressive lord. Because of the necessities of agriculture (manure, tools, capital), complex relationships among holdings of various sizes developed. The larger holdings were, the more they relied on wage labor with all its hierarchical complexities. Only seasonal work gangs or specific kinds of nonrural and protoindustrial work (not textile manufacture but rather seasonal activities such as fishing, shipbuilding, and mining) led to different workers' identities, with a higher degree of mobility or collective action of workers.[35]

THE MYSTERIES OF TRADE

If the travelling gangs of harvest workers were characterized by high levels of mobility, high wages, gendered working patterns, and a proper working identity, other specialist workers also developed such attitudes, linked as they were to a lifestyle of movement, specialist skill, and a specific workshop culture. No other group has been as famous as the craftsmen who built the medieval cathedrals, belfries, and castles. Skilled workers at these huge building sites, from architects to stonemasons, were often recruited from distant places, and their skill as craftsmen constituted their identity and prestige.[36] Stonecutters and building masters started to use their own signs and marks to distinguish themselves as specialists. They boasted about having been employed at particular sites, and they developed their own collective identity with rules and practices that not only guaranteed the excellence of their work but were designed to transfer skills and status, in short, the mysteries of their trade across generations of craftsmen.

Building workers were not the only ones to develop their own collective identity. Travelling groups of entertainers similarly acquired a distinct work identity as did those engaged in intellectual trades, such as teachers and scholars, for whom migration and mobility were key elements (see Figure 4.1).[37]

Less known is the fact that also the most important medieval manufacturing industry was characterized by movement. Textiles workers developed a group identity in part

FIGURE 4.1 Musicians playing at a banquet. The Beaupré Antiphonary, vol. 2, Flemish, 1290. Baltimore, Walters Art Museum, MS W.760, folio H. © The Walters Art Museum, Baltimore.

because clerical elites, who had a disdain for this type of manual labor anyway, viewed their activities with great suspicion. The monks of Sint-Truiden near the river Meuse in present-day Belgium called textile workers "the most presumptuous and arrogant of all." But in their disdain, they recorded at the same time what must have been the first examples of industrial collective action and workers' rituals in northwest Europe. They described how in the early-twelfth-century travelling weavers gathered in a ritual around a ship on wheels that was rolled into town and how they kept watch over the ship, a watch that turned into a celebration for a substantial part of the town's population. Workers were also linked to all kinds of heretical movements. Some decades later the "wretched weavers" of Arras, another important cloth city of the Low Countries, were suspected of belonging to Manichaean sects. Clerical authors explained how they gathered in their huts and cellars to practice their heretical ritual and described these weavers as highly mobile, moving from place to place, and as uncultivated and dangerously greedy. Undoubtedly these testimonies reveal the existence of a sense of group identity around 1100, long before any formal association came of age.[38] Weavers did not hesitate to associate their work with the deeds of Christ and saints.[39] As such, the nature of manual work became an intricate part of an emerging common identity. But it was still far from generally accepted yet.

URBAN WORK: GUILDS AS ARTIFICIAL FAMILY?

Undoubtedly the most important institution regulating cultures of work was the family, in the countryside as well as in towns. The relationship between work and household is discussed in Chapter One, but in short, little agreement exists about when the so-called nuclear household, the single most important transition allegedly associated with the second part of the Middle Ages, came of age. Many authors claim that it was the Black Death that finally decided the fate of the extended family in large parts of Europe, while others state that the success of the nuclear family dates from a much earlier period.[40] What is increasingly clear, however, are the strong differences across Europe. If the demographic cataclysm of the successive plague epidemics had a great impact on European marriage patterns, which resulted in small nucleated households, they were not the only cause. In some regions, even before the plague's arrival, nuclear families were at the heart of the organization of work, and other factors seem to have triggered the pivotal role of the nuclear household. It is striking that, in the second half of the thirteenth century, almost one hundred years before the Black Death, with the appearance of craft guilds, households, as focal points for organizing work, entered craft regulations in the Low Countries, never to leave again.[41]

Because of the inherent demographic fragility of the nuclear family in a period of high child mortality and migration, the permanence of the family as a beacon of social stability and security for each individual could not be guaranteed over the long run. As a result, other types of solidarity became necessary. Modern guild historians have often considered these associations to be "artificial families." The triumph of the companionate marriage and the declining importance of the extended family in the course of the late Middle Ages are understood to have boosted this phenomenon. It made intergenerational solidarity within the context of the extended family more difficult. According to the so-called nuclear hardship thesis, the elderly were particularly at risk, because of life cycle mismatches when solidarity and care were directed toward the immediate offspring.

Hence alternatives in society needed to be organized, and guilds were instrumental in the process because of the complex institutional framework they created for providing health care, social security, retirement homes, and so on.

For a long time, guilds have been understood as political and economic tools against a hostile feudal aristocracy and an oppressive commercial elite. But recent scholars have seen guilds as positive instruments for organizing solidarity, charity, and devotion. Some scholars even go so far as to state that guilds primarily embodied the values of brotherhood and mutual assistance in urban society.[42] So-called poor boxes (or purses) were designed to help guild members who were too old or sick to work. They were financed by contributions of guild members who wanted at a later stage profit from the guild box. This practice created a network of solidarity within the guild. In some guilds only a part of the guild community was allowed to participate (usually the masters), but in others the system was much more inclusive. But whether inclusive or exclusive, the poor box added another layer of solidarity, a community within the community.[43]

Some of these institutions were already active at an early stage from the thirteenth century onwards, but they seem to have become more numerous over the course of the fifteenth century, particularly in northwest Europe. The fact that guilds developed this institutionalized system of health care and assistance relatively late strengthens the claim that brotherhood and solidarity were core values when guilds made their appearance. In the early periods formalization would not have been necessary. And, indeed, most guilds had started as charities over the course of the thirteenth century, and from their beginnings many were anxious to develop various, often informal systems of social security.[44] The charter of the cloth weavers' guild in Mechelen of 1270, that started this chapter, was issued not by the guild authorities but by the mercantile elites of the city. Yet it states prominently how weavers, who were not able to work and earn an honest income, could rely on their guild brothers for assistance. They were allowed to visit all the weavers' workshops where they would receive a fixed amount of money to help them through their difficult period. The charter was, however, also keen to limit the number of times disabled workers were allowed to exercise these rights, and it is not at all certain if these limits were set by the urban elites. The internal regulation of the guild seems to have been, even at this early stage in Mechelen's guild history, the prerogative of the craft guild officers themselves.[45]

But guild solidarity of course targeted more than financial support. Guilds were foremost institutions of sociability. Collective rituals cemented guild solidarity. The collective nature of devotion, celebration, guild administration, transition rituals, and death molded guild ideology and identity. Social bonds between guildsmen were constantly being renewed in weekly masses and in the decoration of guild chapels, and they were present in most guild activities. In almshouses, old guildsmen or their widows could spend their final years. Secular pageants and religious processions were organized, and in many cities ritualized political action was also organized, for example the so-called call-to-arms when guild members paraded through the city with their armor and banners. In many cities of northern Europe guilds provided the backbone of urban militias, a notable practice in a period when organized and disciplined foot soldiers were gradually gaining the upper hand over aristocratic mounted knights on the battlefield.[46] But daily events also helped to reinforce bonds among guildsmen. The guild officers organized tours in the cities from workshop to workshop to control the activities of their members and take out free-riders. Guild tribunals dealt with internal matters. Meals and drinking events celebrated the admission of new members or promotions to mastership. Impressive guild houses holding charters and weaponry served as visual reminders of prestige and political power. In short guilds became a cornerstone in the body politic of urban society (see Figure 4.2).[47]

Guilds also provided the framework in which individual members could organize their lives. Their regulation fit the normal life cycles of average craftsmen. The guild organized the transfer of skill during adolescence and took care of disciplining young members; it facilitated the establishment of social networks; it allowed entrepreneurial continuities after the death of a guild master by allowing widows to continue the businesses of their deceased husbands; and, finally, it assisted guild members and members of their household in their old age.[48] It would be going too far, however, to state that associational life entirely replaced family life.[49] In late medieval cities, even in those where associations became strong pillars of society, family relations remained at the heart of the circles of sociability surrounding everyone. Whether they were craftsmen, beguines, or single women, it was to family members that most turned in their hour of need.[50] Surviving wills from this era testify to this practice. When, for example, beguines of northern European cities felt the necessity to draw up wills to dispose of their possessions after death, they always put their own blood ties first. Although they were part of a strong religious community with its own institutional organization and with well-established relations of work, friendship, or shared devotional experience in the community, it was to their children or parents, to nieces and nephews, and to brothers and sisters that they gave their wealth, and if fellow beguines were among the beneficiaries, they tended also to be family members. Similar patterns appear in the case of other town dwellers. Certainly gifts to guilds and their social institutions were

FIGURE 4.2 Cloth Hall, 1200–1304. Ypres. Wikimedia Commons.

plentiful, but these gifts, however important for the guilds, do not point at their role as alternative families, nor is there any contemporary discourse which claims they are taking on this role.

FORMALIZING WORK

The economic actions of craft guilds are much better known than their cultural role. In most European cities, guilds came of age in the course of the thirteenth century as solidarities of people exercising more or less the same occupation. But guilds included wealthy entrepreneurs linked to the mercantile and even aristocratic elites of the cities as well as impoverished workers working for piece or time wages. And work hierarchies were increasingly formalized on the work floor. Guild masters could develop their own activities, while journeymen were by definition limited to working for entrepreneurs as skilled craftsmen and apprentices, usually underage and under the protection of the masters who trained them. But guild hierarchies did not necessarily reflect economic success.[51] Masters could work as wage earners for other masters; journeymen could, if they possessed skills which were in demand, use their bargaining powers to earn relatively high wages and apprentices, certainly at the end of their training, and seem to have been used as a source of cheap skilled labor. Besides these formal guild categories, masters often made use of the labor present in their own households by involving their wives, children, and servants in the activities of the workshop. Complex systems of subcontracting could complicate things further, leading to networks of workshops that were organized to meet the demands of particular entrepreneurs or merchants.

Until recently, scholars have been reading guild statutes in very legalistic ways. A superficial reading of guild statutes can present a seemingly egalitarian ambition linked to a carefully crafted and hierarchical world where various thresholds limited entrance into the guild and molded patterns of social exclusion. But guild regulation was carefully drafted in order to allow entrepreneurs to achieve economic success through the loopholes of strict statutes. Although there was a tendency to curb extreme competition by stimulating access to skill and raw materials for all masters and by limiting the negative impact of asymmetric access to information for guild members and consumers alike, this did not stop competition within the guild.[52] Economic success did not only depend upon membership in the guild; access to social and financial networks was just as crucial.

All of this, of course, directly affected the work floor. Medieval artisanal activity has sometimes been described as static and not open to much technological innovation. Although this may be true in comparison to the dramatic changes of the Industrial Revolution, the argument is less convincing in light of everything that went on before. Medieval industrial development was not without its technological earthquakes. The introduction of the broad loom, of the windmill, and of new mining techniques must have had shattering consequences for the organization of labour.[53] It certainly had dramatic consequences for the status and the identity of the workers involved. If anything, organizational innovations triggered most changes in the workplace, and guilds seem to have been paramount in these developments. A striking feature of the organization of the workshop in the late Middle Ages is the labor market's much higher level of formalization. Entrepreneurs in the twelfth and early thirteenth century did not seem to have been much concerned with carefully regulating labor markets and setting wages. On the contrary, they profited from flexible labor relations. It was quality standards that they cared about, and these could be achieved through their own organizations (the merchant guilds or the city governments they controlled). Before 1300, merchants tended to leave the initiative of manufacture to guild masters. They could mobilize only limited amounts of capital in order to control manufacturing chains, but they could rely on the collective actions of their guild. The craft guilds filled the institutional gap in many places, and from this moment on, labor relations on the work floor became meticulously regulated.[54] Formal labor markets were organized to bring entrepreneurs into contact with a floating work force, both skilled and unskilled; hierarchical relations between employer and employee were drafted; labor time was carefully regulated and publicly announced with clocks and bells. The late Middle Ages developed a standardized and predictable labor market, well suited for less powerful employers. Guilds were not only, and certainly not primarily, about consumer or worker interests. They were politically dominated by (albeit often small) entrepreneurs and, as such, they served chiefly their interests.

Market transparency was seen as crucial both for the continuity of the premodern economy and to guarantee guild solidarity.[55] Free riders had to be taken out by implementing complex systems of fines: low for infractions that were only scratching at the surface of guild regulation, heavy for those that broke the essence of guild solidarity and jeopardized the guild's reputation. Only rarely did guild courts assess breaches of guild solidarity to be so great that removal from the guild was deemed necessary. They did so mostly when the position of the guild itself in the city as a whole was threatened. The result was an avalanche of sometimes seemingly petty rulings, which in the past were inevitably interpreted as conservatism and rent-seeking, stifling entrepreneurial initiative, and economic growth, and of course guilds did, as we have seen, put up barriers in order to shield their activities.[56]

Yet the inflation of petty rules also served other goals than providing an impregnable fortress of guild exclusion. If anything is proven by the endless cases of litigation before guild and city courts about countless infringements on guild regulation, it is that these rules were constantly being negotiated, changed, and adapted, and that only rarely did they really allow strict monopolies or provide a waterproof system of exclusion. On the contrary, if the inflation of guild rules and their attempts to define all circumstances, from production and exchange to leisure and sexuality of guild members, may seem intimidating, the dense regulation is nonetheless full of inconsistencies, even outright contradictions.[57] Moreover as research on guilds in the Low Countries, England, and Italy shows, not all regulations were actually enforced all the time.

It is striking how high levels of product innovation characterized the late medieval economy. It allowed, for example, guild masters to follow the accelerating fashion cycles of the late Middle Ages, related to everything from dress to art, and thereby to produce fashionable new types of dress, panel paintings, tapestries, brocaded silks, and armor, as well as the right kinds of hats, gloves, belts, sleeves, and so on. Skill was paramount in this process of adaptation, and guilds were extremely attentive to the transfer of skill. It created the value of the product and guaranteed the income and reputation of the guildsmen. It constituted their collective identity. Through all the minutiae of regulation of commodities and commercial exchange, it is this concern that seems paramount.

The concern for skill and constructed value came, however, at great expense for some of the workers. Non-guild workers, who in many cities constituted the majority of all city dwellers, were relegated to a less formalized economy of makeshift: less protected from the adversities of the market, less able to profit from its benefits. Most also became second-rate townsmen, as full citizenship increasingly was linked to access to political power and membership in one of the corporate bodies in the city. But entrance into the guild system still seemed feasible in the late Middle Ages. In the cities of Flanders half of all guild members had no pedigree in the guild whatsoever and many, if not most, were newcomers coming from outside the city.[58] Guilds were still open institutions. Thresholds for outsiders were rising nonetheless. More importantly masters' sons and native-born citizens profited from better social networks and access to capital to start businesses of their own. They had opportunities to climb the ladder of political power in the guild and city administration. Stories of extremely successful newcomers are abundant from London to Gdańsk, but one must remind oneself that success stories were still to a large extent exceptional. Guilds and their effects on the work floor were not always inclusive; they even tended to become increasingly exclusive after the Black Death.

It is probably women who paid the highest price of all.[59] Well before the Black Death they were banned from formal training schemes in the guild (foremost through apprenticeship). There were, however, exceptions. In some cities there were female guilds, where, usually under the guidance of male supervisors, women made up the bulk of the workforce. In Paris silk weavers were usually women, and the same is also true for silk manufacture in some Italian cities. In Cologne there were several female guilds.[60] Yet, as a rule, women were ousted from the regular guild curriculum of apprentice, journeyman, and guild master in most manufacturing guilds from the late thirteenth century onwards. Before 1300 the statutes of cloth towns in Flanders still mention female weavers or dyers together with their male counterparts; after 1300 this became rare, and the practice disappeared almost completely around 1350.[61] The process is simultaneous with the move toward manufacturing more luxury fabrics, whose reputation for quality was linked to expensive raw materials and, above all, to skill. Women outside the guild training schemes could no longer be associated with the end product. This does not mean that women disappeared from manufacture. Their role was, however, gradually limited to non-guild-organized stages of production (in cloth manufacture, for example, spinning and cleaning fabrics, which was badly paid and low-status work), while labor on the other more prestigious steps of production was gradually drawn into the patriarchal household of the guild master. Strikingly, these changes occurred at the same time that guild statutes started to contain many references to the household as an economic unit.

GUILD VALUES AND WORK ETHICS: A CULTURE OF CONTROL AND REPUTATION

The ideology of guild sociability and solidarity was also apparent in new work ethics. It was work and membership in the guild that constituted the worker's identity. In the process workers adopted a set of values, which focused on moral behavior and strict hierarchy. With the increasing formalization of labor markets and the nexus of quality and transparency, new labor mentalities came to the forefront. Public morality and respectability became the core values for every guildsman, and as such they penetrated into the value system of the rising urban middle classes. Guildsmen were not allowed to live with a concubine while being married to another woman; they could not get involved in prostitution; they were not allowed to gamble or be found in improper situations when being drunk; they had to be dressed properly in the colors of the guild and honor the public engagements of the guild; they had to assist in public guild ceremonies.[62] Some guilds went as far as forcing their members to dress properly for work. The Mechelen statutes of the cloth weavers around 1300 mention that workers should wear decent woollen clothing. It is striking how pictorial representations of urban middle classes even in a merchant city as wealthy as fifteenth-century Bruges always show citizens dressed in fine woollens, rarely in silk, which remained the fabric of the nobility.

Guilds were permeated with a culture of respectability. There are, of course, also economic reasons for this. Reputation was an important asset in developing businesses and guaranteeing their continued success. Being disreputable meant being dishonest and not worthy of trust. Guilds tried actively to weed out possible infractions. In particular, the workplace itself was increasingly regulated.[63] Teams of guild officers went from workshop to workshop, inside the privacy of the home, to see whether guildsmen abided with the quality regulations of the guild. The workshop was by no means a purely private space; it was a space shared by the craftsmen and their family, by the guild and consumers. Trust and control went hand in hand. Social control became even more important toward the end of the Middle Ages, when all kinds of disreputable behavior of guild members were considered more and more threatening to the guild's reputation as a whole.

But the focus on reputation was not only enforced by the craft guilds and their officers; it was also deeply lived by the guild members themselves. It belonged to their way of life. This can be seen in court cases, when guildsmen had to develop lines of defense before a judge. While asking princely pardon for a sentence from the duke of Burgundy in the fifteenth century, guildsmen in the Low Countries fashioned themselves as loyal subjects of the prince and as victims of unbridled passion and circumstance, like all other supplicants did.[64] But guildsmen usually added other elements to their self-fashioning strategies: they were not only loyal subjects, they were also loyal brothers to their companions, the notion of brotherhood and solidarity being among the core values of the guild. They were living from their own means and from their own work. Finally, they had a reputation for being honest and utterly respectable as contributors to the urban society in which they lived as well as to the common good, which inevitably could only be beneficial for the prince as well. In short, they proclaimed, even at a moment of extreme tension when sometimes life or death was at stake, their guild identity as being the essence of their actions. They were no longer despicable trades.

CHAPTER FIVE

Work, Skill, and Technology

VALERIE L. GARVER

Modern popular culture often takes the view that the Middle Ages were a backward era; yet the period from 800 to 1450 saw many major technological advances, the development of new forms of skilled labor, and increasing expertise in long-standing areas of work. One would not want to overstate the rate of these changes, especially in comparison to the last century. Indeed, greatly because of modern expectations concerning change in the workplace, medieval technology remains a subject of significant controversy. The field took off with the publication of *Medieval Technology and Social Change* by Lynn White, Jr. in 1962, an influential book whose conclusions have raised varying degrees of dispute but whose overall argument—that technological innovation has broad social and cultural repercussions—remains a hallmark of the field.[1] Published at a time of low unemployment, optimism concerning technological change and a desire for time-saving devices, White's views can seem old-fashioned as many now face the environmental repercussions of technological growth and increased skepticism concerning the economic and cultural benefits of technology.[2] Although few would credit technological change for causing far-ranging medieval societal changes to the degree that White did, most medievalists agree that new technologies brought innovation to those who labored.

One scholar has noted the danger of thinking about medieval technology in the same way modern people consider technology in their era. Because workers and those who wrote about labor thought of technology in varied ways that do not always match present-day assumptions, it is crucial to examine technology (and the skills to employ it) contextually.[3] The problem frequently is that it is hard to know why medieval individuals adopted or improved some technologies quickly, but others only slowly despite their ability to improve work conditions and productivity, and why they employed still others alongside or in alternation with less effective technologies. Some scholars studying late medieval use of agricultural technologies in England note that locations and periods of high rent seemed to correlate with intensive use of technology to increase yields, but the incomplete nature of the evidence makes it difficult to be sure this connection was causal, especially when sources can make it appear that the English were sometimes less apt to adopt new technologies than their counterparts across the English channel.[4] In addition, only England and the Italian peninsula have been subject to systematic study in regard to technology.[5] Studies of other areas will eventually help flesh out the broader medieval view and provide greater context for local studies.

A paucity of written sources, especially for some types of production, has hindered research into the transmission and development of work skills and technologies. Craft production in rural villages throughout much of medieval Europe, for instance, has long been difficult to document, but careful analysis of material remains shows potential in uncovering the nature of that labor and its cultural implications.[6] Archaeology and scientific analysis promise to open up increasing information about these subjects. Work practices in stone sculpture workshops have left virtually no written traces, but analysis of stone types, particularly with attention to geologic data, has helped to clarify the skills and technologies involved. Geologic study has identified a specific type of Lutetian limestone known as *liasis de Paris*, which, although only available in the Paris Basin, was used in large-scale sculpture in Paris and across much of north-central France, particularly in locations with waterways. As a result, it is probable that these stones arrived by boat, a practice attested to in some medieval documents. The similarities in sculpting these stones suggests that the artisans were in touch with one another, perhaps even meeting sometimes at the quarry where they may have directed the selection of stone. A stained glass window at Chartres Cathedral depicts the sculptors at work in a group, a widespread practice and another opportunity for the artisans to pass on knowledge, skills, and ideas.[7]

INNOVATION AT WORK

The cultural value of technological change varies from one society to another. Scholars long assumed that craft guilds, which lasted relatively unchanged in structure for five hundred years, hindered technological innovation because of the strict controls they tried to exert over output, price, labor, and access to training. Recently, historians have challenged that view, noting that it accords guilds too much power and too little flexibility.[8] Instead technological change occurred as a means to increase production or to improve the quality of finished goods so that proprietors could earn more money. Evidence for thefts of inventions and secrecy concerning techniques survives from the fifteenth century, a transformative period that saw increased emphasis on innovation. Statements concerning secrets in craft recipes reflect this new cultural milieu. By the late Middle Ages, innovation began to take on a positive value, especially in certain places such as late medieval Italy where craftsmen sometimes wrote manuals that could spread technical innovations across significant distances.[9]

Some technologies, once thought to be medieval inventions, in fact had longer histories. Many scholars once argued that the wheelbarrow appeared in Europe only in the twelfth century. Although they recognized the increasing evidence for their use from the 1170s in southeastern England and northwestern France, medievalists now realize that this technology existed in the ancient eastern Mediterranean. Whether its use persisted in either the East or the West or whether the wheelbarrow was reintroduced from China, where it had a much longer, continuous history, medieval workers used it, especially at building sites, from the thirteenth century.[10] The absence of archaeological remains of wheelbarrows and the ambiguous references to them in written texts make their origins obscure. Pictorial depictions from the thirteenth century on comprise the primary evidence for them alongside textual references, the earliest of which also dates to the thirteenth century. One scholar has suggested that the multiplicity of wheelbarrow designs in the pictorial record means that the "idea" of this technology was what mattered in its transmission over time and space.[11]

Technological changes sometimes altered gendered divisions of labor. During the early Middle Ages, most weavers employed warp-weighted vertical looms, which were relatively narrow and cumbersome to set up. A recent study of ninth- to eleventh-century textile tools, including those related to vertical looms, found at the Viking-era sites of Birka (Sweden) and Hedeby (Germany) emphasized the many work hours such cloth production required.[12] Early medieval women carried out the vast majority of textile work, but starting around the eleventh century with the development of the horizontal loom with pedals, men increasingly took charge of and carried out textile work, particularly the manufacture of woollen cloth. This new technology made cloth making more profitable because of its efficiency; yet that same productivity required more spinning to produce the requisite thread. Because it was the lowest form of textile work and to a lesser degree because women were traditionally associated with spinning, many women spun while men wove.[13]

Some technological advances failed to be taken up in certain locations. In the Othe Forest on the border of Champagne and Burgundy, iron working, once a prominent industry there, had all but ceased by the end of the fifteenth century. In part, some operations failed to adopt new practices and lost out to those that innovated, but perhaps most decisive was the price of timber which could bring in far greater revenue. In this case, medieval people did not "fail" to innovate; other factors made innovation a moot point, and iron working shifted to the Vanne River where forges and mills grew, sometimes working in conjunction as when some mills sharpened iron implements.[14]

MINING AND METAL WORKING

In addition to mining for metals, medieval people dug salt mines in the Alps, especially in what is now Austria. By the thirteenth century, salt mines existed in the Berchtesgaden and Salzburg regions. Digging a salt mine required horizontal tunnelling, carried out mainly by hewers and their assistants using chisels and hammers. To make the hewing easier, some specialized mine workers' job was to bring in firewood. After allowing a fire to burn, miners doused it with water causing the stone in that area to become brittle. This process made hewing easier but more dangerous because sometimes noxious gasses resulted and portions of the tunnel ceiling fell. To avoid the latter, expert timbermen felled trees to make boards that could line the tunnels while blacksmiths created metal joins to hold the boards in place. Surveyors then kept track of the tunnels to avoid collapses and to ensure the property rights of the mine owners, at times by marking them on the surface and at others by drawing the interiors of mines, aided, at least by the fifteenth century, by compasses. In sum, salt mining required many specialized laborers working together, and one finds evidence that others recognized and rewarded their expertise. In Hall, in 1345, for example, mine workers successfully stopped working in order to gain concessions. Because salt mines competed for the best workers, it is likely that miners earned high wages.[15]

The Holy Roman Empire became important for mining, especially as demand for metal, including gold and silver, increased in the thirteenth and fourteenth centuries. The Harz Mountains and Bohemia were particularly important mining regions. Yet learning about mining remains difficult because medieval authorities rarely described it. Historians therefore often rely on archaeological evidence, but most mining sites were destroyed when medieval miners filled in old mines or built new ones on top of old ones. As with salt mines, those who dug mines for metals used hand tools and similar methods. These techniques kept medieval mines quite shallow in comparison to modern ones, and initially shafts did not extend below the level of ground water. The supply was sometimes exhausted quickly and resulted in efforts to dig deeper, sometimes up to hundreds of meters below ground, forcing mine workers to find ways to drain water. These included using a series of waterwheels, which moved water to the surface. Such pump installations often required teams of horses or men to operate them, but some employed a waterwheel on the surface.[16]

Other medieval technologies intersected with mining, shaping its practice and providing new innovations to workers. Mining often spurred or appeared in conjunction with watermilling. Thirteenth-century forge mills in England, France, and Sweden are among the earliest cases, but the use of waterpower for bellows and pumps developed in Italy in the thirteenth and fourteenth centuries and for bores in German lands in the fifteenth century.[17] Clocks became key to regulating the labor done in mines, particularly because miners were underground where measuring a work period by daylight was unhelpful. As clocks helped to develop Europeans' understanding of abstract time, they aided in spurring regulations and agreements about how many hours the miners would toil below the earth's surface.[18]

AN AGRICULTURAL REVOLUTION?

Some scholars have accepted a set of technological changes to the practice of agriculture, which they allege dramatically improved yields across the central Middle Ages (c. 900–c. 1300), as a "revolution." Whether this is the best term or not, food production inarguably soared, and many farming practices changed in the medieval era in no small part due to the increasing availability of metal.[19] Historians have questioned the causes and mechanisms of this agricultural growth because of both new archaeological finds and reassessment of the periods of late antiquity and the early Middle Ages. These new views on the transformation of agriculture have resulted in less certainty concerning the timing and geographic origins of changes, and skepticism that this was a period of entirely new innovations. Instead, what consensus has emerged emphasizes continuity from the ancient world, incremental change, novel practices that responded to environmental, social, and cultural conditions, and technological innovation that occurred more in fits and starts than in sweeping strokes. At the root of this reassessment is cultural history, which has caused medievalists to look at technology within varied contexts.

A range of inventions and technological transformations in agriculture increased productivity, which both responded to and promoted growth in the population, the economy, and cities. Gone are the days when historians could pinpoint the start of this "agricultural revolution." Rather new archaeological evidence has caused a reassessment of the transformation of agricultural technology in the Middle Ages. Among such changes was the invention and growth in use of the heavy moldboard plow, including those with fixed moldboards that could toss dirt in only one direction and swivel plows whose moldboards could move to either side as well as those with wheels and those without. Moldboard plows could dig up the earth and turn it over unlike the ard, a lighter instrument, used for centuries prior to the Middle Ages, that could only tear up the soil. Scholars once argued about whether the moldboard plow replaced the ard around 1000 or some centuries earlier, often during the Carolingian era (c. 700–c. 900). Recent archaeological finds have demonstrated that the heavy plow was in use in some places as early as the late Roman period, even those using a floating iron coulter, once thought a later innovation.[20] At the same time, medieval farmers continued to use the ard alongside or instead of the moldboard plow; for example, in Denmark, Sweden, and Norway use of the ard is attested through the end of the medieval era. Agricultural workers chose the best tools for the type of soil, were only motivated to adopt the more expensive moldboard plow if their fields were large enough or their soil hard enough, or simply employed what they had at hand.

Other medieval agricultural tools similarly continued in use or developed slowly and perhaps haphazardly from earlier Roman tools—including the long scythe, the flail, the hoe, the iron-shod spade, the sickle, both toothed and non-toothed, and the harrow. Roman farmers had used the harrow for weeding, but it appears to have had a surge in use around the tenth century as it was also effective in breaking up and evening the ground and in covering back up seed that had been sown (Figure 5.1).

The development of new forging techniques in the thirteenth century permitted the construction of scythes with blades that joined at about twenty-five degrees, which allowed for more effective striking of crops and expanded use of the tool, but sickles nevertheless remained common harvesting instruments into the modern era. One brand-new tool was the Flemish hook, a short-handled scythe that spread through Flanders, Artois, and Hainault in the late thirteenth century.[21] These developments transformed the average agricultural worker's day, making certain tasks easier and thereby opening the possibility that he could engage in other forms of labor more easily.

In addition to the moldboard plow's metal-tipped coulter, better mining techniques and equipment made possible metal-covered wheels, horseshoes, and more effective tools.

FIGURE 5.1 Two horses draw a harrow guided by a man while another man plants seeds. Glass panel, c. 1450–75. England. © Victoria and Albert Museum, London.

Horseshoes made a number of conveyances viable, including four-wheeled wagons that allowed many workers to be more efficient, but horseshoes were not medieval inventions, for the Romans had utilized them. Their apparent decline in use during the early Middle Ages may have resulted from the difficulty of obtaining the requisite metal in some regions, or perhaps relates to the vagaries of evidence survival. In medieval Denmark, for example, horseshoes only appear in the archaeological record from the eleventh century.[22]

A number of medieval inventions related to the horse. Among these were the horse collar and a new type of harness that made increased use of horse-drawn wagons, harrows, and plows possible. By 800, the combined breast-strap harness and horse collar came into use in western Europe, and by the twelfth and thirteenth centuries it had become predominant. This system took the weight away from the neck, for earlier harnessing could choke horses, and placed the weight instead on the chest and shoulders. Swing bars, made of wood and attached at the ends to the animals' traces (rope or leather harnessing) and at the center to the vehicle or plow, also aided horses in pulling heavier loads more easily, though these were not a medieval invention. By the tenth century, a driver could harness horses and oxen in files, allowing them, particularly the oxen, to pull enormous loads.[23] Oxen continued to be used for many of the same purposes as horses across the Middle Ages. In German lands, for example, farmers did not employ horses as much as in England and at first only used them for harrowing. More commonly, horses drew conveyances, but it is impossible to know how much new horse-related technologies helped to drive the growth of urban markets and how much those same markets increased demand for and use of the new horse-related technologies.[24] Horses drew both two-wheeled carts and four-wheeled wagons across much of Europe, although over time the wagons became predominant, probably because of the revolving front axle, an important thirteenth- and fourteenth-century development.[25]

Agricultural practices also necessarily had to respond to geographic limitations and local environmental conditions which changed over the course of the Middle Ages. As other chapters in this book demonstrate, many other cultural changes were afoot that aided and abetted the spread and increasing sophistication of agricultural technology, not least changes to the organization of laborers, the laws governing them, the value placed upon hard work, and the position of "those who work" in the ideal scheme of medieval society. By the thirteenth century, many French villages were able to organize their planting of specific types and rotation of crops on the parish's cultivated land in order to maximize grain yield for livestock through a system known as *assolement*.[26] Social cooperation also made possible the system of "micro-fields" that many cultivators in central Flanders used in order to maximize flexibility in terms of crop choice from the twelfth century on and in the reclamation of fields in sandy inland areas and along the coast in the thirteenth to fourteenth centuries. With the growth of Flemish cities, farms of all sizes in Flanders appear to have responded to increased urban demand for grain and specialty crops, especially flax.[27] The construction of dykes along the coasts and rivers of the Lowlands as well as the draining of peat moors near the coast, required substantial cooperation, particularly because those living in these areas had to continue to deepen drainage ditches and build further dykes in order to retain the new fields they created and to protect the region from flooding more generally. Large and small landholders funded these projects proportionally based on the size of their lands, which helped to preserve smaller farms in the region that may not otherwise have survived. By the fifteenth century windmills became key components of this system of flood control, drainage, and reclamation (see Figure 5.2).[28]

FIGURE 5.2 Medieval windmill. Gotland, Sweden. Wikimedia Commons.

In the Mediterranean, cultivation of olive groves continued, just as in the ancient era, in order primarily to produce the lucrative and highly desirable commodity of olive oil. Although the average life of an olive tree is five to six hundred years, growing one to maturity over about twelve years and then maintaining it for optimal productivity required irrigation and a great deal of ongoing labor. For that reason, mainly only large landowners and monasteries could afford the investment of resources necessary to cultivate olive groves in the Byzantine world. Those pressing olives for oil required considerable skill and knowledge, such as determining when to harvest the olives, controlling the duration and degree of pressure applied to the olives, and maintaining and operating the requisite equipment. Olive mills generally stood close to olive groves, but it is rare to find them associated with monasteries. Because monasteries often had grain mills, this absence of large-scale olive pressing underlines the high level of skill involved and the need for many workers. Therefore, private owners in towns and on large estates were better equipped to run them.[29]

The "agricultural revolution" did not necessarily lead to a proliferation of agricultural treatises in the Christian West, but in Islamic al-Andalus the growth in productivity was accompanied by the composition of a number of texts concerning agricultural techniques, tools, and practices between the eleventh and the thirteenth centuries. Drawing from Roman, Islamic, and eastern tracts and practical knowledge, these texts sometimes display an "experimental" approach based on direct observation in how best to grow crops and on knowledge of and expansion upon earlier technologies such as watermills.[30]

HARNESSING WIND AND WATER

Windmills and watermills multiplied in the medieval era. Both provided efficiency in grinding grains and other tasks and supported other technological innovations. Their cultural, social, and economic implications have long been recognized. In his 1934 cultural study of technology, the American historian Lewis Mumford argued that during the second half of the Middle Ages, Europe saw a major increase in the number of watermills and windmills, which led to a social transformation and laid the ground for the Industrial Revolution.[31] One year later, and independently, the French historian Marc Bloch outlined the spread of watermills from the eastern Mediterranean to the north and west, where they proliferated in France and England from the central Middle Ages onwards. He identified adoption of this technology with the lack of slave labor from the ninth century on and the concomitant need for labor-saving devices. At that time lords from the Carolingian Empire began to have them built and used in earnest.[32] In the ensuing decades scholars have questioned various aspects of these influential models, particularly in light of new archaeological evidence concerning Roman watermills which were far more common than once realized. Watermills had spread throughout the Roman Empire, and in both the East and West. Evidence suggests, however, substantial variety in the degree to which medieval people employed watermills. Regional studies therefore hold great promise in expanding understanding of the medieval watermill's cultural implications.[33]

Employing Italian evidence, one scholar has pointed out that the increased survival of agricultural contracts starting around 750 may account for the "apparent explosion in the construction of hydraulic mills around that time."[34] In some parts of Italy, though not all, peasants and townspeople wanted watermills, built them, and employed them for grinding grain, moving a typically female form of labor performed at home into the male sphere, for men were most likely to transport grain to the waterways where the mills were located. In this sense, watermills changed the conditions and types of labor more than they saved time spent working. What may instead have spurred construction of Italian watermills was the ability to collect tolls for grinding grain, the prestige of having a mill, and a desire for more finely ground flour, which could produce more nutritious, better-tasting bread.[35]

Watermills and windmills were prevalent in England and Ireland during much of the Middle Ages. Irish sites have produced rich archaeological evidence of mills from the seventh century on, and various medieval Irish texts mention the use of waterpower.[36] Watermills were also in use in Anglo-Saxon England, as at the well-excavated site of the Tamworth Mill, where two successive mills were dated to the ninth century using dendrochronology.[37] Completed in 1086, the Domesday Book, a survey of England that King William I (d. 1087) had produced following his conquest of England in 1066, recorded 6,082 mills, which meant that watermills were not unusual sights. The references in Domesday were almost certainly to watermills because windmills are difficult, if not impossible, to date prior to the 1180s, and they spread slowly over time in England because, according to one leading scholar, only those lords without water resources turned to the new technology of the windmill in the thirteenth century, and their use declined following the Black Death.[38]

Archaeologists have found relatively few remains of watermills in formerly Byzantine territory, though written texts confirm their use. Watermills played a role in the daily life of monastic communities, cities, and farming regions, and Byzantine legal and religious texts attest to their social and economic value. The specifically Byzantine-style watermill was replaced, however, with western-style ones in the twelfth century after Crusaders arrived bringing this technology with them.[39]

Archaeological remains demonstrate that irrigation systems and grist watermills spread throughout much of rural al-Andalus, but scholars debate the reasons for and mechanisms of their diffusion because a lack of textual evidence concerning rural areas makes explicating their cultural use difficult. Although these technologies drew from Indian, Persian, Arabic, and Roman precedents and paralleled developments in the Christian West, social differences almost surely made their use differ.[40] Some scholars have argued that the hydrotechnology of al-Andalus matches well to patterns of peasant work, including the layout of their fields and communities, but it is clear that civic and aristocratic authorities also funded and employed various forms of waterpower. Peasant mills often sat at the ends of canals, a good location if one did not want to interfere with irrigation systems critical to the agricultural work of peasants. In contrast, mills installed by lords, which are less studied for this polity, were sometimes placed at the head of irrigation systems.[41]

Mills ground more than grain. Production of oils required the pressing of poppy seed, hempseed, and olives, and mustard required the grinding of mustard seeds. Dyers had plants such as madder ground at mills as did leather workers tanner's bark. In addition, by the thirteenth to fourteenth centuries, mills could sharpen blades, operate turning lathes, move tilt hammers via cams, and thereby contribute to various trades, including fulling, forging, lumber processing, and paper making.[42] Aside from grinding grain, forging and fulling may have been the most common purpose of mills.[43] Watermills provided an excellent means to felt cloth, especially in comparison to doing so by hand or by feet in a trough. Cams raised and lowered pestles which churned the woollen cloth in vats of water and other products. They first appeared in Italy at Abruzzi in 962 and in Normandy as early as 1086–7, and by the twelfth century had spread through much of Europe but were especially prominent in England. Yet the use of mills to mechanize other areas of work was limited; changes to the ways artisans carried out tasks in workshops almost certainly had a greater influence on production. For example, the introduction of the spinning wheel in the thirteenth century helped to transform textile work.[44]

MARKING TIME

In order to analyze increases in efficiency and productivity it is useful to consider how medieval workers and those who supervised them understood and measured time. The proliferation of mechanical clocks across much of Europe from around 1100 to 1500 changed workers' lives and broader understandings of the nature of work itself. Devices that measured time had existed in antiquity and the early Middle Ages and appear in the historical record across Eurasia. Some early and central medieval monasteries had time-telling devices, including water clocks, that often essentially functioned as alarms so that monks would know when to pray, and medieval Muslims often employed water clocks to ascertain when to pray.[45] Clocks seem to have been more common in the Arab and Byzantine worlds than in contemporary western European early medieval polities. *The Royal Frankish Annals* report that, in 807, the Abbasid caliph Harun al-Rashid sent Charlemagne presents, including a brass clock the annalist describes as "a marvellous mechanical contraption."[46]

By the thirteenth century, public clocks, that is time-marking devices, whether mechanical or water clocks or some other apparatus, that marked time visually or aurally for a city, town, or village and often the surrounding countryside, became more common. These clocks were often connected to the ringing of bells or some other signal to indicate the passage of time to those in the local area. No standard form of telling time existed in the medieval era; localities determined the ways to mark the passage of hours, a fact that a number of travellers noted. The reasons for the spread of public clocks related to varying local factors, although the increased prestige that structures such as clock towers and belfries brought to their communities seems to have served as a strong impetus. In contrast to older arguments that have had a lasting influence on popular modern conceptions, merchants were not the sole driving force behind their growing presence.[47] A range of community members wanted public clocks, and their acquisition and funding varied by locality. Civic authorities, one of the most common groups to advocate for the construction of clock towers, for example, appear to have desired them not only to compete with neighboring cities but also to mark time on notarial documents and to delineate council meetings and the like.[48] They therefore wished to harness public clocks to help organize those particular forms of work.

Clocks spurred workers and supervisors to think differently about the workday. In the early Middle Ages, when public clocks were unusual, most measurements of time related to labor referred to half days, days, weeks, months, or years, or work was associated with the completion of a certain task. Polyptychs, monastic inventories of dues, often listed certain quantities of time that dependents owed in labor and products they were to deliver on a regular basis. Measurements of cloth that servile women owed, for example, did not stipulate the amount of time the textile workers were to spend on fabrication.[49] As clocks came into use, weavers, among many other city workers, began to use the bells of public clocks to determine when to start and stop work. Guilds began to use the bells and other signals to delineate an accepted workday. Breaks or shorter periods of time, however, were often measured through use of a sandglass. At first the new public clocks did not much alter working hours, but eventually both supervisors and workers employed clocks as means to argue for what they believed should be the length of the working day. Yet only in the fifteenth century and only rarely did medieval workers earn an hourly wage. Most casual work was still done by the day or by completion of an assigned task. More unusual still was the employment of periods of time in explaining manufacturing processes in written texts. A good example is the fifteenth-century text known as the *Feurwerkbuch* (*Fire Workbook*) which designated rather specific times in manufacturing explosive powders. Only gradually then did working conditions change as a result of better, more visible, and more common mechanisms for telling time.[50]

CONSTRUCTION

Relatively few documents concerning the design of buildings survive from the medieval era until the advent of more technical writing in the fifteenth century. Even the most famous example, the thirteenth-century sketchbook of Villard de Honnecourt, does not offer information on building techniques. Rather it provided partial views of some contemporary buildings and drawings of stone cutting, timber framing, applied geometry, and some machines. Most construction workers learned from experience and from one another (see Figure 5.3). Indeed, some scholars have argued that this lack of written instruction allowed for substantial creativity and innovation in construction, particularly in regard to Gothic architecture. Changes in architecture, such as the development of the flying buttress in cathedrals, almost certainly resulted from consideration of earlier building projects and the costs associated with moving heavy material such as stone. The flying buttress allowed for the construction of tall buildings that used far less stone than if the walls had been solid. (In addition, of course, they allowed for the insertion of large-scale programs of stained glass.)[51]

Across the medieval era those in charge of building large stone structures, especially churches, increasingly employed prefabricated and standard masonry.[52] A recent study also indicates that stone workers at times operated an assembly-line mode of production. In this instance, carved shafts from the cathedral at Chartres show signs of different specialists working in separate stages upon the same piece of stone. The identification of individual carvers from their repetition of unconscious small details makes clear that they did not work in set teams. Rather a given "finisher" may have completed the sculpting of a range of different carvers. This practice suggests a high level of consistent and specialized skill across these laborers because they could work with one another interchangeably.[53]

Scholars have also reassessed the degree of skill involved in wood construction. From a modern vantage, twelfth- to thirteenth-century northwestern European carpenters, for example, appear to have "over-built" large structures in an effort to prevent collapse. Carpenters, owing to a lack of mathematical knowledge, were unable to calculate the size of timbers efficiently and instead planned the large timberworks of some surviving buildings based on experience. They generally chose large trees to fell and square in order to ensure structural stability. Yet it is clear that these carpenters equally made aesthetic and technical choices intended to impress and to contend with specific conditions at an individual site, such as wind, planned building use, or ease of construction.[54]

In the second half of the fifteenth century, artisans began to write about their technical knowledge, preserving and disseminating certain technological innovations. In a treatise the Florentine notary Mariano Taccola (1382–1453) wrote that the influential architect Filippo Brunelleschi (1377–1446) cautioned innovative artisans to guard against those individuals who would steal new inventions and achievements. Brunelleschi was well known even in his own day for architectural innovation, especially for the massive dome of the Cathedral of Santa Maria del Fiore. The context of his admonition included committees of workmen with whom he had to share plans in order to carry out work and those approving funding for the work. In his concern over technological theft, he was therefore most concerned with maintaining the integrity of his design.[55]

FIGURE 5.3 St. Hedwig directs the construction of a new convent at Trebnitz, 1353. Silesia, Poland. Los Angeles, The J. Paul Getty Museum, MS Ludwig XI 7, folio 56. © The J. Paul Getty Museum, Los Angeles.

THE TRANSMISSION OF KNOWLEDGE AND SKILLS

The transmission of skills was crucial to the development and continuation of new technologies. The main means of acquiring technical skills in the second half of the Middle Ages was apprenticeship. Because no medieval polity enforced compulsory schooling or developed complex bureaucracies similar to those of the modern states, no centralized means of educating children or young adults existed. Rather, if a parent or young person wished to acquire certain work skills, the most common approach was apprenticeship. One reason the contracts drawn up between masters and apprentices appear extremely complex to a modern reader was their purpose of dealing with various possible situations in which either the master or the apprentice could take advantage of the training relationship. An unchecked apprentice might have wished to leave one master for another who offered better conditions, leaving the first master with the costs of his initial training while the subsequent master had a well-trained apprentice to help without having borne that expense. Equally, contracts often protected apprentices from labor exploitation, insisting that masters provide a minimum level of education lest the master dismiss the apprentice once his labor might become more costly or create competition. In this manner some have argued that craft guilds were far more interested in cost sharing than in fixing prices.[56]

Transmission of the knowledge of specific work skills often took place as medieval workers plied their crafts side by side. Early medieval Frankish girls learned to sew from women more expert than them, often in groups.[57] Late medieval stonemasons acquired skills in a similar way, for guild regulations often indicated that a master mason would have learned the requisite skills for his craft by having served for years as an apprentice. Different types of masons worked closely with one another. Quarriers freed up raw material while freemasons, who worked free stone, that is free from sedimentary strata and fossils, labored in cooperation with wallers, pavers, and setters who prepared door and window frames. Each worker employed the correct tool. "Roughmasons shaped rubble with hammers, hewers dressed ashlar with an axe, cutters did so with a chisel."[58] This kind of labor doubtless created a work culture in which individuals could observe others' techniques in the field and potentially pass on "tricks of the trade" in addition to basic skills.

Some technologies in contrast showed significant continuity. Although the horizontal loom sped production substantially, it sometimes coexisted with the vertical loom as at Winchester, where excavations revealed the use of both types of loom from the twelfth to fourteenth centuries.[59] Archaeometric analysis of surviving tenth- to fourteenth-century pottery from southern Tuscany determined that a change in glaze did not result from technological advances; in fact, ceramic production there showed marked continuity, indicating that potters' technical ability remained much the same over these centuries.[60]

Some industries tried to cultivate the development of skills and knowledge but discouraged their spread beyond an established group of experts. Glass making in Venice took place solely on the island of Murano from at least the end of the thirteenth century onwards. Venetian glass workers became expert in producing luxury glass of a consistently high quality partly because of the development of a new occupation, the *conciatore*, whose job involved overseeing the raw materials melted together to make glass. Each *conciatore* had to pay close attention to the melting process and add materials as it proceeded in order to ensure high-quality glass for the masters who made the final products. This stage of manufacture was crucial because the raw materials imported into

Venice were of mixed quality and chemical composition. Essentially the *conciatore* had to react on the fly. Because Venice had no raw materials for glass, the development of this occupation was a response to the contemporary situation, and it underlines the way glass involved the work of a group.[61]

The guild governing the glassmakers understood the value of its workers' specialized knowledge. Unscrupulous individuals could steal it. A monk named Gian Antonio wrote in a eulogy for a Venetian glassmaker that he had taught a student some secret recipes. That student subsequently entrusted them to his daughter who left them out one day. Giorgio Ballarin copied them, and lacking the right pedigree, he sought out a rival glassmaker with an eligible daughter and obtained permission to marry her so that he had the right to start his own workshop where he used the recipes to his advantage. He became a leading glassmaker in Murano.[62] Such recipes facilitated internal transmission of skills and knowledge as, for example, in the first known Venetian glassmaking recipe book from 1446.[63] By the mid-fifteenth century the guild began to fine and imprison any glass workers who left the city and taught others their skills. Some Venetian glass workers did this temporarily, but others settled elsewhere permanently, eventually resulting in the development of high-quality glass manufacture elsewhere in Europe during the early modern era.[64]

MILITARY TECHNOLOGY

The scholarship on military technology in the Middle Ages is vast, and it is clear that various technological developments changed and shaped the work experiences of medieval soldiers. When employing certain tactics or weapons that required a relatively high level or certain types of skill, combatants most likely felt the repercussions of such changes quite sharply. For example, the use of bows in warfare marked the entire medieval era. During the early Middle Ages both Vikings and Franks, particularly from the eighth century on, employed longbows with great success. Because the Carolingians, the dynasty that ruled the Franks from 751, fought both Slavs and Avars, they adopted the composite recurved bow, a technology familiar to both of those eastern cultures, while continuing to use the longbow. By the twelfth century, most western Europeans, aside from those in Iberia and England, began to use the crossbow instead. The armies associated with the Reconquista in Iberia used composite bows, perhaps drawing upon their knowledge of Islamic military tactics.[65] Such adoption of the tactics and weapons of opposing armies underlines the ways in which medieval soldiers could adapt and implies the training necessary to this occupation.

Skill played a key role in success on the medieval battlefield. The ninth-century chronicler Regino of Prüm offered an example of what could happen to the unskilled combatant when discussing Vikings who came to plunder the region around Prüm in 882.

> In that place a countless multitude from the fields and farms gathered together on foot as one crowd and approached the Northmen as if they were going to fight them. But when the Northmen saw that this crowd of common people was not so much unarmed as bereft of military training, they rushed upon them with a shout and cut them down in such a bloodbath that they seemed to be butchering dumb animals rather than men.[66]

The widespread western European use of mounted shock combat from the twelfth century onwards involved mounted men holding spears or lances under their arms to charge at an opposing army, which necessitated training.[67] In England, use of both the longbow and the composite bow continued even as the crossbow became predominant in the twelfth century in many other western European cultures, so controversy remains among military historians as to why fourteenth-century English armies that included significant numbers of longbowmen successfully defeated French forces. Most historians believe that English archers changed tactics, not technology. These highly skilled individuals shot at charging armies in order to cause their lines to break and to prevent flank attacks. Yet by the fifteenth century use of the longbow began to decline. Among the principal reasons was a lack of trained archers. This problem underlines the ways in which weapon technologies shaped the labor of soldiers; practice was a necessity for military success.[68]

In terms of the culture of work, however, arguments against technological determinism in warfare should prevail. Understanding the labor of individuals in the past requires studying their conditions and motivations, not merely arguing that a weapon or technology dictated the experience of armed combat. In that light, it is useful to consider the alleged medieval military revolution tied to the introduction of gunpowder. Gunpowder of course contributed to the obsolescence of the longbow in combat over the course of the fifteenth century, but it appears to have done less to transform most soldiers' work life than to change the work of those who built and relied upon the walls that protected medieval cities and fortifications. Beginning in the fourteenth century, at least from 1374 onwards, gunpowder was used to destroy such walls, and by the fifteenth century, civic authorities and lords of castles knew they had to take defensive action against cannons, a medieval technological invention. As early as 1347, the English began to build gunports in walls so that they could fire against enemy cannons; by the end of the fourteenth century, the French, Germans, Iberians, and Italians were also constructing gunports. Other defensive efforts, such as earthen ramparts to strengthen walls, also began by the end of the Middle Ages.[69] These developments began slowly and somewhat haphazardly, similarly to the technological changes affecting agriculture, milling, and clocks. Changes resulting from the introduction of gunpowder seem far more gradual than some early modern historians have presented them, and such slow transformations argue for the utility of examining technological change and work across long periods, cutting across traditional periodization.

VARIETY IN THE CULTURES OF WORK, TECHNOLOGY, AND SKILL

This investigation of work, technology, and skill has come full circle, back to an emphasis on a long period, similar to the approach that Lynn White, Jr. took in his seminal book mentioned at the beginning of this chapter. Yet local studies also provide a way forward in understanding changes and continuity. A study of the decreasing use of limestone in construction in Autun in France provides an example of a fruitful combination of both approaches. Because it was common in the early Middle Ages to find building materials by reusing stonework from older structures, nearby limestone quarries went out of use, and over time workers naturally lost the necessary skills to quarry this material. This shift in construction subsequently led to a continued low rate of use of limestone in this region. Limestone was mainly limited to decorative purposes. In part, this use related to cost; the transportation costs would have been prohibitive had it been the main building material. Yet it was still a desirable material because it readily recalled an antique past given the long reuse of older limestone in Autun and surrounding regions.[70] Here a study of a single region over much of the medieval era helps to explain how cultural, practical, and work-related factors played a role in shaping the degree and application of skill and technology. This interplay among various forces helped to produce the demonstrable variety of working conditions and their results across the Middle Ages. Further, it underlines that historians have much still to study, with the excavation of new sites, discovery of artifacts, and application of new methods. The cultural history of work and technology remains a work in progress.

CHAPTER SIX

Work and Mobility

NICHOLAS DEAN BRODIE

In a number of respects worker immobility was once seen as a defining element of the medieval period. Historians formerly looked back on the "Middle Ages" as a time largely wedged between the barbarian invasions that despoiled classical antiquity and the frenetic movement of the great age of exploration and colonial empire building that eventually followed. The tent maker St. Paul could travel the Mediterranean in relative peace, and the sailors under Columbus could crisscross the Atlantic, but people of medieval Europe were expected to be almost superstitiously still. Mobilizing events such as the Crusades and the Hundred Years' War were seen as anomalies—relatively brief, localized, or peripheral movements that saw elites and their immediate servants moving in contrast to an essentially static peasantry who simply endured these difficult generations in their hamlets and villages until freed from such bondage by modernity. Similarly, the raids and expansion of the Vikings and then the Normans into France, England, and the Mediterranean could be dismissed as the last vestiges of the great age of migration that ended antiquity, when the narrative of expansion gave way to one of settling. Then, disrupting the settled high medieval world of the fourteenth century, the Black Death theoretically carved out a new dynamic whereby peasants could more effectively bargain their way out of bondage and simply move away from one place of servitude to a more conducive option. In reaction, medieval elites supposedly imposed increasingly harsh rules upon what has been seen as a tide of vagrancy. This "class struggle" dynamic, a tension between oppressive stasis and freeing mobility, has come to be seen as one of the defining structural features of the late medieval world.

This seemingly agreeable two-part narrative, of slowing ethno-migration followed by increasing individual movement, serves a broadly useful purpose but masks a much more complex reality. Partly a retrospective construct based on the limitations of sources, influenced by postmedieval notions about the medieval world and occasionally reinforced by scholarly research techniques and interests, such a narrative is beginning to look dated. Even relatively simple questions give way to exceedingly complex answers. In the absence of census data, for instance, how can the movement of laborers be discerned, far less comprehensively tested? Should literary examples serve as real-life exemplars or just idealized and class-based projections or prejudices or even deliberate inversions where readers no longer have the cultural coding to get the jokes? Or how can the daily commute of a peasant be measured in any way that makes possible regional comparisons, say of Wales versus Westphalia? Does the *Reconquista* of the Iberian Peninsula simply reveal the steady movement of political authority, or was there a concomitant advance of working people into the conquered territory? These and similar questions make a general query concerning medieval mobility and work into an almost unanswerable conundrum. Yet, excitingly, questions of mobility are at the cutting edge of historical research.[1] At present the effect of this historiographical turn toward mobility as a subject remains to be fully seen, however, and so this inquiry must largely seek answers from bodies of research centered on other concerns.

As such, any attempt at a broad chronological narrative will fail in the face of regional variability or research suitability or be drawn into replicating the old two-part metanarrative simply by using a similar range of sources and general impressions. So to remedy these methodological problems, this chapter is more of a surveying foray than a tight synopsis of several generations of dedicated research. What follows is a focus on some leading questions, at times arbitrarily creating conceptual boundaries to provide overall structural guidance. This chapter approaches the mobility of medieval workers through a simple binary: their movement to work or with work. The first part will address questions and patterns of migration, essentially focused on those vectors of human movement that preceded work. The second part will address those elements of human movement that were direct products of work, such as seasonal movements or other trends that were structural to medieval society. Many of the great works of literature to have come out of medieval Europe dealt with human movement, so the general picture of mobile workers should be familiar. In Geoffrey Chaucer's *Canterbury Tales*, for instance, the very recitation of its stories was predicated on the movement of a diverse group of people undertaking pilgrimage.[2] More particularly, moving workers drove some of its subplots, as when a carpenter went to the woods to gather wood in *The Miller's Tale*, clerks visited from the north in *The Reeve's Tale*, various merchants undertook journeys and messengers conveyed information as in *The Lawyer's Tale*. These characters, going about their daily routines, exemplify the mobility of the medieval world: its scale could be local or regional; it could define borders or cross them; and it could be in the service of self, community, or master.

Whether moving within a locale or journeying across regional borders, work and workers were rarely static. But even when worker mobility can be discerned in various records, there is the overarching problem of interpretation in context. The very size and structure of medieval populations are poorly known, complicating any attempt to assess mobility in proportion to a medieval "whole." In part this is simply a lack of source material. The great chronicles of the medieval world mainly focused on elites or large collectives, leaving quotidian life generally undescribed in the sort of detail social and cultural historians would like. Also, while we should not fall into the trap of assuming early medieval societies neglected to produce records pertinent to the administration of their farms, towns, and kingdoms, we also have to recognize that such documentary evidence survives in much greater part toward the end of our period, creating something of a social documentary bias. Workers in 1450 are apparently more mobile than their counterparts from 800, but that is not surprising, because they are more observable.

Perhaps the most important example of how sources and research interact concerns the fundamental question of population. At 800, population estimates are little more than educated guesses. Moreover, such guesswork is made harder because this was a period of demographic flux, increasingly known as the great migration period (which spans late antiquity and the first part of the early medieval era). As a recent volume of essays addressing the "neglected barbarians" of Europe reveals, determining the characteristics of theoretically distinct people from fleeting mentions in chronicles and artifactual assemblages is hard enough, whereas working out their numbers, origins, and end points are near impossibilities.³ These "barbarian" peoples' mobility, at least as perceived by commentators, often thwarts their ready identification. Even the social features of the early medieval period can be unclear, with regional power structures apparently developing fairly organically but prone to the sorts of "varied localisms" that make generalizations difficult.⁴ At the other end of the spectrum and period, in a long-studied and relatively settled landscape such as late medieval England, the total picture is not necessarily significantly clearer in all respects. The population of England has been the subject of intense study over multiple generations of scholarship, but only with the turn to the early modern era and its widespread use of individual parish records of births, deaths, and marriages (mostly from the mid-1500s onwards) does the complete picture appear with any great resolution.⁵

Medieval records are not without some use, however. Various taxation assessments, manor accounts, court records, and the like facilitate investigation into medieval populations, at least giving some relative measures of segments of the population, from which the wider picture can be estimated. Yet, in part because of this relative lack of easily quantifiable sources, the medieval era has become something of a testing ground for theoretical constructions of human societies and economies, in ways that still affect (and afflict) research into the period.⁶ The economic structures of the medieval era, seemingly gradually transitioning toward modern forms of agriculture and capitalism, have fascinated researchers for the better part of a century. Of particular scholarly influence has been the study of wages and inflation in connection with population, such as twentieth-century studies that charted the changing cost of food relative to builders' wages to produce an indicator of the real buying power of workers' income.⁷ This approach has in turn been used to extrapolate population dynamics, the theory being that a major unseen variable driving real wages up and down is population. From these sorts of research interests and projects one can derive much of the general picture of medieval society against which to assess worker mobility, but it is worth bearing in mind the way that this context is often more theoretical than demonstrable and is mostly concerned with other economic trends and indices.

One last caveat is worth addressing. Two evidentiary specters afflict the study of medieval social demography: migration and poverty. Rarely quantifiable, they can be hard to factor into research in comprehensive ways. The builders' wages used to chart inflation are day payments to workers at a given site, for instance. Whether it was the same builders or a moving selection is not always clear in such sources. Similarly, the taxation records that are used to help estimate urban populations usually only recorded the tax-paying segment of the population. Historians assumed that working-class families and paupers existed in some sort of proportion to the taxed men and used such small family and local estimations to construct larger regional and national ones. The case of the English town of Exeter reveals the problem, where relatively regular, fairly complete, and surviving assessments give various numbers of individuals and households which may be indicative of shifts in the records as much as in the population.⁸ By factoring in an average family size and untaxed proportion of poorer inhabitants historians arrive at an estimated population of some 3,000 people in the late fourteenth century, with a firmer estimate of approximately 8,000 people by the early sixteenth century. The extent to which earlier records may be unreflective of the total population, has, of course been contested.⁹ The rate of population growth is therefore highly conditional on the reading and analysis of such limited evidence. The complexity of the whole medieval demographic scene is perhaps best exemplified by noting that Exeter is one of the best-documented towns in this regard. The population for the city in the early medieval period is little more than guesswork, and even the later medieval period is contingent on layers of estimation.

Scaling such evidence up to develop a general European picture compounds the problems with evidence many times over, especially when we consider the limitations to examining worker mobility. While potentially useful for charting genetic movement across counties and centuries, DNA analysis lacks the detailed resolution of the day-to-day. Archaeology offers many insights into the ways of living and working and the cultural and economic landscape upon which workers of the medieval era trod, but rarely charts the full range of movements for individuals. Documentary analysis allows for a foray into the structures of medieval societies, but such evidence often emerges from reading sources against the grain of the use for which they were intended and produced. Tax assessments were for facilitating the extraction of money, for instance, not for charting population trends or familial movements in a certain locale, even though they can be used for that purpose to some extent. Moreover, sparse records can be indicative but should not necessarily be taken as representative. Yet this complex picture can help us gain a better idea of medieval society, because it forces us to think beyond preconceptions about a world in stasis. In the evidentiary darkness we can put the meanderings and movements of medieval workers into the proverbial spotlight.

Innumerable factors determined worker mobility in medieval Europe. From the simple fact of migratory settlement to expert masons travelling between major building projects to the seasonal peregrinations of harvesting operations, the workers of Europe moved with a regularity that possibly surprises later ages. Because research into mobility often requires lateral thinking about the evidence, it can be useful to focus not only on evidence of movement itself but also on contextual factors of encouragement versus restriction. What opportunities or situations encouraged workers to move, and what structures inhibited or facilitated the movement of workers? Here, as ever, research processes can limit the objects of inquiry. Answering questions often raises more problems. Although there are some well-founded assumptions about medieval migration, for instance, they frequently hew rather close to historiographical supposition. Yet if treated under four major headings some generalizations can be arrived at, dealing with structural and experiential aspects of movements for work: peasant bondage, urbanization, group migration, and vagrancy.

PEASANT BONDAGE

Much of the medieval world was essentially agrarian. Despite migrations of people, various networks of trade, and intergenerational wanderings from village to village, we are often faced with the impression of a world seemingly in situ. A way of life that is distinctly medieval is, at least in popular memory, decidedly dull and dreary. Indeed, drawing on early Marxist historiography, the social stratification of the medieval world furthers this image. Medieval societies are often framed as pyramids of power: kings and popes at the top, broadening through bishops and barons, priests, and knights, to a mass of peasants beneath. This tidy structure sometimes, but rarely neatly, works as a broad model. Social mobility, after all, was as important and real as physical mobility. In fact, various medieval theorists, most notably Ælfric of Eynsham, advocated a threefold division of society based on role—those who prayed, those who fought, and those who worked—dividing humanity into three distinct orders or estates. To an extent this conception worked as a model for understanding (and administering) medieval society, even though the neat characterizations it presents blurred at their edges. Either way, the medieval theory and the postmedieval "pyramid" conception share the assumption that a large body of workers supported the prayers and fighters in the most rudimentary sense of ensuring they were fed, and in this the models are probably correct, but hardly unique to that epoch. The production of food was the great necessity of all societies, and the medieval means of production were the peasants, but they were not all always as dutifully still as foundation stones.

Medieval farming methods and technology, as well as preparing fields and planting, tending, and harvesting crops, all meant that workers had to reside near enough to that land in sufficient numbers on a permanent basis to ensure food supply. This necessity explains the main patterns of medieval settlement, with manors and villages being common reflections of this phenomenon, each a small clustered and essentially local workforce. Individual peasants were often also legally tied to a specific plot of land, either directly or at the will of a master to whom they were bonded, which suggests that the medieval peasant was forced into remaining static.

Peasantry came in many varieties, however, and "peasant" is quite a malleable term. In England, legal bondage has generally been called serfdom, although the term "serf" (from *servi*) covers a wide spectrum of technical terms or forms of bondage. Long the subject of incidental study, as part of wider social and economic trends, medieval English serfdom has recently been the subject of detailed research, such that the picture has become much clearer.[10] Serfs could be bonded directly to their lord, typically through inheritance, which meant they had to work the lord's land and give the lord his dues. Alternatively, serfs were bonded to the lord by virtue of their tenure on his land, a situation generally known as "villein tenure," where a serf owed certain dues to a lord because of the land he occupied, rather than by virtue of his innate status. Either way, English serfs could be obligated to their lords in several ways, generally deriving from older traditions that belonged to the earlier part of the Middle Ages but which perceptively dropped off in usage toward its end. With regional inflections and various applications, serfdom was not universally experienced in the same way by every serf, but some peasant obligations reveal various restrictions upon the movement of English serfs in the medieval countryside which help reveal their mobility.

Merchet was a serf's obligation to get his or her lord's permission to marry. Chevage was a fine for living away from the manor. Theoretically, these obligations should have inhibited movement to some extent, but they also provide rare evidence for peasant movement in the medieval countryside by virtue of the manor accounts that record associated fines. As often, the evidence is open to interpretation, particularly over whether increasing evidence of payments reflects an actual increase in serf movement away from manors or simply a seigniorial shift in administration of that particular servile incident. Although the immediate aftermath of the Black Death did see an increase in chevage fines, those fees also fairly quickly fell away and became relatively uncommon within a few generations. In other words, the notion of increasing serf freedom and therefore mobility in the wake of the Black Death is not quite borne out by the latest English study, at least not in the traditionally understood sense (and there is no discernibly universal seigniorial reaction). It seems that serfdom was already in decline, and the Black Death may not have been the main catalyst for its gradual disappearance in England. The real overriding pattern was one of gradual changes with regional variations. As with so many other areas of medieval Europe, analyzing peasant movement pushes at the limits of the source material. When late medieval landlords attempted to restrict servile mobility, as was the case for England and Sicily, these actions were more about extracting fines and remedying landlords' accounts than necessarily dealing with any actual movements of workers.[11]

At the level of individual peasant movement, however, local case studies across Europe generally reveal a fairly fluid social reality. In the valley of Valldigna in Valencia, for instance, there was a remarkably mobile peasant society.[12] This phenomenon seems more astounding when one considers that these were post *Reconquista* Muslim peasants living in an enclave of Christian-controlled territory. Other evidence from the early medieval period hints at the movement of people, as elite documentation mentioned people further down the social strata. An Arabic traveller visiting the Volga in the early tenth century witnessed a large regional market, for instance, evidence for the movement of people and goods in what he saw as the wilds of northern Europe.[13] Other medieval travellers, such as the cleric Gerald of Wales, captured the interconnectedness of parts of regional Europe even while detailing their own journeying.[14] The boatmen, carters, and innkeepers they relied upon all point to otherwise undocumented human mobility.

In some contexts, however, there is more direct evidence of peasant and worker mobility. The evidence of English surnames has been used to chart migration before the Black Death, for instance, suggesting relatively high rates of local movement.[15] In early medieval Iberia, differential pottery distributions suggest greater foreign immigration (or at least cultural influence) to towns than cities and a deep conservation of cultural attributes in peripheral geographies that harken back to late Roman times, suggestive of areas where immigration may have been low.[16] This distinction between areas of high and low emigration or immigration still needs further study, but in some settings the fact of migration is easily demonstrable. For instance, as far as historians can tell in relatively well-documented medieval England, individual migration was relatively normal in the century before the Black Death. A study of fourteenth-century Essex indicates that roughly one in twenty adult males left or entered their villages each year.[17] Where detailed local studies of serf migration have been conducted, they reveal movement of considerable distances. One study of Suffolk manors charts 65 percent of the serfs of a manor permanently moving over twenty miles away.[18] Yet while individual migrants can often be linked through familial names, probate records, and court cases to their home village or manor, revealing intergenerational movements and potential rural migratory patterns, one of the main medieval migratory trends was simply the movement of people from country toward towns and cities.

URBANIZATION

Towns and cities tend to be better documented than rural areas, so focusing on urbanization can help assess the acceleration of migration or wider drifts of population in the early medieval period. It reveals, for instance, that most major English towns had been established by the time of the Domesday survey in 1086.[19] In part this growth of townships probably reflects the general growth of the European population during the central Middle Ages, particularly during the medieval Warm Period (c. 950–1250) when favorable climatic conditions fostered a growing European population. Many major cities such as London, Trier, and Rome, however, had premedieval foundations, so the phenomenon is often more concerned with urban growth than the spread of towns as such. Although the European population was overwhelmingly agrarian, the larger cities of Europe had a disproportionate economic effect and demographic pull on their regions.

It is a common historiographical refrain that many of the larger towns and cities of Europe in the medieval era were not self-replicating, but in fact relied on immigration to maintain and expand their populations. But this could be another case of medieval modelling getting ahead of the evidence. One study of later medieval cities found that the devastating effects of the Black Death were fairly quickly restored by accelerated immigration.[20] Sudden labor shortages drove wages up, which increased immigration from the surrounding country. Yet this rebound effect was not universal. Trier, for instance, may only have reached 83 percent of its pre-plague population in the century and a half after the plague wiped out perhaps half of its inhabitants. Europe-wide generalizations are hard to come by. Regional economics or wars, like plagues, could determine mortality and immigration rates in ways at which the sources can often only hint.

It is also worth noting that migration was not necessarily unilinear. Although plague-ridden towns undoubtedly attracted migrants, killed many with disease, and drew more migrants, less attention has been given to out-migration from towns or to movements within the urban environment. This focus is essentially a product of the documentary record. It is much easier to assess migration into a place than to follow emigration, because the disappearance of a person is rarely immediately explicable. As already seen, serf fines allow peasant movement to be charted, but no such fines exist in bulk for town dwellers leaving for the country. Similarly, civic records before the early modern period generally do not have detailed catalogues of working people's addresses. Yet, if we expand our period slightly, poor relief records from the city of Exeter reveal that poor people moved about the city at a relatively high rate, at least as indicated by movements among the city's parishes and wards.[21] Approximately 15–20 percent of those receiving poor relief had moved across parish boundaries within the prior two years (while still drawing relief), a minimum figure that probably reflected a common experience in late medieval urban society, especially among those who rented accommodation, and does not even account for nonpauper or intraparochial movements.

Of course not all movement into towns was necessarily economic migration or rather may not have been seen that way by the migrants themselves. Familial connections and social networks most likely go a considerable way to explaining much personal movement. Furthermore, a distinction between work and personal identity may not have been quite as clear-cut for medieval workers as it is for modern observers. Medieval guild structures, for instance, formed workers through apprenticeship and training into specialized craftsmen whose social identities could be regulated or culturally determined by their working arrangements. The persistence of occupational surnames highlights this intertwining of work and domestic identities. One of the many opportunities that towns and cities offered migrant workers was the possibility of becoming apprenticed to a trade. As such, the phenomenon acted as a pull factor to towns, while also becoming a restrictive one for the duration of the apprenticeship, because apprentices were theoretically under the control of their master, generally living in the master's house. But guilds and trades also offered opportunities for further migration. A study of Venice and Altare revealed that while some guilds tended to restrict or forbid emigration, essentially making stasis part of the guild's identity and tying a worker to a particular place, other guilds took a more managerial approach to migration, even facilitating interregional guild expansion or the ready introduction of new skills, technologies, and product tastes through the welcoming of migrant workers from other areas.[22] In towns by the Baltic Sea, merchants and craftsmen were known to send their sons abroad deliberately so they could learn languages and make advantageous business and social connections.[23]

GROUP MIGRATION

The phenomenon of guilds, or even town councils, making arrangements to encourage collective immigration, or families sending their children away, raises an unusual medieval conundrum: the links between locality, identity, and ethnicity. Migration and identity could be intertwined in complex and interesting ways, although with the attendant downside of making generalizations nearly impossible. The history of the Middle Ages, in part because of its relationship with early modern and modern state formation, coupled with nineteenth- and twentieth-century ethnic nationalisms, has often been represented in terms of ethnic movements. From mobile Goths and Franks to static Germans and French, the connections have frequently been either accepted relatively uncritically, aggressively rejected, or simply ignored. Moreover, popular understandings often derive from postmedieval reimaginings, such as the patriarchal "Anglo-Saxon man" of nineteenth-century scientific and racial discourses.

The discipline of archaeology particularly struggles with questions of the connections between people, ethnic or cultural identities, and material culture when studying the early medieval period.[24] In some ways all large movements of collectives of people could loosely be ascribed to economic imperatives or at least affect our reading of work and mobility. Arguably any people that moved in order to settle, even if such movement followed from conquest, were migratory workers, leading to debates about how to characterize certain phenomena. The movement of Germanic settlers into neighboring territories during the last half of the Middle Ages, for instance, is a sensitive subject, especially considering its role in later nationalist discourses.[25] In general terms we can point to the movements of a certain group such as the Vikings into the British Isles, western Europe, and the Mediterranean and confidently assert mass movements at the commencement of the period, but discerning when invasion becomes immigration is not always straightforward. It was probably the case with many wars and conquests throughout the Middle Ages that conflict precipitated some sort of colonial migration. For example, when the English invaded Ireland, English and Welsh workers were encouraged to move, changing agricultural practices and building patterns in the process.[26] Similarly, the crusader kingdoms of the eastern Mediterranean encouraged religious orders to migrate and settle, providing administrative workers that sustained colonial enterprises.[27] Below the easily documented level of warring and colonizing elites was a whole gamut of workers supporting and driving economic, social, and political shifts.

Alternatively, we could point to occasional expulsions as forces mobilizing workers, including the persecution of minority communities, such as the expulsion of Jews from England in 1290.[28] Other movements that fit a similar analytical frame, albeit with an entirely different motor and expression, include the resistance of invasion and purging of invaders, most famously the turning back of the Mongols and the extended conflicts between Christian and Muslim powers in central Europe. There were also clear cases of ethnic expunging, where people were either pushed aside or made to engage in significant cultural adaptations. In the Iberian Peninsula of the *Reconquista*, Moors and Moriscos provide an example of shifting religious-ethnic identities, the actual migratory correlatives of which are relatively hard to subject to easy characterization. The story for each decade, region, class, and family could be quite different. Moreover, beyond straightforward expulsions, various restrictions could operate upon such "other" collectives. There were a variety of such restrictions upon Muslim groups in the Middle Ages, for example. Shifting restrictions in Valencia are revealed by decrees that allowed free movement for Muslims, required licenses for such movement, and restricted the marriage of Muslim women in relatively quick succession.[29] Yet there were risks involved in making restrictions too comprehensive, because populations could flee if they felt too oppressed, leading to depopulation and attendant economic malaise. Even where there were ostensibly repressive regimes, therefore, it is wise to consider the question of application as another element to the equation. As with serfdom, the theoretical capacity to restrict a worker's movement did not always ensure stasis.

Navigating questions of ethnic migration, restrictions, or opportunities for movement and perhaps typifying the potential mobility of medieval workers more than any other were the Romani peoples often referred to as Gypsies. Linguistic evidence suggests an origin in Asia, with some indicators of a sufficient Grecian sojourn to adopt various language markers.[30] But precise origins aside, the fact that these people were identified as recent migrants from the Near East (Gypsy ≈ Egypt), points to the strong likelihood of continued collective migration into Europe during the medieval era after the nominal waning of the so-called "migration period" and despite often hostile or repressive official reactions that could be taken to indicate a late medieval obsession with unbonded laborers.

VAGRANCY

In one respect Romani people seem to link neatly with a late medieval concern with unemployed vagrants in the sense of providing a phenomenon to which various governing authorities reacted while complicating a tendency to see ethno-migration as an early medieval phenomenon. Just, as with the study of population trends, a complex historiographical relationship among the phenomena of vagrancy, unemployment, underemployment, idleness, and work history complicates easy readings of these seemingly straightforward things.[31] In the later Middle Ages, an abundance of local regulations and ordinances, various national or royal laws and decrees, and a series of literary stereotypes all seem to suggest a growing problem with nonworkers freely wandering about, living by idleness rather than by their own labor. At the least the documentary output of governing authorities suggests a potential shift in attitudes toward work and idleness such as to mark a major cultural worry or a sort of criminal panic. In part this apparent change may simply reflect a selection bias, a product of the surviving written records. Increasing laws regulating social movement may simply match the greater use of codified written law for social regulation; the development of stereotypical rogue varieties reflects shifting literary conventions as much as social realities; and the apparent increase of regulations in towns and courts is probably partly reflective of the historical context, but also often these records derive from a mixture of increased recordkeeping and better source survival (for more on these subjects see Chapter Eight). Centuries of documentary loss separate the early and late medieval records of vagrancy, giving a sense of increased concern or worry that is perhaps overstated at times. In a similar way the topic of "vagrancy" itself as a discrete object of study is as much a product of historiographical isolation as it is a concoction of medieval governance. For instance, vagrancy's association with the (un-) working classes was strongly affirmed by the first historians to address it, themselves largely nineteenth-century social reformers, who set the agenda for several gestations of scholarly discourse.[32] Nineteenth-century unemployment did much to define the study of medieval vagrancy.

That is not, however, to say there is no basis for seeing an increase of vagrancy or a concern about it. As already mentioned, medieval documentary evidence suggests that societies experienced quite substantial rates of migration and a considerable "urban pull" factor which could explain unemployed persons moving to towns in search of employment. If not finding it, or arriving in too great a number, the situation in a given town could conceivably produce a hostile administrative reaction. Urban act books are filled with such generic instructions to punish foreign beggars and vagabonds, often without any obvious contextual explanation. They are generally assumed to be in response to fluctuations in local conditions. This historiographical connection underpins the widespread assumption that vagrancy increased during the later medieval era throughout Europe. However, sometimes the context of such records is more immediately observable, revealing that unemployment-vagrancy was not always the main issue. A copy of a royal order in the Salisbury General Entry Book for August 1452, for instance, orders the punishment of vagabonds and beggars.[33] The town had just agreed to supply twenty soldiers to fight in Aquitaine in the Hundred Years' War, had discussed the means of paying for this contribution, and then transcribed the royal order. There were seemingly bigger social control issues at stake than simply an excess of beggars. Vagrancy regulations worked as convenient catchall laws, suitable for addressing a range of problems, from genuinely bothersome beggars to the threats of spies or insurgents in wartime.

When examined in a longer sweep, the case of English statute law is quite instructive of the methodological problem that vagrancy presents. Parliamentary statutes facilitating the arrest or punishment of strangers, vagrants, or beggars can be charted easily through 1285, 1349, 1383, 1388, 1495, and 1504.[34] On the surface they could simply be taken to illustrate a particular clustering of concern about vagrancy in the generation after the Black Death, which neatly matches older historiographical modelling of the plague's effect, and which was followed by a growing problem at the close of the medieval era as populations rebounded, evidenced by several statutes passed in the 1500s. An alternative reading, however, could point to differences in the execution of royal authority. Of these laws, one each was passed by Edward I and Edward III, traditionally seen as stronger kings, with two passed by Richard II, often considered a weaker king, and two by Henry VII, perhaps an attempt to bolster a new dynasty. Henry VII's two laws were, however, essentially the same law reissued, which points to another potential reading, and highlights the wisdom in reading source material with sensitivity to its context as well as to the research topic. The legal and legislative context explains much about the statutory changes, rather than immediate socio-economic concerns. The rapid growth in Tudor vagrancy law can be read as part of the general explosion in statutory lawmaking during the sixteenth century. Moreover, whichever interpretation of this relatively discrete legislative regime is favored, the conceptual underpinnings of the whole were relatively static throughout the medieval period; laws facilitated the easy punishing of vagrants, attempted to regulate begging at a local level, and encouraged local relief of local poor. Yet in some respects this is the same methodological conundrum that affects studies of peasants and population, the tensions between theory and actuality, stasis and mobility, and historical suppositions and empirical demonstrability. In some ways, all historians can reasonably do is develop and test models, work out reasonable limits, and identify discernible minima for advancing wider trends.

MOVING WITH WORK

Leaving the mass movements, methodological concerns, and historiographical debates behind, it is now time to move from macro to micro history and focus more closely on the local picture, even if generically constructed. The most common forms of worker movement in the medieval era were those that, like vagrancy itself, occurred beyond ready documentation in the everyday. Here, in this quotidian world, the majority of medieval workers were in motion: going about their daily routines and labors. Undoubtedly, certain glimpses of their movements can be seen and others reasonably supposed. Going to fields, taking livestock to market, or attending upon building sites, the farmers, servants, and wage-laborers moved about their locales and regions for a variety of work-related causes. It would be easy to catalogue a long list of specific tasks identified one way or another by historians and archaeologists, but it is perhaps more useful to break these down into slightly arbitrary groups for the purposes of ready analysis and to provide a frame for further research.

Workers moved with the seasons, even if only in the sense of moving to and focusing their activities on particular parts of a given landscape, so it is possible to speak of seasonal mobility. Written records of daily farming regimes are rare survivors from the period, however, so archaeology provides much of the new information on agriculture in the medieval era.[35] Such evidence reveals the material results of humans in the landscape, such as field structures and domestic and industrial buildings, or technological artifacts.[36] As archaeological work progresses, wider landscape trends continue to become clearer.[37] For the later medieval period, when farming ledgers and accounts can provide more of a window into the annual economies of medieval farming, and therefore something of their operation, research is largely focused on questions of regional variation and temporal change. As with questions of migration, the particular structures of medieval farming have been examined with a focus on macrohistoriographical concerns with changing farming regimens over time, queries about market operations, capitalization, consumption, production, and so on. Nevertheless, through the study of the changing landscapes, economies, and social structures of the rural medieval era, some appreciations of the mobility of rural workers can emerge.

It is easiest to start at the end of the annual cycle. During harvest time, workers naturally moved to a particular crop, and then along its length, because the mainstay crops were generally sowed in strips in dedicated parts of the rural landscape. This process drew workers to a particular holding. Farmers would often hire extra labor; family members were expected to help; and intracommunal assistance could occur as neighbors assisted each other. On larger holdings, landlords could often compel their serfs to come perform such work. The mainstay grain crops such as wheat were cut and bundled into sheaves before being taken for threshing (the process of knocking the grains from stems and husks; see Figure 6.1).

Meanwhile, the fields were "gleaned" by people who picked up remnants of the crop left after the main processes. Often these were local poor, and this opportunity to gather remnants was considered a form of charitable relief. The harvested field could then be turned to pasture, with the shepherds and herders potentially moving in to the area while tending to their animals. This movement modified over a longer period of time because the fields were rotated for different uses over seasons and years, creating multiyear oscillations in the use of landscape and attendant movement of workers. A

FIGURE 6.1 Two men threshing a sheaf with flails. Luttrell Psalter, c. 1325–35. London, British Library, Add. 42130, folio 74ᵛ. Wikimedia Commons.

commonly held approach was the three-course system, using some fields to grow grains, others for legumes or other supplementary crops, and leaving more fallow, and rotating the fields' uses to maximize the extraction of resources from the soil. Of course, there were variations on this scheme, depending on regional conditions and specialization. As a study of Flanders indicates, however, more fragmentary systems could be used on the ground than these neat theoretical divisions of the landscape might at first suggest.[38] Yet, despite the lack of European-wide clarity, the general principle should hold that harvest mobility within the landscape reflected local cropping practices, which were significantly determined by geography and climate, as well as different farming methods. Variability, not unity, was the hallmark of medieval farming and associated labor movements.

That is not to say there were no parallels across Europe. In general, the main late summer harvest was undoubtedly a time of great worker mobility, where competition for wages could create problems for employers struggling to keep their employees on task. The window for harvesting was relatively small and needed to be completed as soon as the crop was ready because a single ill-timed storm could do severe damage. Moreover, the grains needed to be picked before they became too ripe, in which case the harvesting dislodged too much grain prior to threshing, leading to a loss in productive quantity. As such, harvest workers were often in a better position than usual to earn good wages and work in fair conditions over this crucial period. In the early sixteenth century a major royal English works program ran into persistent trouble with workers absconding from service to get better wages at harvest time, and such problems were most likely quite common in earlier periods.[39] A study of the diet of medieval peasants suggests that the consumption of increasingly bigger and better meals by harvest workers over the later Middle Ages highlights the importance of these workers within the rural economy and probably hints at the competitive nature of working conditions.[40] The essence of their work was mobile, so their opportunities for bargaining or simply leaving for another employer were concomitantly high.

At the other end of the agricultural cycle, several months prior to harvest, various operations also moved workers on the landscape. Plowing the soil was less labor-intensive than harvesting, but it was nonetheless a task that required people to move through the landscape. So too, the actual sowing, done by hand, drew workers to and across the fields, as did the harrowing of land afterwards to settle plowed soil.[41] Similarly, the preparation of the fields and their maintenance during crop growth necessitated continued weeding, bringing workers into and through the crops. Medieval farmers and laborers were not entirely idle in the months between sowing and reaping, although there were periods of greater and lesser activity. Even children could find work in this environment as living scarecrows during the growing seasons who were kept busy throwing rocks to ward off the birds and other pests. Other agricultural products of the European medieval human ecosystem all had their own demands, from turnips to grapes to beans, and each also required workers tending them, and moving about the landscape to do so.

After agriculture, animal husbandry was most likely the main cause of worker mobility in medieval Europe. It is also conceptually important for bridging and blurring the distinction between workers moving by seasons and occupations, but in doing so it highlights a useful category of occupational mobility. Shepherding flocks of sheep or tending herds of cattle kept workers very mobile, for instance, although few traces of their activities remain well documented. Yet it is possible to know that many of the large English manors employed specialist head shepherds in charge of hundreds of animals, and in the hillier territory of Scotland sheep rearing was often a better use of land than cropping.[42] Importantly, shepherding could also be another activity in which children were employed. Although the gendered division of working roles was not quite as universally held as sometimes imagined (shepherdesses were relatively common, for instance), there was nonetheless often a tendency for boys and girls to be given differentiated tasks once they reached certain ages. At about seven or eight years old, girls could find their tasks more focused on domestic chores, while boys may have been given oversight of a small flock of sheep.[43] Their workplace training was, of course, highly mobile. Such boys could reasonably have been expected, with their fathers, older brothers, or whoever was training them, to have spent considerable time away from their nominal home, living either by camping or in simple shepherds' huts that could demographically dot peripheral landscapes. Such transhumance, "a move of [the] whole or part of a community," can be observed in the English and Welsh moorlands, where occupation of such territory while pasturing cattle could even occupy a third to half a year.[44]

Some of the movements associated with tending animals could thus range from the relatively minor, contained within a small region, to effective seasonal migration that was sometimes quite extreme in its extent. Spanish cowherds, for example, could take herds on journeys of up to four hundred miles between summer and winter pastures.[45] Yet pastoral mobility was not simply a matter of tending a feeding herd through various pastures but also involved taking stock from field to market, and this often required considerable travel. It is a reminder of the ways in which medieval societies and economies were knitted together from processes of movement which demanded human involvement. Once driven to markets animals could then be butchered for food, and other by-products, such as textiles and leather, could be manufactured. Thus at the other end of the mobile animal sector was a relatively static urban workforce, waiting for the key product to arrive before deconstructing it through labor for consumption or further export.

Yet even an urban and ostensibly static manufacturing workforce reveals, on closer reflection, medieval worker mobility. Certainly the putting-out system of textile manufacture, where wool was spun into cloth, facilitated and perhaps encouraged workers to be relatively contained in a single workspace, often the domestic home. Similarly, the necessary physical requirements for tanning operations and the advantages of scaled economizing favored urban operations. Urban manufacturers were therefore supported by the movement of raw materials, transported both to and within the locality concerned, which required mobile human labor. Such operations also extended back out into the surrounding country, and more broadly connected other towns and regions, networking the whole of medieval Europe (even into Africa and Asia) with a series of creaking carts and ships and mobile humans supporting the efforts of horse, oxen, waves, and wind. At their extreme, the journeys of such traders linked society over thousands of miles. For example, Iceland was connected with Yorkshire through trade in fish, while even Marco Polo's perhaps atypically lengthy sojourn from Italy to far eastern Asia was not entirely without precedent or parallel because it was his merchant family's connections that got him a good portion of the way (see Figure 6.2).[46]

In fact some segments of the medieval population specialized in long-distance trading, such as the Radhanites, who were Jewish merchant traders connecting the Middle East with Europe and serving the economic needs of Islamic and Christian polities alike. Often encouraged to settle in the early medieval era as a means to facilitate such trading

FIGURE 6.2 Marco Polo sailing from Venice in 1271, fifteenth century. Oxford, Bodleian Libraries, MS Bodley 264, folio 218ʳ. The Print Collector / Alamy Stock Photo.

connections, this role declined during the later medieval era for a variety of reasons, more often than not because of a mixture of rivalry and prejudice.[47]

Finally, Europe was also connected by information. The nineteenth-century tendency to examine social history through reference to "class," isolating manual labor from the wider phenomenon of work, was largely carried through the twentieth century by the long shadow of Marxist analysis. As such, those workers not employed in an easily collectivized and narrowly defined and economically productive sense (peasants, laborers, miners, manufacturers) have frequently been overlooked in discussions of medieval work more firmly focused on the major industries that developed or declined as they approached early modernity. Yet quite structural to medieval society was information, and crucial to its role was the messenger, whose journeying connected Europe on micro and macro scales. The most important messengers could expect to travel over sixty miles a day on horseback, while less crucial messengers travelled on foot, perhaps the ultimate expression of mobile human work.[48] While some were undoubtedly men in service sent by their masters, others were clearly messengers by trade. The well-known letter collection by the Paston family in England, for instance, reveals a complex mix of delivery modes for their correspondence, with some messengers named or their point of origin mentioned.[49] While much of their communication relied on servants, they also clearly used established courier services at times.

CONCLUSION

Other examples of medieval worker mobility abound, whether the peregrinations of preaching friars or the campaigning of archers and knights. The threefold division of medieval society into workers, prayers, and fighters is an artificial construct that often fails in the face of detailed analysis. The Benedictine motto of *ora et labora*, pray and work, perhaps best highlights how the often unwritten medieval everyday transcended the scholastics' easy theorizing. In some ways it is the main lesson to take from a survey of medieval work and mobility. Human movement generally operated at the fringes of ready documentation and is now mainly observed through inference and effect. Whether serfs paying fines to live in the next village or town ordinances compelling vagrants to leave or entire peoples settling into a landscape, the picture of medieval Europe that emerges is that it was a place of great mobility. The Romani, Radhanites, and Moriscos complicate models of slowing ethno-migration, while also highlighting the development of territorially and culturally defined entities that subsequent ages would see as nascent nation states. The apparently greater freedoms of individual movement and concern with vagrancy of the later medieval era certainly highlight a growing economic complexity, but also reflect the growing resolution the period offers historians as it draws toward its close.

There is, however, one more specific group worth ending with, precisely because of the long cultural resonance of their movements: the masons. As already seen, medieval construction work provides some of the best evidence for work in the Middle Ages, simply because of its tendency to produce financial accounts which offer windows into wages and conditions. As with manorial accounts, construction sites have therefore had a perhaps disproportionate effect on the directions and content of the wider historiography of the economy and society of the Middle Ages. Yet, despite this, they rarely capture much specific detail about the movements of individuals over time and through landscapes. Some efforts have been made to use masons' marks in building stonework to chart the movements of individuals whose lives have otherwise left little trace (see Figure 6.3).[50]

FIGURE 6.3 Stone cutter's mark on a tower in the medieval Louvre, Paris, France. Wikimedia Commons.

Yet in the face of this sort of detailed research it is perhaps worth standing back from the scene a little and observing the broad commonalities of medieval European material culture. From castles to cathedrals to mills and fields, even with regional variations and particularities factored in and allowing room for sizeable minorities with their own particularities of expression, a distant perspective makes it obvious that a lot of people moved about quite a bit, even if they each remain hard to follow for terribly long.

CHAPTER SEVEN

Work and Society

HOLLY J. GRIECO

This chapter addresses the theme "Work and Society" from 800 to 1450, focusing specifically on social welfare within European Christendom. In this lengthy span of time, Europe experienced major changes in the balance of rural and urban populations. Although the overwhelming majority of people still lived in rural areas throughout these years, towns and cities became increasingly important in the eleventh and twelfth centuries and remained critical within medieval society, even after the population contracted following the Great Famine and the Black Death in the fourteenth century. In some cases, social welfare took similar forms across rural and urban environments, but sometimes urban centers and the institutions they nurtured gave rise to distinctive forms of poor relief. At the beginning of the ninth century, western Europe was on the cusp of a great period of technological advances, including the development of the heavy plow, which enabled the cultivation of rich, heavy northern soils in addition to the sandy soils that could be tilled with a simple scratch plow. Land clearing known as assarting expanded agricultural production and aided or drove urban expansion. Great political changes marked this period, which witnessed, among other events, the beginning of the Carolingian dynasty, the expansion of the Holy Roman Empire, the Christianization of Iceland and other Scandinavian countries, the founding of the Capetian line in what would become the kingdom of France, the ongoing *Reconquista* in the Iberian Peninsula, and the development of independent communes and city-states in the Italian peninsula and elsewhere.

Although it is difficult to generalize across more than five centuries and the span of the European continent, nonetheless we can safely say that issues of hierarchy and status within society played key roles in shaping and determining the kinds of assistance provided for those at or near—and in some cases, well beyond—the margins of respectable medieval society, as well as the kinds of assistance that were provided to those experiencing temporary need that was not owing to material poverty. Medieval charity and social welfare were not intended to reweave the fabric of society to make its rigid social boundaries more flexible. In order to understand better the variety of forms such assistance took, this chapter will provide an overview of the work in medieval communities across Europe that sought to address the basic needs of people in society.

Attitudes toward wealth and poverty provide a valuable and compelling entry into thinking about human labor in the Middle Ages and the institutions and practices medieval people developed to address poverty and to heal the sick in their society. To that end, this chapter will examine social need and charitable work within the context of traditional and reformed Benedictine abbeys as well as within communities of other religious, such as the Hospitallers. It will look at the role that bishops and secular clergy played in providing for the needs of the vulnerable in medieval society. It will examine the work of lay confraternities—that is, mutual aid societies in medieval towns and cities often organized by trade or profession—and lay penitents, or laymen and laywomen dedicated to a life of penance, sometimes members of groups such as the beguines or *Humiliati*. Finally, it will look at the role that secular governments and leaders played in providing social welfare. Aid within medieval Christian society took many forms, funding the symbolic distribution of alms as well as endowing hospitals that provided for a range of needs medieval people faced. Over the period from 800 to 1450, individual laypeople and municipal governments increasingly stepped into roles of financing and administering social assistance that previously had been dominated by clergy and religious.

HIERARCHY, THE PLACE OF POVERTY, AND ATTITUDES TOWARD THE POOR

Poverty could be alleviated but not eliminated; this was the typical view between the years 800 and 1300 and beyond that resulted in inflexible hierarchies delimiting the ranks of each person within so-called feudal society. The exact customs varied by location, but the underlying principle remained a society in which vertical relationships connected members to each other, with obligations of service for those at the bottom of the hierarchy, and obligations of protection for those at its top. When members of the medieval intellectual elite considered the world in which they lived, they imagined it divided among three orders or estates, composed of those who prayed, those who fought, and those who worked with their hands—*oratores, bellatores, laboratores*. That, men could be categorized as clerics, knights, or peasants. The tripartite structure described by the historian Georges Duby (d. 1996), in his classic study that focused on northern France, resonated with some modification across medieval Europe. This approach to understanding divisions in society differed greatly from the focus on citizens and noncitizens in late antiquity, or the period from roughly the middle of the third century until the sixth century. Citizens might be eligible for a distribution of grain, not because they experienced need, but because they were citizens, whereas poor people who could not prove their citizenship were ineligible.[1]

What is most important for this chapter is the rigidity of these categories. Some men were born as peasants, and spent their lives working with their hands, subjected to the rule of others. Other men were born into the nobility and bore arms and exerted power in the secular realm. Some of these men were called to serve as clerics, taking the topmost position in the earthly hierarchy. Each of these three orders had a role within society and thus contributed to it. A peasant, however, had no hope of ascending this static hierarchy; he would remain among those who worked with their hands. Such a rigid view of society and the idea that each person was born into a particular "estate" or "order" had an effect on the way medieval people viewed and addressed material need.

The growth of towns and cities beginning in the eleventh century and continuing into the thirteenth century complicated, but did not eliminate, the hierarchical nature of society. Along with the demographic growth and urban renaissance in former Roman towns and cities such as Milan and Paris and the foundation of new ones, like Prague, an important center of trade by 965, and Montpellier, founded around 985, the eleventh and twelfth centuries witnessed the development of a monetary, profit economy in western Europe. The shift to a profit economy rooted in the exchange of coin, from an economy of exchange of goods, affected medieval wage-laborers profoundly. Local and regional rulers could affect the process of exchange and compensation through the manipulation of currency. Such practices had a disproportionate effect on those at the margins of medieval society who might have been able to barter but who lacked access to hard currency. This new way of doing business blossomed at the same time that voluntary poverty became a prominent feature of religious devotion in medieval Europe, the latter of which may have been a response to the former.[2]

Some scholars have drawn a distinction between charity and social welfare, associating the first with a religious motivation and the second with a secular one. Other scholars find it difficult to break medieval charitable practices into a strict binary. Medieval people intended charitable practices to address material need and serve the common good within society, but such generosity also provided a spiritual benefit to individual donors. From the High Middle Ages to the late Middle Ages a demonstrable shift occurred in the practice of charity, which changed from something one did as an individual (or as a group of individuals, such as members of a monastery) to something one did as a society for the good of society. Nonetheless, we cannot describe charity before a certain period as wholly religious and after a certain period as purely secular in motivation.[3]

Many forms of charity and social welfare existed in the Middle Ages, but not all of these charitable provisions were for the materially poor. Benedictine monasteries typically provided travellers, poor or otherwise, with shelter and food—a temporary form of aid. A pilgrim or poor person receiving such aid is depicted in the refectory of the Old Cathedral of Lleida in Catalonia, as seen in Figure 7.1.

In some cases, recipients of hospitality were royals or noblemen travelling with their household. Similarly, *leprosaria* such as Mont-aux-Malades and Salle-aux-Puelles outside of Rouen required an entrance gift. These foundations provided an important service to lepers, but because only the wealthy or someone with a wealthy patron would have been able to live in either leper house, these charitable foundations reinforced the traditional strata of medieval society and did not aid the most vulnerable lepers.[4] Institutions did exist to aid the poor and marginalized who faced serious (and sometimes ongoing) need, but their assistance was shaped by the way medieval society viewed poverty and the place of the poor.

Attitudes toward poverty and the poor in the Middle Ages developed out of early Christian texts and traditions. In particular, the Greek Fathers focused on the intentional poverty of monastics and other ascetics, rather than the poverty of the economically disadvantaged. Perspectives such as this one shaped the medieval view of poverty as a category that existed outside the bounds of economic need and as one tied to concerns about ascetic virtue and salvation.[5] Passages such as Matthew 26:11, "For the poor you have always with you," affected medieval attitudes toward poverty, which in turn led to particular responses to the poor in society. Such texts influenced the view that poverty was inevitable within society. Other passages, such as 2 Thessalonians 3:10, "[I]f any man will not work, neither let him eat," sowed the seeds for articulating an understanding of work ethic in which material aid was restricted to those deemed deserving according to certain criteria.[6]

In the eleventh and twelfth centuries, voluntary poverty reemerged as a spiritual value in western Europe. In the thirteenth century, mendicant friars such as the Dominicans and Franciscans identified voluntary poverty as the primary means of imitating Christ, whom they believed to have embraced poverty both in a theological or spiritual sense, as God-become-man, and in a material or economic sense, as someone who had been

FIGURE 7.1 A poor person or pilgrim receiving aid. Refectory of the Old Cathedral of Lleida, Catalonia, Spain, around fourteenth century. Photo: PRISMA ARCHIVO / Alamy Stock Photo.

poor during his earthly life. The popularity of voluntary poverty correlated positively with increased practice of charity; yet it also complicated the question of who the true, deserving poor were within medieval society—who had the right to beg for and accept alms? Motivation for individual charitable actions was complex; though compassion played a role, such generosity was also spiritually pragmatic. Giving alms, founding a hospital, or endowing a college for impoverished students helped to redeem one's sins and purify one's wealth. Indeed, this view made the poor part of God's plan of salvation for the wealthy. The rich man benefited more from this exchange than the poor man, since the rich man exchanged material goods for the prayers of the poor and, ultimately, treasure in heaven. More ominously or insidiously, such a view of wealth and poverty had the effect of sanctioning social inequality as part of the divine will. If poverty was natural and intended by God as part of his plan for humankind, then people needed not make an effort to eliminate poverty from society or alleviate the suffering of the poor.[7] The redemptive value Christians placed on earthly suffering also did not help matters.

Charity cannot be studied in medieval society divorced from contemporary ideas about property, community, and salvation. Of equal importance, economic circumstances must be such that people have excess income or goods to give away. But the economic ability to give alms did not guarantee that people would do so, nor did it predict the form such assistance would take.[8] Rather, assistance depended upon society's view of poverty and the poor considered in tandem with the social hierarchy. Andrew Brown has observed that we would do well to consider "charitable giving and regulation on poverty within the darker context of repression: social discrimination may well lurk behind the pious handout, civic hierarchy behind expressions of community."[9] Far from eliminating or equalizing material differences in society, medieval charity sought to reinforce differences between those who gave charity and those who received it.

Generalizations about poverty and the poor in the Middle Ages are challenging because the poor did not constitute a monolithic group. Medieval people distinguished two basic categories of the poor in society: *paupers* and *indigents*. Paupers were free men who were not necessarily landless, but the size of whose holdings subordinated them to large landholders and left them vulnerable in times of economic, social, or environmental stress.[10] Indigents formed a subset of the poor who had fallen beneath their station economically. A knight who had lost his fortune, for example, could be impoverished but he did not cease to be a knight.[11] In other words, the poor did not constitute a separate *estate* within society; rather, poverty designated the condition of a person at a particular moment.

Poverty placed an individual at risk within society. Indeed, poverty sometimes led the poor to enserf themselves or their children. These poor men and women preferred to barter their personal rights for the promise of greater security than to remain free and impoverished.[12] Poverty humiliated a man in the eyes of others as well as in the view of the social group to which he belonged.[13] If he had official responsibilities as part of his role in society, poverty was more than an indignity; it was also an obstacle that affected his ability to perform his office and perhaps disqualified him from holding it. Poverty rendered men unfit to rule because society perceived it as a disability. Similarly, according to Pope Innocent III (r. 1198–1216), the clerical estate was incompatible with poverty. Leaders in Christendom, whether clergy or laity, could not properly speaking be poor and remain in positions of authority.[14]

Innocent III spoke out against clerical poverty at a time when mendicant orders were growing in popularity across Europe and challenging traditional attitudes toward clerical wealth and poverty. The mendicant model of fraternity fit well with horizontal ties developing within medieval towns. The Franciscans in particular fostered this horizontal social structure in part because they rejected a vertical hierarchy that subordinated and denigrated some men while holding up others. The early friars rejected the traditional economic framework of Umbrian society, refusing to participate in an exploitative economy. They worked like other manual laborers but refused to take more than what was necessary as compensation. Mendicants posed a threat to secular clergy because their visible poverty and identification with the poor put the secular clergy, who justified ecclesiastical wealth through their service to the poor, in an uncomfortable situation. Secular clerics often accused the friars of taking alms intended for the involuntary poor.

In the *Decretum*, the twelfth-century Bolognese canonist, Gratian, distinguished between *hospitalitas* (hospitality) and *liberalitas* (generosity), in the way that twenty-first-century people might distinguish between alms and welfare: the former provided to all without distinction and the latter dependent upon the worthiness of the potential recipient.[15] The lexical valence of the word *liberalitas* raises an important point about how medieval people understood poverty and the status of the poor. *Liber*, the root of the word *liberalitas*, means free or independent, in the sense of not being a slave. Someone without full legal rights could not be considered poor in the Middle Ages, perhaps because his lord was expected to meet his needs, or perhaps because as an unfree or semi-free person the slave or serf did not have the right to benefit from the generosity of others since he or she did not fully participate in society in a legal sense. *Liberalitas*, then, was aid or generosity provided to free people in medieval society who needed and—more importantly—merited such assistance. By contrast, *hospitalitas* was provided to all with a particular need, whether society would consider the person worthy or not, and whether or not the recipient was materially poor, or simply experiencing a temporary need.

Generosity to the poor not only provided material support, it also helped the donor's quest for salvation. But the generosity of benefactors did not negate the pervasive attitude of scorn toward the poor. Gifts to the poor tended to be basic: if the poor had the bare necessities, they ceased to be considered as such. Alms should be moderate, medieval people counselled, in keeping with the constitution of the poor. Gifts of fine food "would not agree with their constitution and ... might excite their senses."[16] Even in giving charity—*especially* in giving charity—preserving the social hierarchy was paramount. By giving charity, the donor exhibited the virtue of generosity; by accepting it, the recipient modelled humility. Considering the balance between *hospitalitas* and *liberalitas*, Gratian and commentators on the *Decretum* tried to reconcile the conflicting pronouncements of church fathers such as John Chrysostom (c. 349–407), who urged blind almsgiving without respect to worthiness, as opposed to Ambrose of Milan (337–97), who developed a hierarchy of preference.[17]

What did poverty look like? In rural areas, a poor person might be a landowner whose holdings were too small to support his family, or he might be someone who held sufficient land but lacked a plow and draft animals to help him cultivate it. He might also be a landowner at a time of famine or at a time when grain prices were low. In cities and towns, the combination of decreasing wages and increasing grain and food prices squeezed urban workers. In other words, many medieval people, rural or urban, were members of the working poor, one crisis away from destitution.[18] That someone who worked might live in such precarity strained the credulity of many, just as it does for many today. The rural working poor—free peasants—were useful in medieval society, growing and harvesting grain and other agricultural products, but those of higher social standing still scorned them.[19] Medieval people seemed to be suspicious of those who worked yet did not have enough to meet their needs. This preoccupation related to another concern about so-called false paupers, who accepted alms intended for the truly destitute. Medieval authors raised concerns about usurpers who used makeup to alter their appearance or who exaggerated physical illness in order to receive alms. Writings about those who were considered unworthy of receiving alms preoccupied elites in the twelfth and thirteenth centuries. Thomas of Chobham, an English cleric and theologian who died sometime between 1233 and 1236, complained about beggars who went to church not to fulfill religious obligations or to nurture spiritual growth, but to make money. Others told stories about a beggar who became rich by begging. Such concerns tell us more about the concerns of twelfth- and thirteenth-century elites rather than about thirteenth-century beggars. These stories also play on the same kind of unfounded anxieties that some people have today about those on public assistance.[20] In general, people agreed that babies, children, and people with disabilities required assistance of some kind, though to whom this responsibility belonged was not always clear. Attitudes differed toward those considered able-bodied. We should not assume, however, at least in the case of late medieval and early modern England, that intellectual and theological hostility to the poor always reflected actual hostility on the ground.[21] This chapter will examine the ways that monastic communities, secular clergy, laypeople, and lay institutions provided for those in need in medieval society through almsgiving and social assistance.

MONASTIC CHARITY

In late antiquity, Christian communities tended to be organized along the same lines as Roman governmental boundaries. Christian life centered around the cities and their bishops, who took primary responsibility for dispensing charity as well as providing pastoral care. With the collapse of Roman cities after the fall of the western Roman Empire, monastic foundations became the primary sites for charitable actions in the early Middle Ages. Medieval religious offered two main types of aid: hospitality and alms. Important within the Benedictine tradition, hospitality typically relieved an immediate, temporary need for food and shelter, regardless of whether the recipient was poor. Monks and nuns provided respite and nourishment for travellers and pilgrims, honoring the charge found in the Benedictine Rule to welcome the stranger as Christ himself. The Benedictine Rule required monasteries to have provisions for such itinerant guests and poor people, to provide food, drink, and shelter in a space separate from the monks' cloister. Even though guests' meals were cooked and served in separate quarters, and they bedded down for the night in a separate guesthouse or dormitory, the brothers served those who arrived at their gates with their own hands. Monasteries became permanent residences for some guests who were homeless. In addition, others sometimes paid a fee to board with the monks. Over time these arrangements within male and female communities became institutionalized and known in England as a corrody—a price attached to room and board which could be purchased for oneself or provided by a patron, or even given as a privilege by an abbot.[22]

In addition to hospitality for those on the road, religious also distributed alms to the materially poor. These forms of charity provided by monastics sometimes took a highly symbolic form, geared more toward the spiritual rewards for the community and its donors than for the material benefits to the poor. For example, on major feast days, the monks might feed twelve (or multiples of twelve) poor men. On Holy Thursday, the monks might wash the feet of twelve poor men, as they reenacted Jesus' actions in John 13:1–17, and then feed them. Some scholars have argued that monks saw themselves as the true poor of Christ, so the poor were less individuals in need of assistance and more players in a spiritual drama acted out primarily for the spiritual benefit of the monks and their donors, and only secondarily for the material benefit of the poor people they served. For Bernard of Clairvaux (1090–1153), this state of affairs was as it should be. He argued that it was one thing to feed the hungry "in service of nature" and another to "have a zeal for poverty" in "service of grace." In Bernard's estimation, the latter, reflecting the contemplative as opposed to the active life, was preferable.[23] Bernard placed greater value on the contemplative life as a model for coenobitic communities, which tended to lead to forms of charity weighted with spiritual meaning more than material assistance. Yet this representation is something of a caricature of monastic attitudes toward poverty and the poor. For many, if not most, monastic communities, charity was not a gesture devoid of concern for its recipients.

The hospitaller orders added further complexity to these models of charity within medieval religious communities. The Knights of the Hospital of Saint John in Jerusalem, or Hospitallers, are primarily known for their crusading activity in the Holy Land. But this aristocratic religious order was also recognized for works of charity. Before the fall of Jerusalem in 1187, the order's main hospital in that city could house between 900 and 1,000 inmates, including the sick and terminally ill of both sexes. They cared for Jews and Muslims in addition to Christians. Within Europe, the care offered varied widely. The order had no hospitals in Valencia on the Mediterranean coast or in Frisia on the North Sea. During the High Middle Ages, the city of Arles in Provence was home to a significant foundation run by the Hospitallers of Saint John. By 1338, the institution's doors were no longer open to people and the brothers only distributed symbolic charity. The fourteenth century did not mark the end of the order and its hospitals, however; even at the end of the fourteenth century, in 1373, the Hospitallers' foundation at Genoa still functioned, boasting a surgeon, physician, separate wards for men and women, wet nurses for foundlings and orphans, and a dowry fund for poor girls. In other words, the Hospitallers at Genoa prospered and played an important role in filling unmet needs of the people.[24]

Religious men and women working in hospitals lived the active life, serving in the world, unlike many traditional and reformed Benedictines who lived as contemplatives in the cloister, as had Bernard of Clairvaux, who disparaged the active life. The various hospitaller orders followed the Rule of Saint Augustine, a flexible rule dating back to Augustine of Hippo (354–430) but not fully articulated until cathedral clergy, among others, adopted it in the twelfth century. As is made plain in the description of services offered at the hospital in Genoa, the charity offered by the brothers there and by brothers and sisters at other hospitaller foundations centered on providing a wide variety of hands-on care and assistance. Such a model of charity was consistent with the contemplative and active life lived by those who professed the Rule of Saint Augustine. By contrast, the vocation of traditional Benedictine monks centered on personal learning and experience, which led to a more ritualistic and spiritualized practice of almsgiving—one that focused more on the spiritual rather than the material value of their actions.[25]

With the rise of the hospitaller orders, Benedictines, including Cluniacs and Cistercians, no longer monopolized medieval charity. Yet monastic charity remained important, and the institution for organizing charity within the monastery setting—the almonry—became more important and more complex over time. With its increased importance, the monastic almonry often received a dedicated building and a special budget, along with a dedicated manager—the almoner. That space may have included a kitchen, dormitory, and even a chapel at larger monastic foundations. The almonry was often situated near the gatehouse through which outsiders passed to receive hospitality. At an abbey like Cluny in Burgundy, a third of the house's income went to assist the poor. As cloistered religious, the monks were limited in what they could do and how they could respond to contemporary social circumstances. With societal change came new religious orders and different means of assisting the poor in medieval society. Templars distributed alms three times a week, unlike a traditional abbey, which until the later Middle Ages would have limited alms to special feast days or the anniversaries of important benefactors. The form of social assistance varied widely with the location. In the Iberian Peninsula, the Mercedarians and other redeeming orders arranged prisoner exchanges during the *Reconquista* and paid ransoms for others.[26] In eastern and central Europe, hospitals and the hospitaller orders began to flourish later on. Around 1220, bishops assigned the Brothers of the Order of the Holy Spirit and the Croziers to serve at hospitals in Kraków and Breslau.[27]

Though monastic hospitality has been described as ritualistic in character, some visitors to the almonry, in addition to being served by the monks—may also have received medical care. In fact, the Benedictines had founded the hospital in Jerusalem at the turn of the twelfth century that would later be taken over by the Hospitallers of Saint John in Jerusalem.[28] The hospital at Jerusalem was not an isolated example. In 1109, Abbot William of Whitby founded a hospice for lepers that later was opened to all people. Cistercian nuns in northern France also cared for lepers, and considered their hospice care a form of manual labor. Cistercian nuns were not alone in adopting this charitable work; other women religious, including the nuns of Fontevraud and the Premonstratensians also adopted the care of lepers as charitable work.[29] The Benedictine Rule authorized many forms of monastic charity. Providing basic schooling to children beyond the precinct did not fall within the purview of the Rule, which only addressed the education of oblates, or children vowed to the monastery by their parents. Nevertheless, many Benedictine monasteries had open schools from 950 to 1150. In England at the turn of the thirteenth century, the Benedictines developed a separate school for nonoblates as part of the almonry, that is, the monks considered the education of children a charitable work. These schools admitted paying students and poor students who had benefactors for teaching and training.[30]

SECULAR CLERGY AND THE COMMON GOOD

We have seen that the charity provided by medieval monastic communities cannot be dismissed as purely symbolic. So-called military and hospitaller orders and redeeming orders, and even traditionally contemplative monastics such as the Cistercians, assisted the poor directly, cooking for them, feeding them, and washing their wounds with their own hands. Secular clergy, by definition, lived and served in the world, leading bishoprics and parishes, providing pastoral care and guidance, and educating young boys, unlike religious clergy who were more firmly bound to the cloister and the contemplative life.

Within early Christian society, bishops played a key role in meeting the material as well as spiritual needs of the faithful. In addition to practical responsibilities for the needy in their dioceses, figures such as Bishop Ambrose of Milan; John Chrysostom,

Patriarch of Constantinople; and Augustine, Bishop of Hippo, also helped to shape and define Christian discourse concerning wealth and poverty.[31] With the fall of the western Roman Empire, the importance of key Roman cities and their prelates waned but did not completely disappear. Although in the early Middle Ages and into the Carolingian period, monastic communities were the primary locus of charitable activity, the influence of bishops and other secular clergy became more prominent in the High Middle Ages as cities and towns once again grew in importance. Bishops, cathedral chapters, communities of canons, and parish priests all engaged in works that fostered the common good both materially and spiritually. This assistance might be relatively anonymous and scripted, such as the bishop feeding the poor on Maundy Thursday, or limited to a particular neighborhood—the confines of a parish—where those seeking alms would be known and evaluated before receiving assistance (see Figure 7.2).

In western Europe, the major hospitals in the twelfth and thirteenth centuries had been founded during the Carolingian period, if not earlier. Foundations dating back to the Merovingian period were more likely to have an episcopal founder and benefactor.[32] During the Carolingian period, monastic charity came to the fore, yet the framework of episcopal hospitals remained in place, even as their importance was temporarily eclipsed. Arles, Rouen, Amiens, Reims, and Metz all boasted episcopal hospitals from the sixth century. The Council of Rheims in 813 instructed bishops to let the poor dine with them, an example of the ideal of episcopal hospitality in the Carolingian period.[33] In Milan, the archbishop founded a hospital for pilgrims and the poor in 879.[34] In Iberia, the

FIGURE 7.2 Saint Louis of Anjou, Bishop of Toulouse serving at the table of the poor. Simone Martini (c. 1284–1344), predella of altarpiece of Saint Louis crowning his brother Robert of Naples. Photo: DeAgostini. Image courtesy Getty Images.

hospital at Mérida dated to 580. In the tenth century, episcopal hospitals were founded at Barcelona and in the Pyrenees. Elsewhere, hospitals developed after the Carolingian period. The cathedral hospital, St. John the Baptist, was founded in Florence in 1040. No such episcopal institution existed beforehand. The Low Countries and the Holy Roman Empire had about four episcopal foundations before the eleventh century, including those at Cologne and Bremen. In England, no episcopal hospitals date prior to the Norman Conquest of 1066. A few English cathedral towns had hospitals like other major European cities—among them, Winchester, Canterbury, and Oxford—by at least the beginning of the thirteenth century.[35] Otherwise, hospitals developed later in England.[36] In some cases, a hospital might begin as a lay foundation and only later come under episcopal control, as at Cambridge, where the bishop of Ely took responsibility for (or perhaps usurped rights to) a hospital in the mid-thirteenth century that had been founded by a townsperson at the beginning of the century. This hospital was not initially an episcopal foundation, and even after it came under episcopal control, it was not primarily administered by the bishop.[37]

Miri Rubin's study of charity in medieval Cambridge illuminates the changing role of bishops across Europe. In England, as elsewhere, bishops sometimes founded leper hospitals. Two miles east of Cambridge, at Stourbridge, the leper hospital of St. Mary Magdalene received an income from the bishop of Ely. In 1227, that sum was equal to the former royal payment to the foundation. Like the hospital at Cambridge taken over by the bishop, this leprosarium originally belonged to the burgesses of Cambridge, who held it from the king. Uncertain circumstances led to the transfer of control to the bishop from the town, which had administered the foundation from as early as 1150 until 1227. After the mid-thirteenth century, the house no longer admitted lepers. In other cases, the bishop of Ely provided spiritual support for a hospital without providing financial patronage. In particular, after a new leprosarium was founded in Cambridge in 1361, the bishop granted an indulgence in 1392 for those who visited and helped the house and its staff.[38] Charitable foundations in the Bishopric of Ely illustrate not only the variety of relationships a bishop might have to local charitable institutions, but also the ways those relationships overlapped and changed over time.

Not all hospitals or hospices offered the same services, provided the same benefits, or had similar staff members. Some hospitals provided only physical care, while others combined physical and spiritual care, including masses, burials, and so forth. Hospitals providing spiritual care required clerical approval usually from the bishop but possibly from the cathedral chapter or the pope.[39] With their primary focus on spiritual care, hospitals run by bishops or cathedral chapters typically did not have physicians or surgeons on staff. In part this was because hospitals, generally speaking, before the fourteenth century, emphasized caring for inmates, not curing them.[40] Treatment more closely resembled today's hospice care than the kind of medical interventions one might expect in a modern hospital. Episcopal foundations especially stressed healing through prayer and penance because of the long-held association of bodily sickness with spiritual sin.[41] This focus reflected the purpose of hospitals to serve as places of shelter for the temporarily homeless, regardless of material need.

Urban hospitals served a variety of purposes to meet a wide range of needs. The hospital in Barcelona founded sometime before 995, was one of the first in Catalonia. As an urban hospice, it served all kinds of people. In 1236, the episcopal hospital merged with a new foundation in Barcelona, En Colom. The combined hospitals sought to serve a transitory population, though hospital documents seem to reveal otherwise. In 1307, the hospital housed ten sick people, four foundlings aged five years, eight nurslings, and two poor boys who received academic instruction. Although some of these people may have been transitory, many of them clearly were not.[42] The list reveals the broad range of aid such hospitals dispensed, including relatively comprehensive care for children, from nurslings to school-aged boys and girls. Such institutions invested in the education and training of abandoned children as both a spiritual and a societal good.

Parishes also bore responsibility for managing charitable services. Bishops had the primary responsibility for running foundations like that in the Crown of Aragon, where the poor at the margins of society—itinerant beggars, the criminalized poor—fell under the charitable auspices of the cathedral. But the local poor in Aragon received aid from parish institutions. The same was true of foundlings in Paris, who were generally cared for in the parishes where they were discovered.[43] In the late thirteenth century, parishioners in the diocese of Valencia elected someone from each parish to serve as the "father of the poor," who would bear the responsibility of distributing alms on Saturdays. On holidays, disbursements included meat and rice; on All Saints' Day, the father of the poor also distributed winter clothes and blankets. A similar institution developed in Catalonia, at Girona. In fifteenth-century Castile, parishes developed an institution similar to the Italian *monte de pietà*, which loaned and distributed money at no interest to the poor. Without such a loan fund, people who scarcely could have afforded to borrow money in any other way would have lost an important source of credit.[44]

Distribution of alms in the parish setting allowed for greater discretion than other means of distribution, permitting the poor to live their lives as much as possible like others in their neighborhoods. Parish institutions, by and large, were intended for those within the parish, whether families, individuals, students, or officials. Parish distribution of material assistance signalled the expansion of charity intended as social welfare or as a social safety net, rather than as a symbolic encounter between donor and recipient. In Barcelona, for example, after 1250, only the local and deserving poor could benefit from parish assistance. Local ties enabled designated parish officials to separate the deserving from the undeserving poor.[45]

LAY AND MUNICIPAL CHARITY AND WELFARE

Laypeople have long made charitable donations and engaged in charitable work within society, but more structured forms of social assistance developed at different moments throughout the Middle Ages. Lay support for those at the margins came from individual donors, including royals and nobles; confraternity members and lay penitents; and municipal governments and foundations. Just because these donors were laypeople did not mean that their actions were purely secular in the contemporary sense of being devoid of religious motivation. In this chapter, I have employed sections for the principal types of social assistance provided by monastics, secular clerics, lay institutions, and laypeople. But these forms did not successively replace each other. Monastic and secular clerical forms of charity did not cease to exist in the Middle Ages when lay forms of charity really began to flourish. Historians cannot identify a clean split between ecclesiastical and lay support for charity. Laypeople donated before the year 1200, but not in the same numbers and not with the same degree of organization. In the ninth and tenth centuries, for example, laypeople were supposed to pay the tithe to the church, and the church in turn provided charity to those in need. Lay elites could and did give alms and make gifts, but typically they did so only upon request in times of local crisis. The Council of Tours reinforced this expectation in 813, declaring that individuals should first care for their households and dependents.[46] Jonas of Orléans, a Carolingian bishop and moralist, wrote that those of means should visit the sick, whether they were rich or poor. But along with material aid, donors should remind the poor and sick that illness indicated divine disfavor. Carolingian nobility did not typically engage in such service to the poor and sick, unlike monastics in the same period. By contrast, the High and late Middle Ages witnessed an increase in the number of lay-founded and lay-directed institutions, particularly those sponsored by municipal governments.[47] In this section, I will focus primarily on confraternities and lay penitents and on municipal institutions and their policies.

Confraternities, or mutual aid societies, provided benefits for members. Caring for those outside the organization was not one of the original purposes of these institutions, but over time aid to others became incorporated. These associations developed very early in the Iberian Peninsula and then faded in importance, only experiencing a revival in the eleventh century. In Languedoc, Provence, León, and the Italian peninsula, confraternities established practices and institutions for paupers in addition to providing support for struggling members.[48] Within a town, confraternities were often associated with a particular trade guild. For many guilds, monetary donations were the primary means by which members participated in charity. Parisian masons contributed the fines they collected to charity. If an apprentice wanted to serve fewer than six years before becoming a journeyman, for example, he could buy out the rest of his time by paying a fine in the form of a donation to the chapel of the guild's patron, St. Blaise. Similarly, guilds in Toulouse surrendered half of their income from fines to support the upkeep of the city's bridges over the Garonne River. Charity expanded beyond the bounds of the guild and its confraternity for fullers at Lincoln as well. Upon the death of a fellow guild member, the other members each gave a halfpenny to buy bread for the poor. These are three examples showing guild members expanding their generosity beyond the confines of the institution to include local churches (under whose care bridges resided) and the deserving poor.[49]

The Confraternity of the Holy Spirit, dedicated to charitable works, was popular at Lyons, Geneva, Freiburg, Zurich, Cologne, and Brussels. In Florence, Franciscan Tertiaries founded the Orsanmichele in 1291, which became a charitable organization over time. Members of the Orsanmichele and other confraternities dedicated themselves to the corporal works of mercy, such as giving drink to the thirsty (see Figure 7.3).

In Florence, the Orsanmichele made offerings to hospitals and to the poor, distributed alms to unemployed laborers, provided assistance to pregnant women and orphans, and gave relief to those in debtors' prison. Almost all of the charity disbursed by the Orsanmichele (94 percent) went to support these causes. But by the beginning of the second quarter of the fifteenth century, the Orsanmichele had ceased to be an important source of charity within Florence. A new institution, the Buonomini, dedicated to helping the "shame-faced poor," developed in the mid-fifteenth century. This organization provided relief to the needy families of craft workers in the city—to artisans and those in the textile industry, to abandoned wives, widows, families with children, and families with a sick or incapacitated wage earner. Later in its history, the Buonomini would shift to providing assistance to the indigent, but at its foundation, the organization dedicated its efforts to helping those who had fallen from their station within fifteenth-century Florentine society. In another Tuscan city, San Sepolcro, fourteen new confraternities had their genesis in the decades before the Black Death. One of them, the Laude de Santa Maria della Notte, though primarily devotional in nature, also distributed grain

FIGURE 7.3 Giving drink to the thirsty, roundel, c. 1430–40. Coventry, England. © Victoria and Albert Museum, London.

and clothing, and provided subsidized dowries for poor girls. In 1417, more than seventy-five years after the first outbreak of plague in Europe, 37 percent of this confraternity's expenditures went to charity.[50] While confraternities played an important role as sources of social support within the Italian city-states and within southern France and Iberia, they were less developed and influential in England and in Germanic-speaking parts of the Holy Roman Empire.

Confraternities and penitential movements flourished in central and northern Italy during the High Middle Ages. Within a group of penitents, members bore a responsibility for the welfare of others in the association. If a member were sick, others would arrange weekly visits, meet the needs of the member and his family, and attend the funeral if the member did not recover. Some penitents engaged in symbolic acts of charity as did religious and secular clergy, by feeding twelve poor men before their Palm Sunday banquet. The members ate separately after they had served the poor in order to emphasize their shared brotherhood. This form of charity also reinforced social boundaries within the community. Hospital work and social service formed part of penitents' activity on behalf of the poor. These kinds of services were a real societal good, yet they necessitated greater organization and corporate activity, putting them in tension with the origins of confraternities as independent lay movements. Confraternity members typically celebrated mass once a month with a dinner afterwards, to which each member contributed. Leftover monies went to provide assistance to poor or struggling members; any surplus beyond what was needed to meet members' needs, the organization donated as alms. Almsgiving was also a traditional facet of the annual celebration of the feast day of the confraternity's patron saint.[51] Interestingly, confraternity members in Bologna served as lay chaplains in the city jail and distributed to prisoners bread that they had baked with municipal funding. Confraternity members, then, were active in meeting the material needs of the incarcerated and keeping prisoners connected to the rest of the city's Christian community.

Many lay penitents dedicated their resources to serving the poor at hospitals. Laymen in Cremona, Lodi, and Piacenza either founded or ran hospitals in those cities. The most well known was Raimondo Palmerio (d. 1202), who founded a hospital in Piacenza. Other penitents served at this hospital, in effect receiving training as social workers. Some of them began at Raimondo's hospital and went on to found hospitals in their own communes. One such example was Gualterio of Lodi (1184–1224) who began to work in the hospital at Piacenza as a teenager. After serving at another hospital, he founded the Misericordia, a hospital endowed jointly by the commune and bishop of Lodi. Another lay penitent, the goldsmith Facio of Cremona (c. 1196–1272), would have been among the most prominent artisans in his city. Yet his personal asceticism and charitable impulses drove him to found a hospital in his city and begin a lay order of penitents called the Società dello Spirito Santo. In Florence, male Franciscan tertiaries ran a hospital beginning in 1229, San Paolo dei Convalescenti. The Orsanmichele also had a hospital in Montelupo Fiorentino, southwest of Florence, and a poor house in Florence that determined the eligibility of those who desired to receive alms from the brotherhood. Such service was not limited to male penitents. The Franciscan tertiary Margherita of Cortona (d. 1297) worked as a midwife, engaged in charitable works, and later founded both a hospital and a charitable confraternity.[52]

Two specific groups with particular regional prominence played important roles as providers of lay charity in the Middle Ages. The *Humiliati* and the beguines each developed primarily within a particular region. The *Humiliati*, penitents in Lombardy, especially in the city of Milan, enjoyed great popularity because they provided a spiritual outlet for men and women who felt a religious calling that went unanswered by the prospect of vowed religious life or ordination. By 1180, these penitents had shelters in place for the poor and pilgrims. Innocent III restructured the group at the beginning of the thirteenth century by dividing the penitents into three groups: monks; canons regular; and laymen and laywomen, including couples and families.[53] Because of their positive attitude toward manual labor, care for the poor and travellers fit within the scope of the *Humiliati*'s understanding of its charism, or the spiritual gifts from the Holy Spirit that defined the way the *Humiliati* lived out their lives.[54]

The beguines, groups of female penitents that first developed in the Low Countries, are better known than the *Humiliati*. Whereas lay *Humiliati* typically lived in their own homes and gathered together regularly, beguines lived in community, either in a stand-alone beguinage or in a court beguinage, a walled complex with many houses, hospitals, and chapels for the beguines and those they aided—a "City of Ladies," as Walter Simons has called it.[55] In the later thirteenth century, some beguines served lepers as well as elderly, ill, destitute, or homeless women; elderly priests; and single mothers. In a prohibition likely related to this last group, some statutes explicitly forbade the women from acting as midwives. Such a prohibition suggests that the beguines were, in fact, playing this role within their communities.

The beguine movement attracted women because it provided them with a way to express religious devotion through caring for others and through manual labor. This life path offered women flexibility, since women took no permanent vows when they joined a beguinage in order to live the active life as caretakers, nurses, teachers, and artisans. The community provided a place where working with one's hands was valued as a part of religious life in addition to nurturing the contemplative life.[56]

Beguines provided for the welfare of members of their own community as well as for those in the surrounding town or city. Able-bodied beguines typically did not live by alms, but rather through their own labor. These arrangements could be reciprocal; some beguines provided room and board and a basic education to young girls, who in exchange cared for elderly beguines. By the 1260s, however, the numbers of indigent beguines required changes in the institution. Some communities established a Table of the Holy Spirit, modelled after parochial patterns of distribution, at which beguines handed out essential foodstuffs, clothing, a small stipend, and sometimes assigned shelter to destitute beguines within a court beguinage. Other communities created a separate convent within the court beguinage for destitute beguines. Finally, new beguinages were sometimes founded especially for indigent women. A number of such communities were founded before or during the last quarter of the thirteenth century, including at Antwerp, Boekhoute, Bruges, Ghent, Louvain, and Ypres. These foundations provided a charitable service as well as a semi-structured religious life for poor beguines.[57]

The beguines had no single systematic approach to charity or welfare, with the exception of beguinages founded especially for indigent women. Within beguine communities we also see, even if not explicitly stated, medieval concerns about work ethic and poverty in practice, through the real-life application of 2 Thessalonians 3:10, which medieval people understood to mean that the able-bodied who did not labor should not receive food. Beguines who were able worked in some way—whether performing manual labor or working at a craft or trade.[58]

From the thirteenth through fifteen centuries, municipal governments became more involved in founding and supporting charitable institutions. Communes supported hospitals for the sick and elderly, foundations for abandoned children and orphans, communal loan funds, and dowry funds. People sometimes identify charity as assistance for the needy that has a religious motivation, whereas welfare is associated with a humanistic appeal to the common good. Such a binary understanding of assistance for the needy plays into a traditional narrative of the Middle Ages as an "age of faith" very different from our own, when juxtaposed with the early modern period as one governed more by secular concerns. Throughout the Middle Ages, assistance to the poor continued to be motivated by religious concerns even as concerns about the common good developed.[59] Almsgiving had a number of purposes for civic governments; in addition to meeting obligations to the suffering and needy in society and providing for the common good, it was also one way to demonstrate earthly authority and to tie that authority to the divine.[60] Ways of supporting the sick and poor, the hungry, abandoned, or orphaned have much in common, whether administered on behalf of a secular government or on behalf of a chapter of cathedral canons, whether by Benedictine monks or lay beguines, although we can still identify trends across the period from 800 to 1500.

Municipal governments sometimes played a role in establishing or supervising hospitals, a trend that accelerated at the beginning of the thirteenth century. Municipal hospitals in France date from 1207 at Montdidier and Angers, and from 1220 at Paris and Cambrai. During a second wave in the fourteenth and fifteenth centuries, it became common for towns to combine smaller hospitals into larger municipal hospitals. This trend developed early in Aragon, at Saragossa in 1425, with the creation of Nuestra Señora de la Gracia, and later consolidation of hospitals in Majorca sometime between 1456 and 1458. Typically, smaller specialized hospitals were combined into a single general hospital as at Barcelona, where two municipal hospitals and two capitular foundations joined to form a single municipal general hospital in 1401. Similarly, in Valencia, hospitals for abandoned children and the mentally ill that had existed in 1409 had been combined to form a general hospital by 1495.[61]

Municipalities recognized the importance of supporting orphans and foundlings. Italian communities boasted the earliest civic foundations for foundlings and orphans, with a foundation at Milan dating to the eighth century, an asylum that remained active until the 1070s. San Celso had a municipal orphanage as early as the late tenth century. Other communal foundling homes developed at Broglio, Florence, Siena, Pisa, and Mirandola (see Figure 7.4).

At Lleida in 1303, an institution provided dowries to orphaned girls to aid their prospects of marriage. In France, municipal shelters were reluctant to take in children. At Troyes and Angers, the municipal government refused to take children into its hospitals on the grounds that there were too many to take care of and that they were the responsibility of the parish in which they had lived or been discovered. In Paris, the Hôpital du Saint-Esprit-en-Grève, founded in 1363, took in orphans but not abandoned or illegitimate children. With a capacity of only fifty children, it provided for only a minuscule number

FIGURE 7.4 Hospital of Innocents, detail from portico decorated with tondos in glazed ceramic. Andrea della Robbia (1435–1525), Piazza della Santissima Annunziata, Florence. Photo: DeAgostini. Image courtesy Getty Images.

of the children needing shelter and care in the city. Other children were brought to the municipal shelter at the Hôtel-Dieu at Notre-Dame or to the parish where they had been found. Shelters for foundlings developed in the fourteenth and fifteenth centuries in Castile. Aragon adopted the French and Italian model of municipal shelters.[62]

Some cities did not institutionalize care for orphaned and abandoned children, but instead organized foster parents for them, as did the city of Montpellier in Languedoc. Finding a wet nurse for an abandoned or orphaned baby or toddler was typically the commune's first priority after ensuring that the child had been baptized. In fifteenth-century Montpellier, local women nursed the children for about a year. In Florence, rented slaves or rural women nursed children for one to two weeks before they were placed with rural foster families until 18–24 months of age.[63]

For older orphans and foundlings, concerns centered around ensuring that children were raised so that they might become useful citizens. Pere III, king of Aragon and count of Barcelona, articulated as much when he sent a directive to city officials in Valencia in which he assumed the responsibility of protecting poor children so they might receive a good upbringing and become useful to society. To that end, he ordered the councilmen to name guardians for the children to guide their upbringing and train them in a craft or prepare them for domestic labor. Communities arranged apprenticeships for orphans and foundlings in hopes that these children would become useful and productive in society. Typically, boys and girls would be sent out to learn a trade or contracted out to perform domestic labor at an age younger than what would have been usual for children of artisans. This practice was also common within Tuscany, though by the 1530s young girls at the Ospedale degli Innocenti no longer were sent out for domestic service because of the very real concern that girls of any age were at risk of being sexually abused.[64] To encourage and promote marriage, communes provided girls with positive assistance, including dowry funds, to make them more likely to find a spouse. Marriage formed the heart of stability in medieval society; an unmarried layperson lost status in society and the probability was greater that he or she would continue to be a burden on society, in the future. Such relief provided by municipal governments was primarily designed to encourage productivity and decrease idleness, and thus also is an example of efforts to channel funds to those considered deserving of such aid.[65]

CONCLUSION

The breadth of medieval European charity and social welfare from 800 to 1450 was considerable. Institutional forms of assistance were more complex by the mid-fifteenth century than they were at the beginning of the ninth century, a trend that we see especially vividly in urban centers. A focus on lay institutions and lay charity in the late Middle Ages does not reflect a wholly secular motivation, however. Those performing charitable works or making donations often did so as part of a lay penitential movement or confraternity. Still, secular governments did increasingly found and sponsor institutions dedicated to the public good—institutions such as hospitals, orphanages, and homes for foundlings, as well as low-cost loan and dowry funds. In the early Middle Ages, charity was seen primarily as a spiritual good for the giver and only secondarily as a material good for the recipient. Charitable gifts were not completely devoid of concerns about the common good in the earlier part of the period from 800 to 1450; once alms and welfare became more firmly rooted in the common good, there seemed to be more interest the worthiness of potential aid recipients, and in discriminating against those deemed unworthy. An examination of work in society, from the central Middle Ages to the late Middle Ages, reveals something of what people valued in society: work and productivity, hierarchical order within society, and generosity and concern for those in need. A survey of society's response to those experiencing need provides an important addition to the cultural history of work in the Middle Ages.

CHAPTER EIGHT

The Political Culture of Work

ROBERT BRAID

The political culture of work during the Middle Ages has been treated very differently by historians according to the country. Virtually all historical studies of medieval England devote a certain amount of attention to the labor laws that appeared after the Black Death. These laws have even been the subject of various articles and monographs, and some scholars attribute the appearance of such laws as marking a major transformation in English society.[1] Despite the importance of such laws in English history, few scholars have attempted to understand the precise origins of the regulations; historians tend to assume that the economic context alone was responsible for determining the content and form of such laws. Historians of other regions in Europe, however, have paid significantly less attention to such labor ordinances, quite often ignoring them altogether. This indifference to the subject is particularly surprising when one observes that some of the earliest examples of labor ordinances appeared in continental Europe long before the English crown intervened in the labor market. Moreover, a quick comparison of these laws reveals the many different ways in which governments reacted to similar situations, leading one to the conclusion that such laws were more than just a necessary response to a given economic context.[2]

The study of these ordinances, both English and European, over a long period, is interesting for various reasons. First, it allows us to understand better the particularities of different countries relative to how they perceived the role of the government in regulating labor. Second, it demonstrates a certain evolution in the role of government throughout the Middle Ages, from virtual indifference to work-related issues at the outset to tight regulation of the labor market by the end of the period. Finally, it highlights the multiple factors that interacted to form labor laws, which are in fact a manifestation of a society's intricate relationship with work, rather than a simple remedy to market imbalance. Although it would be unreasonable to attempt a comprehensive analysis of all labor regulations around Europe for such a long period, especially because of the lack of historiography on the subject outside of England and even in England for the pre-plague period, it is necessary to place the English post-plague labor ordinances into a broader geographical and chronological context.

Despite the broad nature of this study, its main concern is to highlight the way in which the ruling classes in Europe went from virtual indifference about labor to very intrusive measures to regulate it, thereby creating a new political culture of work. This chapter will, therefore, focus on the various ways in which different authorities around western Europe attempted to impose controls on how people performed their work, the justifications the ruling classes used to do so, as well as their methods and their major preoccupations. It is also important to remember that not all governments were secular during this period; the church also instituted a certain number of norms relative to labor and markets in general that were sometimes influential when other authorities set up labor regulations.

This study brings to light three steps in the evolution of the political culture of work. First, from roughly 800 to 1200, although various royal ordinances shared many points in common with the post-plague laws, authorities did not attempt to control labor directly, keeping perfectly in line with church doctrine which favored a strong work ethic, but did not condone meddling with markets. Second, starting in about 1200, one observes the emergence of source material which suggests greater intervention of local authorities in England as well as central authorities in Castile and France in controlling the labor market. These regulations tended to contradict church doctrine which continued to favor free markets. Finally, once the Black Death arrived in Europe in about 1348, causing huge mortality, both central and local authorities around Europe attempted to institute wage controls and force people to accept employment. Once these wage caps were in place, however, certain authorities continued to enforce and improve them by issuing other ordinances regulating work hours, the types of payment that were authorized, length of contracts, and so on. Moreover, by the end of the fourteenth century, theological texts began to create justifications for government intervention in labor and other markets. Overall, across Europe, by the end of the Middle Ages, a general political culture emerged that accepted that one of the primary functions of government was to establish rules to regulate work.

800–1200

During this period it is often difficult to distinguish legal and moral obligations, as the crown often enforced religious precepts, and this applies especially to the issue of work. Numerous theological texts from the Middle Ages required men and women to work. According to the Bible, the obligation to labor for a living was one of the first orders given by God to humans.[3] In the fourth century, Saint Ambrose criticized merchants, who often amassed great fortunes without actually working, and praised the honest labor of farmers.[4] Although sloth was not yet one of the official seven deadly sins, in the ninth century, Hrabanus Maurus, abbot of Fulda and archbishop of Mainz (d. 856), believed that idleness was at least a serious vice.[5] In the eleventh century, certain penitentials (books intended to help local priests hear confessions and impose appropriate penance) recommended physical labor as a means of purging one's soul of sin.[6] In the early thirteenth century, Saint Francis of Assisi (d. 1226) proudly performed manual labor and recommended the same to all his brothers.[7] Across all of Christendom and from the earliest days, all subjects were supposed to work for a living as well as for the salvation of their soul, although this obligation was not formally codified in any secular ordinance. At the same time, both church and king formally banned work on Sundays and other religious holidays.[8] In the ninth century, King Alfred of England (d. 901) specifically indicated over forty official annual holidays on which it was forbidden to work, in addition to every Sunday.[9] In the eleventh century, Ferdinand I of Castile (d. 1065) also prohibited working on religious holidays, unless it was an act of charity, also applying this Christian obligation to the Jews living in his realm.[10] In the same legislation, Ferdinand also barred workers from leaving work early on Saturdays and ordered them to take their meals at reasonable hours.[11] Gratian (d. c. 1160), the twelfth-century canonist, drew up a precise list of the thirty-six religious holidays that ought to be respected.[12] So, although church and secular leaders clearly promoted a work ethic, people were not to pursue only earthly endeavors and had to reserve at least a part of their time to focus on more spiritual matters. A lengthier discussion of this issue can be found in Chapter Nine.

The Bible also indicated to a certain degree how masters were to treat their workers. The Old Testament forbade masters from exploiting laborers, in particular by withholding their day's wages until the next morning.[13] Workers were clearly associated with the humble of the world who deserved the Lord's protection.[14] Even God gave a wage to the just for their labors.[15] The New Testament contains even more references to labor and wages. Both Matthew and Luke indicate that the worker deserves his wage.[16] In his first letter to the Corinthians, Paul indicates that each will receive his own reward according to his labor.[17] A different passage from Matthew, however, suggests that the masters could of course give more to whomever they wished and that others should not be jealous and demand more.[18] Although the authors of the New Testament used references to labor and wages as metaphors for good deeds and their just reward in Heaven, and not as mandates to be respected on the labour market, they clearly associated virtuous deeds with physical labor and heavenly reward with a just wage. For much of the Middle Ages, peasants working on their own land or on their lord's land as part of their feudal obligations were responsible for the vast majority of production, so early medieval commentators on these passages limited themselves to the metaphorical explanation. Commentary about how to constitute a just wage did not appear until population growth led to an emerging labor market in the thirteenth century.

There were some early texts about government intervention in economics in general, mostly in favor of free markets. The earliest legal and theological texts in Europe dealing with the question of economic regulation generally stipulated that markets should remain free of government control, as long as the parties involved in an exchange respected certain principles.[19] A transaction was theoretically considered valid so long as there was an absence of fraud and constraint, meaning that sellers could not fool or force their clients into buying their products. Relative to wages, Roman Law treated hired labor like a rental contract.[20] English Common Law treaties did not include employment among the various types of rental contracts, but did not treat the question of workers and wages elsewhere either. Like Roman Law, however, Ranulf de Glanvill (d. 1190), chief justiciar of England under Henry II, clearly indicates in his treatise on English Law that the crown had no jurisdiction over private contracts, therefore suggesting that the government had no business regulating any economic transactions, including the labor market.[21]

But legal theory did not always prevent authorities from intervening. In 794, the future emperor Charlemagne (d. 814) imposed a universal monetary system throughout his kingdom, and added fixed prices for various grains regardless of their abundance or scarcity (see Figure 8.1).[22] After the city of León was sacked by Moors in the early eleventh century, Alfonso V (d. 1028) established laws to rebuild what was then the capital of his kingdom, including measures limiting prices and wages.[23] The exact tariffs were not outlined in this text, but authority was granted by the crown to the local authorities to establish justice in economic transactions, suggesting that this was not generally a power wielded by the town government of León at this time and only granted because of the desperate situation of the devastated community. In general, before the thirteenth

FIGURE 8.1 Carolingian coins, first half of the ninth century, from the Roermond hoard, discovered in 1968 in gravel from the Meuse River. Archeological collection of Centre Céramique, Maastricht, the Netherlands. Wikimedia Commons.

century, in Europe, there are practically no traces of any government intervention in price or wage fixing, or in any aspect of labor other than respecting the Sabbath. This situation changed remarkably in the thirteenth century, at both a central and a local level.

1200–1348

Transformations in Europe's economy and society led to shifts in political structures. Starting in the eleventh century, a decrease in armed conflict in Europe allowed the population to grow and production and trade to flourish, which in turn gave greater resources to monarchies and local governments. Moreover, increased specialization led to more trade and mobility, as well as greater recourse to wage labor, which often required heightened oversight. The thirteenth century, therefore, witnessed an astonishing rise of government activity and sophistication of political structures, and at the same time a rapid evolution of economic structures that relied increasingly on hired labor, both in urban trades and in agricultural production. Crown, Parliament, municipal governments, and village courts began to take a more active role in determining the organization of various aspects of society, and the archives bear witness to this evolution by overflowing with rolls and registers recording their decisions. Many of these decisions concerned the way people worked.

In the kingdom of Castile and León, central control of labor markets began in the mid-thirteenth century. In 1252, the Crown and the Cortes established several dozen articles attempting to limit inflation, including caps on wages and prices, indicating the exact amounts to be applied according to the region, but also limits on exports and consumption, as well as a ban on worker associations.[24] Many different professions were concerned, from agricultural servants and construction workers to wet nurses. These measures were reiterated and refined in 1256 and 1268, suggesting that the authorities were serious about enforcing them and were developing more sophisticated methods for dealing with the complexity of economic regulation.[25] Indeed, after capping wages, legislators realized that, to avoid fraud, it was necessary to control the various forms of remuneration, and consequently they forbade feeding certain workers. And just as in virtually all labor laws after the Black Death, it was forbidden to remain idle; all members of the working class were to accept employment at official wages or face prison. Castilian legal scholars also codified the relationship between workers and their masters at this time. Clearly associated with family members, servants were not allowed to testify against their masters in criminal cases, and masters were entitled to physically discipline their workers so long as it was without cruelty or injury. Yet workers could still take their master to court for disagreements relative to their wages.[26] Clearly, a new political culture began to emerge in Castile in the mid-thirteenth century in which the government was allowed to intervene in labor issues.

The French monarchy became quite invasive in markets starting in the early fourteenth century. The greatest intervention in markets, particularly in labor markets, came as a result of currency fluctuations. After devaluing the currency in 1305, Philip IV the Fair (d. 1314) passed a series of invasive measures to control inflation.[27] He issued another ordinance regulating both prices and wages in Poitiers while he and the pope sojourned in town.[28] In 1330, Philip VI (d. 1350) did the same after strengthening the currency.[29] Once day wages were limited by law, however, workers began to modify the hours they worked or worked less efficiently, leading the Crown to impose official work hours.[30] Right before the plague, another ordinance clearly demonstrates the authority of the Crown over private contracts, including labor contracts, particularly when currency fluctuations upset markets. Because many workers apparently accepted projects for fees and expected to cash them in at a stronger currency, all contracts established but not completed prior to the shift in currency had to adapt to the new value.[31] This ordinance highlights not only the authority of the Crown over private contracts, but also the complexity of controlling markets when people changed their normal practices to adapt to a new situation (see Figure 8.2).

The English Crown and Parliament were significantly less invasive in labor markets than those of Castile and France during this period. The only workers whose remuneration they regulated were bakers and brewers, through the Assize of Bread and Ale. Established at a central level, it was enforced by local authorities around the realm who probably had already passed similar measures but who were keen on having royal approbation to fine bakers and brewers.[32] Many scholars have misinterpreted this legislation as a form of price fixing. On the contrary, the Assize in fact established a very broad scale that allowed the price of bread and ale to fluctuate in accordance to the market price of grain, and therefore only limited the remuneration of bakers and brewers. Other central ordinances from this period resemble post-plague labor legislation, for example forced military inscriptions and quickly abandoned caps on livestock prices.[33] Weights and measures were centralized very early in England relative to the continent, and representatives of the Crown were present in every shire, which would have made centralized economic regulations more effective. Overall, however, the Crown and Parliament in England were relatively indifferent to labor and markets in general, leaving such matters to local authorities.

FIGURE 8.2 Construction of the Tower of Babel, c. 1400–10. Regensburg. Los Angeles, The J. Paul Getty Museum, MS 33, folio 13. © The J. Paul Getty Museum, Los Angeles.

Although village courts did not generally outline precise regulations controlling the labor market, they did handle disputes between employers and their workers, and even between lords and their serfs. In the late thirteenth and early fourteenth centuries, village courts in England fined numerous people for not performing their feudal services, for failing to work diligently, for refusing to labor for wages during the harvest, for leaving the village to work elsewhere, or for just being lazy.[34] Villagers who were physically capable of working were forbidden from gleaning the fallen grain in the fields, a right reserved for the poorest members of the community ever since biblical times.[35] Village courts also defended workers against their employers who unjustly withheld their wages.[36] Although certain historians have asserted that village courts had established maximum wage rates and therefore created a precedent for the royal courts after the plague,[37] there is no trace of such ordinances in the archives. Nevertheless, village courts, at least in England, were clearly active in forcing people to work and settling wage disputes.

The municipal government of London also began regulating markets at this time. After a fire ravaged the city in 1212, a number of measures were instituted to rebuild and protect the town. In addition to regulations about the types of construction materials that could be used, several articles limited the wages of various types of construction workers.[38] Another ordinance later that century also limited the wages of construction workers, indicating different rates according to the season as well as various dispositions for its enforcement.[39] Another ordinance granted the authority to the city council to cap the wages not only of building workers but of any laborers, though the rates were not stipulated and this is the only mention of such authority over non-construction trades.[40] The mayor of London also heard pleas relative to the fees charged by weavers, grain porters, and wine brokers, though this type of case was rare.[41] Most labor issues in London were handled by the guilds, which set relatively strict rules for the employment of apprentices and their ascension to the status of master, established work days and hours, but generally refrained from fixing wages.[42] In contrast, the city of London passed numerous measures to avoid price and wage fixing.[43] The mayor was in charge of maintaining social order and as a result reprimanded citizens for immoral activity, though not with any intention of enforcing religious precepts, much less canon law.[44] In general, throughout the thirteenth and early fourteenth centuries, the city government of London intensified its control of labor issues, settling disputes and limiting abuses in times of crises.

Towns in other regions of Europe also began to intervene in labor markets during this period. Numerous small towns in Provence, for example, integrated various regulations concerning labor in their statutes. In Tarascon and Arles, all servants hired on annual contracts were only to be recruited on the same day of the year, and municipal courts had jurisdiction to enforce labor contracts.[45] Agricultural workers had to finish all jobs that they accepted and in the time agreed.[46] The city of Marseille forced sailors to respect their contracts and forbade all masters from mistreating their servants.[47] Marseille also banned worker associations which intended on striking or collectively bargaining wages and forbade shipbuilders from leaving town.[48] Various communities forced masters to pay day wages promptly.[49] Towns also forbade work on Sundays for all citizens including Jews.[50] A post-plague ordinance indicates an earlier regulation in Aix-en-Provence concerning working hours.[51] Yet very few texts suggest any establishment of official wages in this region. In Avignon, no workers were to accept any remuneration other than their cash wages.[52] The value of the meals of certain workers was limited by law in Marseille,[53] and various regulations controlled the wages of people working for the court, but there was no clear attempt to cap wages of workers in general.[54] Considering the relatively numerous measures concerning other aspects of the labor market by local communities in Provence, the absence of wage controls may be due to a lack of need to cap them rather than a lack of jurisdiction to do so. The economic context would change drastically after the Black Death, inciting authorities to take new measures.

In other regions as well, both central and local authorities attempted to control labor. In Norway, for example, King Magnus VI prohibited the mobility of landless peasants in the countryside in order to keep them available for wage labor during the harvests in 1274, and also forced all able-bodied men and women to accept employment for wages in 1291.[55] In the Low Countries, city authorities capped fullers' wages in the thirteenth century.⁵⁶ This general overview demonstrates that, across Europe during the thirteenth century, in a context of increased economic activity, both central and local authorities began to accept responsibility for labor issues by settling disputes between workers and their employers and even issuing various regulations to control workers, both in urban trades and in agricultural labor.

Many of these laws, however, were in clear contradiction to church doctrine, which for the most part had not changed since the previous period. The twelfth and thirteenth centuries witnessed a surge in intellectual production, notably on theological and legal matters. Thanks to the reintroduction of ancient texts, such as Justinian's Code and the philosophical works of Aristotle, medieval authors developed more sophisticated arguments relative to the valorization of work and the issue of economic regulation but did not change their overall position until the end of the fourteenth century. Many theologians treated at some length the issue of the Just Price, generally advocating the free interaction of supply and demand without any outside intervention.⁵⁷ Although they paid significantly less attention to the question of the just wage, that is because it was considered a mere extension of the theory of the just price. At the same time, theologians continued to promote work as a virtue, even a moral obligation, although the work performed did not always have to be manual labour.⁵⁸ Church doctrine clearly favored a strong work ethic and denounced the sin of avarice, but church authorities did not openly advocate forced labor or authorize secular authorities to establish wage caps in order to curb workers' demands; the lazy and the greedy would answer for their sins on the day of the Last Judgment. The French and Castilian central legislation as well as the various ordinances in place in London and elsewhere, which openly capped prices and wages and regulated other aspects of the labor market, were therefore clearly at odds with contemporary church doctrine, although church authorities did not openly seek to invalidate such legislation. Perhaps paradoxically, church authorities were often members of many of the same institutions that adopted economic regulation, yet their theological training did not seem to interfere with their secular responsibilities.

1348–1450

According to some historians, the Black Death represented a major transition in the legal structure of England by instigating a new political culture that accepted central legislation regulating work.⁵⁹ This epidemic was introduced into Europe by Italian merchants coming home from the East in early 1348, and swept across the entire continent taking with it roughly 40 percent of the population.⁶⁰ As the number of consumers in any given region was cut nearly in half within the space of a couple of months, demand for basic goods declined dramatically. Survivors received the property and cash of the victims, causing a sharp increase in the per capita money supply and therefore rapid inflation. While the plague ravaged Europe, individuals were more concerned with protecting themselves from contamination, or at least in saving their souls in the face of imminent death, and were not particularly eager to spend what looked like their last days on earth working for extra cash. Moreover, people tended to seek to enjoy the finer pleasures that this world had to offer, eating better food and wearing nicer clothing than what they had been accustomed to.⁶¹ The balance of supply and demand in all markets was therefore radically upset, and roughly in the same proportions across Europe, yet the reactions of governments differed significantly.

Edward III of England was one of the quickest to react to the situation. He called Parliament twice during the winter and spring of 1349 to deal with the crisis situation, but in vain as many nobles and clerics had already died of the plague, or were afraid of the risk of contagion that mingling with other people from across the country represented. He therefore acted on his own authority, though not unassisted, issuing the Ordinance of Laborers in June 1349, which was finally ratified and amended by Parliament in 1351.[62] The major thrust of this legislation was to force laborers to accept employment at pre-plague wages, oblige artisans and retailers of basic staples to charge pre-plague rates for their goods, and to ban almsgiving to able-bodied beggars who could work for a living. The authority to enforce this law was granted to local authorities, who would be punished by royal judges if they neglected this new responsibility. Even before it was debated in Parliament in February 1351, there were numerous amendments and correspondence concerning its enforcement.[63] Such legislation cannot be considered as a mere stopgap to control the immediate crisis, because the English Parliament and Crown continued to impose new measures to control the workforce on a regular basis for the rest of the period: regulating worker mobility, imposing harsher penalties, forcing the landless to remain in agricultural service, and preventing them from becoming urban apprentices. Such measures even served as a basis for much central legislation in early modern England. One may be tempted to conclude that this marks a clear transition of work issues to the central government. Indeed, village authorities continued to impose exactly the same economic policies as before the plague, and seem to have allowed the newly appointed Justices of Laborers and Justices of the Peace to hear cases against the labor laws. The city of London, on the other hand, issued a great number of ordinances setting wages and prices, limiting worker mobility and banning illegitimate begging, and enforced these measures rather enthusiastically. The transition of jurisdiction over labor issues from local to central authorities, therefore, was not as clear in England as some studies would suggest.

In other regions, political control over work issues reverted right back to local authorities after the immediate crisis had subsided. Raymond d'Agoult (d. c. 1353), seneschal of Provence, was also quick to react to the situation, drafting legislation as early as September 1348.[64] This extremely detailed ordinance was mostly concerned with setting prices and wages but did not seek to force individuals to accept employment or to condemn idleness, despite the very harsh moral criticism of workers who charged excessive rates. Prices were set for a wide variety of goods, from meat and fish to nails and chamber pots. There were limits on the numbers of workers one could hire and wages were set according to the season. Workers were forbidden from engaging in collective bargaining to increase their wages, or risked having a hand amputated. There is no evidence that the precise measures of this initial ordinance were ever enforced, and no new laws were enacted at a central level; however, numerous local ordinances attest to heightened concern about work issues. The city of Marseille officially suspended the central ordinance on labor, yet on its own authority forced laborers to accept employment, set wage rates, forbade agricultural workers from leaving the town, and regulated work days.[65] The town of Brignoles modified all the rates established in the initial ordinance.[66] The town council of Sisteron dispatched laborers around the territory to work at statutory rates, forbade the payment of wages in kind, and regulated work hours.[67] Most communities, however, were primarily concerned with attracting skilled laborers and artisans by offering them particular advantages. Doctors, bakers, tile workers, weavers, locksmiths, tailors, and carpenters were offered cash, interest-free loans, tax exemptions, free housing, and equipment by numerous municipal councils if they agreed to set up shop in town for a certain number of years. Because of the absence and relative weakness of the counts and countess, who generally resided in Naples, control of economic activity was best handled by the municipal authorities. In fact, the existence of any central legislation on the subject in this region is most likely owing to the fortuitous presence of Countess Jeanne (d. 1382) in Provence who was fleeing Hungarians who had invaded Naples at the same time that the Black Death was beginning to take its toll. In England, where a strong royal administration was already in place, coercive central labor laws were possible, but in Provence, individual communities who were in competition with each other had to develop a different type of labor policy based on attraction rather than coercion. The type of political culture of work that developed after the Black Death in each region, therefore, depended on structures already in place before the epidemic.

Despite the precedence of royal regulation of labor in Castile and France, the monarchies in these countries were surprisingly sluggish in their response to the crisis. It was not until January 1351 that King John II of France (d. 1364) issued an ordinance concerning Paris, which was under his direct authority, and not until February 1352 that he ordered his representatives to enact similar legislation around the realm.[68] Central authorities issued further labor ordinances in 1354, 1355, and then again in 1360.[69] Like the English ordinances, these French laws focused on condemning idleness, regulating worker mobility, forcing people to work for set wages, and obliging retailers to sell their goods at reasonable prices (see Figure 8.3). And like the legislation in France before the plague, they also imposed traditional work hours and forms of remuneration that were no longer respected as workers tried to get around the new laws. The imposition of branding for those who dared to act contrary to the law, although there is no proof that this punishment was actually carried out, suggests that the Crown had strong feelings about the behavior of workers. Afterwards, however, it would seem that the only royal acts dealing with labor merely approved local initiatives.[70]

The Crown and Cortes of Castile were even slower to respond to the situation, taking roughly three years before addressing the problems caused by the Black Death. After the death of his father, who had died of plague himself, Peter I (d. 1369) issued extensive legislation controlling prices and wages in the kingdom of Castile.[71] Like the laws in Provence and France, these measures were extremely precise relative to the prices and wages to be established, stipulating work hours, imposing heavy fines and even public whipping for transgressors. Despite the violent overthrow of Peter I in 1369, his successor to the throne, Henry II of Trastámara (d. 1379), immediately drafted new laws along the same lines as the previous labor legislation.[72] Elsewhere on the Iberian Peninsula, rulers were quicker in their responses to the crisis. Peter III of Catalonia (d. 1387) adopted laws regulating the labor market for his territory in Catalonia as early as July 1349, although they were rather vague.[73] For his territories in Aragon, it took him another ten months to institute similar regulations.[74] These measures were quite similar in essence to laws elsewhere, regulating prices, wages, and work hours and imposing whipping for those who refused to serve. But these new measures were abrogated by 1352 because it was found that they limited the wages of workers who could no longer make a living because of the high prices.[75] In Portugal, on the other hand, the central measures controlling workers instituted after the Black Death remained in effect long afterwards.[76]

Italian city-states also drafted rules to limit the effects of plague on the labor market. Orvieto capped wages as early as September 1348, only a few months after the arrival of plague in the city.[77] In August 1349, Florence instituted very harsh measures on agricultural

FIGURE 8.3 Buying and selling of wares in a silverware shop. French, fifteenth century. Rouen, Bibliothèque municipale, MS 927, folio 145. Image courtesy of Getty Images.

labor, while almost completely ignoring urban trades which were already controlled by the guilds.[78] In general, however, despite some initial attempts to curb wage inflation, and in a similar vein to what one observes in Provence, most Italian communities sought to attract skilled workers, rather than punish greedy laborers. Such policies began as early as October 1348 in Siena and Pisa and can be observed almost as quickly in Orvieto and Venice, although not until 1364 in Florence.[79] It seems obvious that when laborers could walk out of one jurisdiction and into another within a day or two, it was in the local authorities' interest to incentivize them to remain in town. Centralized control of labor issues could only appear in places where the Crown had the legal jurisdiction and the proper administration to enforce such laws.

Most importantly, however, it is interesting to observe that across Europe, despite regional differences, there was a generalized reaction to the epidemic that spurred central and local authorities to adopt various measures to control the situation within a few years. In general, they capped wages and prices, limited worker mobility, forced the idle to work for wages, and regulated work hours and forms of remuneration. Similar laws were also enacted after the Black Death by local and central authorities across German-speaking regions, the Low Countries, Bavaria, Tyrol, and Norway.[80] To what extent such regulations were pursued, if at all, depended on the complex economic and political mutations that followed the demographic disaster, yet virtually all authorities attempted to deal with the situation by instituting new laws. Although only a few governments had already started to intervene in labor markets prior to the plague, it was clearly in the political culture of the secular authorities to wield such jurisdiction when needed. The political culture among intellectuals, on the other hand, had not yet accepted that the role of government was to regulate markets, but their views on this matter soon changed.

Perhaps the greatest impact the Black Death had relative to the political culture of work concerned the way intellectuals perceived this role. Indeed, although all theological treaties prior to the epidemic clearly frowned upon government intervention in markets, by the second half of the fourteenth century, some scholastic authors were actively in favor of government control of prices and wages. Prior to the Black Death, theologians generally treated wage earners as poor individuals who deserved particular protection from cruel masters. This view changed dramatically shortly after the plague. Echoing the numerous criticisms of workers' avarice in the preambles of labor legislation, moralists such as John Gower (d. 1408) and William Langland (d. c. 1386) harshly criticized the excessive demands of workers in the 1370s.[81] Some theologians used an argument, developed in the thirteenth century, that a contract was not legitimate if one of the parties was in distress in order to denounce the excessive demands of laborers who, it would seem, jeopardized the well-being of their employers by negotiating high wages.[82] It is not surprising, therefore, that many intellectuals also saw the relevance of secular control of wages and prices. Starting in the second half of the fourteenth century, many theologians such as Henry of Hesse Langenstein (d. 1397), Jean Gerson (d. 1429), Bartholomew Caepolla (d. 1475), and Gabriel Biel (d. 1495) began to support the role of governments in setting the Just Price to prevent producers from demanding too much for their goods.[83] Bernardino of Siena (d. 1448) recommended that local authorities set prices and wages for the common good. This new attitude among intellectuals is in clear contrast to theologians' stance on government intervention in economic matters prior to the plague. It is possible that this new view among intellectuals resulted less from the plague and the subsequent labor legislation than from the fact that universities came under the direct control of secular authorities during the fourteenth century. Whatever the cause, intellectuals now firmly accepted that governments should play an active role in regulating markets and in particular work.

This is not to say, however, that tight government control of work hours, wages, and worker mobility was gleefully accepted by all. Indeed, the workers themselves were particularly hostile to such measures and it would seem that, at least in England, the new central measures forcing people to work for wages was one of the main causes of popular protest. The Justices of Labourers who were in charge of the enforcement of the legislation were a particular target for hatred and aggression.[84] During the Peasants' Revolt of 1381, rebels called for an end not only to serfdom but also to forced employment. When the rebellion was crushed, King Richard II (d. 1400) reportedly addressed the rebels: "You wretches! ... You who seek equality with Lords are unworthy to live. ... You will remain in bondage, not as before, but incomparably harsher. For as long as we live, we will strive to suppress you."[85] Wage earners, therefore, had very little say in how they were to be treated. During the Middle Ages, and for a long time afterwards, all government bodies, from town councils to Parliament, were comprised of the employers of labor, not those who actually performed the work. In this respect, the vast majority of the population was excluded from political culture insofar as they had virtually no means to influence it.

CONCLUSION

This brief examination of the political culture of work is very revealing of a transformation of political culture of the Middle Ages in general. Throughout this period western political culture did not promote the view that it was the government's role to maintain market equilibrium but rather to enforce proper moral behavior, whether by forcing people to respect the Sabbath, adopt a healthy work ethic, or curb their avarice. Often, the economic behavior of large numbers of people was upset when there were dramatic shifts caused by external factors, such as plague, a devastating fire, or modifications of the currency. But it would also seem that the general rise of economic regulation, and in particular that of labor, accompanied an increase in overall economic activity and the friction that such growth usually creates. The emergence of a political culture relative to work that favored tighter control over labor emerged gradually starting in about the thirteenth century. At this time both central and local governments became increasingly sophisticated and extended their authority over various sectors that had previously been left unregulated, and the labor market was not exempt from such oversight. Capping wages, controlling the forms of remuneration, regulating work hours and holidays, settling disputes between workers and employers, enforcing labor contracts—practically no aspect of labor escaped the scrutiny of government. The Black Death did not, therefore, entirely transform the political culture relative to work, but rather acted as a catalyst for regulation by certain authorities who had not previously intervened directly in labor markets, including the English Crown. The measures adopted after the plague were not radically different from those set up beforehand. Nor did the Black Death immediately transform political structures in all regions to favor greater central oversight of markets. Considering the gravity of the situation, it is not surprising that most governments attempted to reestablish some form of order in markets through various measures to control labor. In England, as it has already been observed by other scholars, control of the labor market generally shifted from local to central authorities immediately after the Black Death, marking another step in the formation of Common Law. But in many instances, such attempts were quickly abandoned and the authority to control wages and other labor practices shifted right back to local authorities in other regions, most notably in Provence. The fact that the labor regulation in the aftermath of the Black Death did not mark a significant break from the past in Castile and France may explain why historians in these regions have not paid very much attention to such legislation. Moreover, such intervention initially had no theoretical justification, since both theologians and legal scholars claimed that markets were supposed to remain free. By the end of the fourteenth century, however, numerous religious authorities finally resigned themselves to the fact that governments had a role in controlling economic activity and developed arguments that supported their efforts. In this sense, the Black Death may have been more influential in convincing intellectuals of the necessity of government intervention than in encouraging the secular authorities to take on this role. In any case, despite the discrepancy between theory and practice that developed in the thirteenth century, and the popular protests that attest to the fact that many workers did not appreciate the way this authority was wielded, by the beginning of the fifteenth century, the political culture in Europe largely supported the notion that governments had a primary role in regulating how individuals performed their work.

CHAPTER NINE

Work and Leisure

JEREMY GOLDBERG AND EMMA MARTIN

There are a number of problems confronting the scholar exploring the concept of work and leisure in the medieval era. Aside from the usual issue of paucity of source materials, especially for the earlier part of our period, the most immediate concern is that of how far the essentially modern concept of leisure may usefully be applied over the several centuries that this chapter considers. Lexicographical analysis, for example, suggests that medieval societies recognized the need to rest from work, but, before the Black Death at least, did not necessarily understand leisure as an activity to be aspired to or consumed. Work is perhaps less problematic insofar as there is more congruence between medieval and modern understandings of work, but we do not necessarily share the underlying premise found from the Christian era that to labor was the lot of mankind as a consequence of the Fall any more than we see rest as divinely mandated since God rested on the seventh day. The boundaries between work and leisure are also difficult to plot. For the aristocracy, for example, activities such as hunting or even playing board games might be considered essential to the training of young men and so part of their "work" whereas we would readily label these as leisure pursuits and presume them to be undertaken solely for pleasure. Inevitably in a survey that ranges so widely both geographically and across time the need to offer generalities will mask real differences in practice, but attention will be given to differences between the pre- and post-plague eras, between different cultural regions, and in terms of when leisure was and was not licit according to its timing and by whom it was undertaken. This chapter will also explore differences of experience between people of differing social status and between women and of men.

LABOR AND REST

The understanding that man's lot was to labor was rooted in Scripture. Punishment was meted out to Adam and Eve following their expulsion from the Garden of Eden for disobeying God's commandment to abstain from eating the fruit of the Tree of Knowledge. In the words of the Rheims-Douay translation of the Latin Vulgate, God spoke first to Eve: "To the woman also he said: I will multiply thy sorrows, and thy conceptions: in sorrow shalt thou bring forth children, and thou shalt be under thy husband's power, and he shall have dominion over thee." The labor of woman was thus the labor of childbirth. Her lot was to raise children. To Adam, however, he said:

> Because thou hast hearkened to the voice of thy wife, and hast eaten of the tree ... cursed is the earth in thy work; with labor and toil shalt thou eat thereof all the days of thy life. ... In the sweat of thy face shalt thou eat bread till thou return to the earth, out of which thou wast taken: for dust thou art, and into dust thou shalt return.[1]

"Labor and toil," then, was the lot of mankind if not of womankind. In fact a non-Scriptural tradition with deep historical roots grew up that understood that after their expulsion Adam and Eve were given tools to enable them to work as God commanded. To Adam was given a spade or a mattock whereby he might till the soil, an iconography established from an early date, but to Eve was given a distaff, an iconography apparent by the twelfth century. Adam wields his mattock in the Grandval Bible of around 840 while Eve sits suckling their child. However, in the early-twelfth-century St. Albans Psalter, and likewise the thirteenth-century mosaics of St. Mark's in Venice, Adam and Eve clutch mattock and distaff respectively. The image of Adam digging the earth while his wife sits spinning, seen in the early-fourteenth-century Holkham Bible Picture Book, or with a swaddled infant at Eve's feet as in the late-twelfth-century Hunterian Psalter (see Figure 9.1), became the standard iconography of postlapsarian Adam and Eve.

As the slogan of the English Peasants' Revolt of 1381 normalized it, "When Adam delved and Eve span / Who was then the gentleman?" Social hierarchy may be challenged here, but gender difference and the compulsion to work were divinely ordained truths.

In fact, the radical cry of the English rebels of 1381 aside, social hierarchy was invariably understood as divinely ordained, but in a way that associated laboring especially with the lowest, albeit majority, social order, those who worked the land and produced crops by the sweat of their brow. An understanding that society was divided into three orders—those who pray, those who fight, and those who labor—had deep historical roots. One of the best-known and clearest articulations was by Bishop Adalbero of Laon in his *Carmen ad Rotbertum regem*, written in the earlier years of the eleventh century, but in fact its roots go back much further. Writing in the late tenth century, Ælfric of Eynsham described how the royal throne was supported by the three props of *oratores, bellatores,* and *laboratores*.[2] Such a model became increasingly removed from social reality with the growth of towns, trade, and craft manufacture. This saw the emergence during the course of the High Middle Ages of self-employed artisans and even prosperous merchants and bankers who scarcely fitted the mold of the *laborator*—the worker—a figure rooted in a predominantly rural, agrarian, and "feudal" society. The model, nevertheless, continued to be expounded and to shape ideas around the meanings of work and nonwork.

The divinely sanctioned reason for work to be punctuated by nonwork was that contained in the Genesis account of the Creation. The work of creation extended over the first six days of the Creation: "And on the seventh day God ended his work which he had made: and he rested on the seventh day from all his work which he had done. And he blessed the seventh day, and sanctified it: because in it he had rested; from all his work which God created and made."[3] It followed that abstaining from work on the Lord's Day was incumbent on all Christians—as observance of the Sabbath was incumbent on all Jews. This was not just a matter of clerical teaching but something that, having been decreed by Constantine, was written into law codes by early Christian rulers in ways designed to protect the laboring population from being made to work on Sundays. Thus the laws of Wihtred of Kent (695) included the clause: "If a servant, by his lord's command, do servile work from sunset on Saturday evening and sunset on Sunday evening, his lord is to pay eighty shillings."[4] Nearly a century later the *Lex Frisionum* (Law of the Frisians) similarly devoted *titulus* (paragraph) XVIII to punishments for working on Sundays.[5] Though protected as a day of rest from labor in such early law codes, this came in time to be seen not as an opportunity for self-indulgence and, in modern parlance, "leisure," but as a time supposedly given over to the worship of God.

WORK AND LEISURE

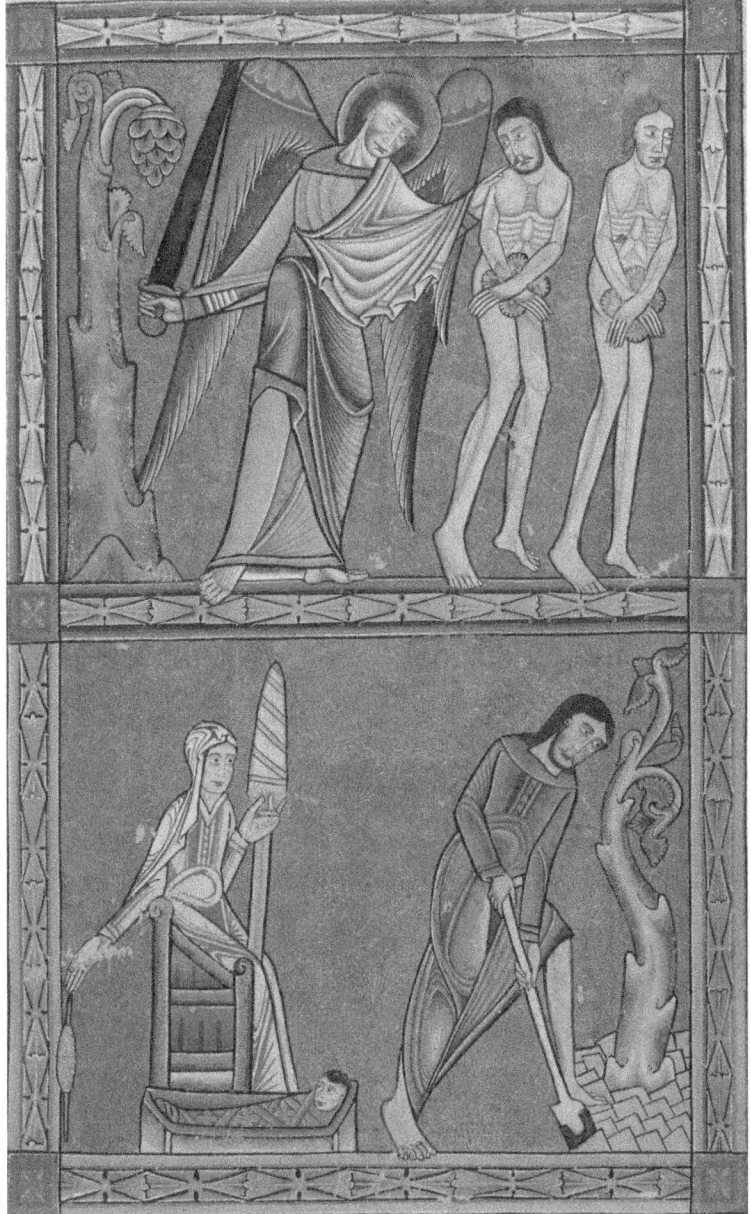

FIGURE 9.1 Adam delving and Eve spinning. Hunterian Psalter, c. 1170. England. University of Glasgow Library, Hunter 229 (U.3.2), folio 8ʳ. © University of Glasgow Library, Special Collections.

From around the beginning of the period covered in this volume, the days customarily observed as holy days—from which the modern English "holiday" ultimately derives—came to include a number of saints' days. It was only in the High Middle Ages, however, following Gratian's twelfth-century codification of key feasts of the church that bishops began to give out instruction as to which saints' days should require abstinence from labor to various degrees according to the importance of the feast in the calendar. These included major feasts of the church but might include diocesan cults and also celebrations of the patronal feast of the parish church. The thirteenth-century Castilian law code the *Siete Partidas* reinforced clerical teaching:

> all Christians should keep them, and, in addition to this, no judge should render a decision, or issue a summons upon them, nor should other men work on those days, or perform the labors which they are accustomed to do on others; but they should endeavor to go decorously and with great humility to the church whose festival they are keeping, if they have a church, and if not, to some other, and listen to the service with great devotion; and, after they have left the church, they should do and say such things as tend to the service of God and the benefit of their souls.[6]

Abstinence from working on the Sunday could be enforced by divine intervention. A hagiographical account of St. Hedwig of Silesia written around 1300 tells of a woman who foolishly ground her grain with a hand-mill or quern on a Sunday. Her hand stuck fast to the handle and when her husband tried to help free it, he managed to tear her arm off. The arm was later restored as a result of an appeal to Hedwig.[7] It could also be a matter for human regulation. The late-ninth-century laws of Alfred of Wessex allowed freemen the twelve days of Christmas and two weeks at Easter in addition to some select feast days including the feast of St. Gregory. The unfree, however, were specifically denied this provision which conflated customary periods of recreation with actual holy days, although how effective such a law was is another matter.[8] In time even the servile came to be allowed much of this provision. Clergy were supposed to announce the week's feast days every Sunday worship and church courts came to exercise sanctions over those who worked on major feast days when most, but not necessarily all, work activity was banned. On some Sundays and holy days plowing might still be permitted and on others only women's work was restricted. The observance of the vigil of feasts was a matter of contention between workers and employers, though Saturday afternoons became generally recognized as a time of rest. Latterly the proper observation of holy days and Sundays was enforced through church courts. When, for example, at the very end of our period Katherine Pykryng and Isabel Hunter were reported—presumably by their scandalized neighbors—for washing linen on the feast of Mary Magdalene, the court ruled that they were to be beaten twice around their church while carrying bundles of linen. Guild ordinances also came regularly to forbid Sunday working. In 1402, the English Parliament even made it an offence punishable with the substantial fine of 20s. to work or to offer work on a holy day.[9]

THE MEANINGS OF LEISURE

The Christian imperative to abstain from work on Sundays and holy days created tensions as to how this time of rest might in fact be used. Churchmen taught that worship was the primary activity of such times of enforced nonwork, but following the Fourth Lateran Council (1215) they increasingly tried to prevent people from engaging in any other pastimes. For example thirteenth-century synodal statutes from the diocese of Aberdeen, as elsewhere, specifically proscribed the use of churches and more contentiously churchyards, hitherto essentially public spaces, for dancing, wrestling matches, or other "base or dishonest" games.[10] In practice, parishioners commonly attended parish mass in the morning but devoted the afternoon to their own recreation. In the early-fourteenth-century miracle account of how little Joan le Schirreve of Marden accidentally drowned but was revived by the intercession of the soon-to-be-canonized Thomas Cantilupe, we learn how the entire village spent their Sunday afternoon at the pub singing, dancing, and, in the case of the older villagers, conversing. Such activity is satirized in a sermon of the Dominican John Bromyard (d. 1352):

> He who starts the love-ditty takes the place of the priest. The place of the clerks is occupied by those who take up the songs and carry them on; and that of the parishioners by those standing or sitting around, who look on and listen with more delight and for a longer time than they would have heard mass or preaching before lunchtime.[11]

The underlying concern was, as an English version of the *Somme le roi* puts it, that those who spent time singing, dancing, playing tables, and other such "fole gemenes [games] ... wasteþ hare time": they waste time because they do not use their leisure productively in good works.[12]

A consideration of the vocabulary of leisure—here focused particularly on Middle English—can offer insight into the way the concept was understood within the culture. While "*werc*," "*weorc*," or variants in a range of medieval Germanic languages and "*labor*," "*labur*," or "*lavor*," and so on, derived from the Latin "*labor*," in Romance languages were very commonly used nouns throughout the period, the word leisure was not. The Old French and Middle English noun "*leisir*," derived from the Latin "*licere*," meaning to be permitted or allowed, first appears in writings from the start of the fourteenth century. Modern usages revolve around rest, recreation, or the ability to use one's time at will. Medieval understandings reference opportunity and permission to carry out activities. From the first it was a concept freighted with resonances of social prescription; it was a permitted activity. "*Leisir*" and related words carried positive resonances: "*leisir*" was not idleness or slothfulness, but sanctioned nonwork activity. Other uses of "*leisir*" have similar positive associations. Lydgate's "Debate of the Horse, Goose and Sheep" argues that leisure is needed in order to come to an intelligent end: "At good leiser / doth the mateer see / Which importith gret intelligence."[13] Another usage relates to the slow passage of time which allows one to heal, prepare, or recoup in some way. In "John Marion's ABC to the Virgin" the speaker asks for "a daye, / laysur and respyte or þat [before] y goo, / So me to arme ayens my mortall foo."[14]

While the concept of "*leisir*" appears only to have evolved in the latter part of our period, "rest," viewed as integral to proper functioning of the body, has a much longer history. "*Rest*," "*reste*," "*rast*," "*rost*," and so on, for example, are found in a variety of Germanic languages over our period. "*Repos*" is likewise found in Old French, "*repaus*" in Old Occitan, and other closely related words in later Romance languages derived from the Lain verb "*repausare*." The vocabulary of rest was mostly used to signify a stepping back from occupation. Rest also represented a more general action of stopping. It is regularly found coupled with moving as an opposite, for example "in moevinges or in restis."[15] Rest did not solely represent change from activity to passivity, but rather the cessation of one activity. To obtain rest there must previously have been movement. According to John Trevisa's late-fourteenth-century translation of the mid-thirteenth-century *De proprietatibus rerum* of Bartholomaeus Anglicus "reste is cesinge of businesse and of trauaille." It was an imperative "for what lackeþ rest amongwhiles is nouȝt durable"; without rest the body is unable to continue to work.[16] Rest both supported and nourished the body after activity. It also carried resonances of peace, comfort, and tranquility as in the phrase "pees and reste in erthe."¹⁷ Much the same resonances are true of the Middle High German "*ruhe*" or the medieval French "*coi*" (derived from the Latin "*quietus*"). Rest was the reward for hard work completed, a recognition of the penitential nature of work. For Bartholomaeus Anglicus rest had greater worth than the act of working; it was the very opposite of unproductive idleness.

While leisure and rest carried many positive resonances that highlight their essential and beneficial contribution to life, they also carried more negative connotations. An excess of rest can have a negative effect on the body and soul. It causes degeneration rather than recuperation. The Wise Man warned his Son in the early-fifteenth-century poem of that name to keep himself "busy more or less":

> Be waar of reste and ydilnesse,
> Whiche þingis norischen slouþe,
> And euere be bisi more or lesse ...¹⁸

In William Langland's late-fourteenth-century poem *Piers Plowman*, the personified vice of Gluttony lists all the people he meets in the alehouse from prostitutes to craftspeople to agricultural workers and servants from all across the social spectrum. Gluttony spends his time in the alehouse rather than attending mass. While his actions directly disregard worship, his idea of time-passing references devotional activity: he "pissed a potel in a paternoster while." His excessive drinking brings on slothfulness as he is put to bed by his wife: "and after al þis excesse he had an Accidie / that he slepe Saterday and Sonday til sonne yede to reste."¹⁹ Gluttony loses two days of productivity in both the secular and the spiritual spheres owing to his unruly leisure.

Langland's characterization of Gluttony may be rooted in clerical notions of the seven deadly sins that go back to the time of the desert fathers; however, anxiety about workers preferring leisure over labor was very current at the time of Langland's composition. Something of the same sentiment is found in Chaucer's *The Cook's Tale*, part of his *Canterbury Tales* written in the late fourteenth century. Here we encounter the character of the significantly named Perkyn Revelour. A London cook's apprentice, Perkyn was easily distracted from his work. He "loved bet [better] the taverne than the shoppe [workshop]." He loved to dance: "At every bridal wolde he synge and hoppe; to hoppe and synge and maken swich disport." He was also addicted to the game of dice: "in the toune nas ther no prentys / that fairer koude caste a paire of dys / than Perkyn koude."²⁰ Perkyn is of course a parody of what an apprentice ought to be, a young dandy who obliviously flouts the terms of his apprenticeship contract. As such he conforms to contemporary understandings of youthful masculinity as undisciplined and given to such vices as lechery, drunkenness, and vanity. But he also signals anxieties about work and idleness that were especially acute in post-plague society and underpin Langland's depiction of Gluttony.

WORK AND LEISURE AFTER THE BLACK DEATH

The European-wide demographic catastrophe of the "great pestilence," known today as the Black Death (1347–50), significantly impacted attitudes to work and to abstinence from work. Perkyn's propensity for what we would call leisure and Gluttony's delight in the alehouse are presented in essentially moral terms, but we can understand them as a consequence of economic change after the pandemic which allowed laborers greater spending power and greater opportunity to purchase leisure. The hemorrhaging of the population in most parts of Europe, following the first pandemic and the lesser, second pandemic of 1361–2—Bohemia and Poland, which were largely spared, Holland and a few other regions are exceptions to this trend—created shortages of labor, corresponding upward movements in the wages workers were able to demand, and corresponding rises in the cost of goods. Such a trend precipitated a legislative response that, though by no means universal, was often fairly immediate. An ordinance to cap prices and wages was issued in Provence as early as September 1348.

Legislation over the immediately subsequent years has been noted particularly in Aragon, Castile, Catalonia, England, Portugal, Florence, Milan, Venice, and other Italian cities, in north German towns, Bavaria and the Tyrol, and, in John II of France's Grand Ordinance of 1352, for Paris and the Île-de-France. In practice, the pattern of legislation varied. The laws in Castile and in Aragon were especially stringent in their attempt to regulate wages and working conditions. The French royal ordinances were primarily concerned with urban employees and with prices, whereas numbers of Italian city-states were more concerned to regulate conditions for the peasantry. The English Statute of Laborers of 1351, which replaced a royal ordinance issued in 1349, is especially striking in that its preliminary statement or preamble adopts a discourse of sin that echoes the sentiment of contemporary chroniclers or of William Langland. The preamble declares that the statute was directed "against the malice of employees, who were idle and were not willing to take employment after the pestilence unless for outrageous wages" and who—motived by "their own ease and exceptional greed—withdraw themselves to work for great men and others, unless they are paid livery and wages double or treble what they were accustomed to receive."[21] This sentiment is echoed in the French royal ordinance of November 1354 that asserted that "greedy laborers" spent their day in the tavern and worked "but two days in the week."[22]

The language of sin lent legislators the moral high ground and so justified their intervention in the operation of a labor market hitherto governed essentially by private contracts negotiated between employer and employee. Of especial interest here is the assertion that laborers "were idle" and cared for "their own ease," apparently an abdication of the responsibility of their estate. In fact the apparent reluctance to work can be understood as a rational response to higher earning capacity and extra bargaining strength in terms of service for laborers. A behaviorist approach would suggest that over time a rise in real wages would have encouraged workers to labor for shorter periods for less money in order to have marginally more control over their lives and satisfaction in leisure.[23] Medieval workers may have set themselves goals in relation to consumption needs and after reaching this point they suspended their labour.[24] Leisure thus became a commodity increasingly within the reach of third estate in the later Middle Ages. This phenomenon of course contributed to the perspective offered by chroniclers and echoed in Boccaccio that the divinely ordained order of society was being overturned following the plague.

ARISTOCRATIC LEISURE

Just as work in the sense of manual labor was deemed the lot of the third order of *laboratores*, so exemption from such hard physical labor was associated with the two other orders of clergy and aristocracy. Such exemption did not, however, imply a license for idleness. For the clergy and increasingly, as hired labor came to displace the monks' own manual labor, members of the religious orders, time free from physical labor was an opportunity for mental labor, that is, time to study. Such purposeful *"otium negotiosum"* was quite distinct from *"otium otiosum,"* leisure for its own sake. Chaucer's *The Pardoner's Tale* comments on activities whereby aristocrats might pass the time: "Lordes may fynden oother manere pley / Honeste ynow to dryue the day awey."[25] The leisure of the upper echelons must not be frivolous or rough, but "honeste," that is, sober and dignified as befitted their status in society. This understanding informs *Master of Game*, a treatise on the "myrthes of huntyng" apparently authored by Edward, duke of York at the beginning of the fifteenth century, but substantially derived from the *Livre de chasse* of Gaston Phébus (late fourteenth century). The prologue works hard to convince the reader that hunting should not be considered idle but rather a productive leisure pursuit, by reason that hunting "causeth oft a man to eschewe þe vii dedly synnes." It does this by engaging mind and body before, during, and after the hunt so that the hunter's thoughts do not linger on sins such as gluttony, lust, wrath, or pride.[26]

Another perspective is offered by the previously noticed the *Siete Partidas* which prescribe hunting as a suitable occupation for a king. The reasons given apply, however, to all men who wield power and authority:

> it contributes much to diminish serious thoughts and vexations … it confers health, as the exertion which is employed in it, when it is done in moderation, causes a man to eat and sleep well, which is the principal thing in life. The pleasure which is derived from it is, moreover, a great source of joy; as, for instance, the obtaining possession of birds and wild beasts, and causing them to obey and serve man, by bringing others into his hands.[27]

The superficially modern sense that exercise is both necessary and health-inducing is balanced against a very medieval understanding that it is men of rank who will have the most "serious thought and vexations" and whose mastery over other men will be reinforced by their mastery over the birds and beasts of field and forest. Langland's long devotional poem suggests yet another justification for hunting. Piers Plowman directs the knight to:

> … go hunte hardiliche to hares and to foxes,
> To bores and to [bukkes] þat breken myne hegges,
> And [fette þe hoom] faucons foweles to kille;
> For [þise] cometh to my croft and croppeþ my whete.[28]

Only the lay aristocracy, particularly males, were permitted to hunt. Aristocratic women might engage in falconry and some kinds of hunting such as shooting from a stand at driven game or coursing deer and hare, but hunting deer *par force* with hounds was primarily a male preserve; women's participation, where it was allowed, was only secondary. This aristocratic privilege did not prevent the participation of other orders in practice. For the peasant, the taking of game—primarily for consumption rather than sport or leisure—constituted poaching and as such was liable to punishment. Peasants might, however, participate licitly in hunts as guides. For churchmen, hunting was frowned upon, but this was no bar on their actual participation. As early as 802 the Carolingian *General Capitulary for the Missi* reproached bishops, abbots, and other senior clergy from participating in the quintessentially aristocratic pursuits of hunting with dogs or with birds of prey. According to William of Malmesbury, Bishop Malger of Rouen was deprived of his see by his nephew, Duke William of Normandy, "because he gave too much attention to hunting and hawking."[29] The Third Lateran Council of 1179 found need to forbid bishops from taking hunting dogs or birds with them when travelling for the purposes of visitation. This suggests that bishops' concern to project their social rank by participating in an aristocratic sport that was otherwise understood as a form of martial training continued to outweigh their duty to shun worldly pleasures. We also find religious castigated at visitation for keeping hunting dogs and abbots for their love of hunting. When, for example, William of Wykeham visited Merton Priory in 1387 he "found some canons and confraters of the Priory to be huntsmen, and, with huntsmen, despising the yoke of the Rule's observance, and employing and keeping hunting dogs, to the danger of souls and bodies, as well as being at much cost."[30] The continued chastisement throughout our period of clergy and religious for hunting suggests that attempts to check leisure pursuits inappropriate to their vocations were generally unsuccessful; it was more important to them to assert their masculinity and social rank than to be bound by such constraints.

Hunting was not the only pastime, aristocratic or otherwise. Indeed, Trevisa's translation of Bartholomaeus Anglicus suggests that there were as many different types of leisure as there were occupations: "In so moche as reste is contrarye to trauaile men schal take hede of reste, touchinge þe effect, in as many maner wise as of trauaile."[31] Returning again to the *Siete Partidas*, the text goes on, still with the needs of the king at its focus:

> There are other pleasures ... which have been devised in order that a man may take comfort when oppressed with care and affliction. These are listening to songs and musical instruments, and playing chess, draughts, or other similar games. We also include histories, romances, and other books, which treat of those matters from which men derive joy and pleasure.[32]

However, such pleasures, the text warns, were only to be indulged in at appropriate times and in moderation. Both the strategic game of chess and board games called tables, which combined strategy with chance, were understood to mimic the strategy of war and as such were singularly appropriate to the aristocracy (see Figure 9.2). Such an understanding of the value of board games in the socialization of boys of aristocratic birth has deep roots that go back well before Alfonso X's law codes. The early Irish law codes, for example, and for precisely this reason, directed that alongside riding a horse or using a spear high-born boys be taught to play *brandubh* and *fidcheall*, games that used checkered boards, whose gaming pieces might signify warfare, and that required a degree of strategy.

Chess became the archetypal aristocratic game of strategy during the medieval period. This is reflected for example in the high-quality walrus ivory Lewis chessmen, possibly made in Trondheim around 1200, but also in the way, as Albrecht Classen puts it, chess "became a significant symbol of courtly society at least since the eleventh century" in European poetry.[33] Alfonso X of Castile—in addition to his concern to codify the law—compiled a *Book of Chess, Dice and Board Games*. At much the same date the Dominican Jacopo da Cessole created his widely disseminated *Liber de moribus hominum et officiis nobilium super ludo scacchorum*, which offered moral instruction through the medium of chess. Malcolm Vale has commented on the way in which the use of terms such as "*familia*" or "*mesnie*" to describe the complement of games' pieces, or king, queen, or knight to describe specific pieces, echoed the world of the court.[34]

FIGURE 9.2 Aristocratic couple playing chess. Ivory mirror, c. 1320–30. France or Germany. © Victoria and Albert Museum, London.

STATUS AND GENDER IN THE MEANING OF WORK AND LEISURE

Pastimes for male youth, including wrestling and ball games, are included in FitzStephen's 1183 encomium for London, but this positive tone is not found in later texts. Youthful and lower-status pastimes came otherwise to attract moral censure in ways that were less true of elite adult males. Despite FitzStephen's praise of ball games, a proclamation, citing noise and disorder, was made against the playing of football in London as early as 1314. Chess and tables, as well as other pastimes, were frequently occasions for gambling. For men of rank this was just another form of conspicuous consumption. Edward II of England, for example, won over £80 in stakes on two occasions in 1307–8. For others, sports and gambling were seen as vices and were persistent sources of clerical and magisterial censure. The founding statutes of 1443 for King's College, Cambridge, intended for the education of poor scholars, forbade not just hunting and the keeping of dogs, but "all harmful, disorderly, unlawful and dishonest games of dice, chance, or ball, and especially all games which may cause loss of money, property, possessions, or goods of any servant anywhere within the College or University."[35] In 1369, and with an eye to the needs of warfare, Charles V of France made an ordinance forbidding "all games of dice, tables, tennis, skittles, ball, football, bowls, and all other such games" in favor of practice with the bow and the crossbow.[36] Almost identical legislation was enacted in the English parliament from the later fourteenth century and in the Scottish in the fifteenth century.[37] The periodic repetition of such legislation over subsequent decades suggests that in practice such recreations continued largely unabated.

Women's leisure activity is much less visible. Dance appears to be one of the few recreations open to most women, though it was not necessarily only women that participated. Communal dancing may be traced back to the early Middle Ages and may have been absorbed into early Christian worship since by the thirteenth century bishops were banning it from churches and churchyards. Women, but sometimes men as well, also danced *caroles*, which were often accompanied by song, that enjoyed wide popularity from the twelfth century. Other than in respect of dance and song, women were more often to be found as observers than participants in recreational activities taking place in public. In Icelandic society, for example, women appear to have been allowed to watch the often violent ball game *knattleikr*, but the game itself was exclusively male. Even as spectators the presence of women could be frowned upon as morally questionable. Concerns about sexual propriety lie behind the advice given in an English mid-fourteenth-century normative text *How the Goodwife Taught her Daughter* that young women "go not to the wrestling or shooting at the cock," occasions where young men displayed their prowess no doubt in part to attract the opposite sex.[38] The Dominican John Bromyard claimed that women dressed provocatively to gain attention on feast days.

Games within the home permitted the possibility of participation by both sexes. Board games allowed men and women to play one another and hence created opportunity for romantic encounters between the sexes. An erotically charged vocabulary—including terms such as "*intrare*" (to enter), "*nudare*" (to denude), and "*ablatio*" (abduction)—was used in both tables and chess.[39] Such overtones are also referenced in a *bas-de-page* image of a king and a noble lady playing backgammon in the Luttrell Psalter of the first part of the fourteenth century. More than three centuries earlier Gunnlaugr Ormstuna fell in love with his host's daughter, Helga Þornsteinsdóttir, while playing board games with her. The late medieval literary fortune games such as "Chance of Dice" and "Ragman Roll" played within higher-status homes might have been played to erotic ends by mixed gender groups or, in the case of "Ragman Roll," a specifically female group.[40] These games reflect an aristocratic culture that came to encourage witty conversation between the sexes, but may also mirror socially more diverse and deeply rooted cultures of courtship such as the riddling games still performed in the Lorraine in the nineteenth century.

The rather more substantial evidence for men's leisure activities than for women's may be explored as a corollary of the greater cultural value and recognition given to men's work rather than to women's. Historical understandings of what constituted work were gendered. Many aspects of the work performed by women were not thought of as work since they were understood as duties given to women by their nature. So far as leisure was the necessary recompense for labor, there may thus have been a perception that men had far more need of leisure than women.

Not only was childbirth—and the labor by which Eve and her daughters were punished—natural to women, but so was early childcare. The *Siete Partidas* reinforced the prescription of nature by decreeing that "mothers should nourish and bring up their children while they are under three years of age."[41] This requirement was doubtless determined by the common cultural practice for mothers to continue to suckle their children for the first three years. Wet-nurses noticed in a case from the York Consistory were hired for a term of three years, though analysis of skeletal evidence from the neighboring vill Wharram Percy suggest children there were nursed for shorter periods. Perhaps the difference lies in the point at which young children became more reliant on solids rather than the point at which mothers finally stopped nursing. The York evidence alerts us to the fact that some women made a livelihood from marketing their ability to produce milk. The aristocracy in particular and the wealthier families in Mediterranean towns over several centuries seem regularly to have employed rural nurses. Whereas numbers of young children were sent to spend time with their, invariably poor, wet-nurses, in aristocratic society the nurse might live with the employer for some years so that the child might be cared for within the family residence. In the case of Thibaut, the infant heir to the county of Champagne, such care proved defective. He was accidentally dropped to his death in 1272 by his live-in nurse from the walls of his parents' castle.[42]

Wives were expected to provide sex for their husbands in a culture that invariably understood sex in terms of performance on the part of the man, but saw the woman's role as essentially passive. Christian teaching came to uphold the concept of the marital debt by which a woman or a man was required to have sex with their spouse if requested. In practice this meant a wife could not lawfully refuse sex. Again, it is unlikely that such sexual services, although expected, were considered work, though of course some women sold sex commercially, and the Paris theology faculty came to rule that it was legitimate for these women to demand payment since they performed work. In the absence of effective forms of contraception most women would have spent much of their married life either pregnant or nursing. Childrearing was again most likely seen as primarily the woman's responsibility, though, aside from Alfonso X's law code, this is in part a surmise suggested by the paucity of evidence—had men been more involved we might expect more of a literature—and extrapolation from the royal and aristocratic custom of leaving sons in female care until they were about seven years of age. In practice, however, the evidence of English coroners' rolls from the later thirteenth and earlier fourteenth centuries is that children were often left to play outdoors among themselves. In artisanal households where the home was the principal location of the main family business, moreover, fathers and mothers could both keep a watch over their children as representations of the infant Christ with Joseph and Mary suggest.

Childbirth, breastfeeding, and childrearing may all have been considered "natural" to women and hence only work when invariably impoverished women sold their services. Other tasks that fell to women within a domestic context were cooking, sewing, spinning, and weaving. The finding of spindle whorls, needles, wool combs, and weaving battens among the grave goods of women in pre-Christian Anglo-Saxon and Viking burials suggests that such understandings again had deep historical roots, but within Christian culture the good wife from the book of Proverbs (Prov. 31:10–31) provided a model of a wife who feeds and clothes her household by her own labor. Spinning was so much part of women's identity—as we have seen in the way Eve is almost invariably represented after the Fall—that in visual depictions the distaff became a sort of gender symbol. The "naturalization" of spinning, which tended to detract from the sense that spinning was really work, is further suggested by its use in the widely found Latin proverb "*fallere, flere, nere, statuit Deus in muliere* [to deceive, to weep, to spin, God placed in woman]."

Once again evidence for women's economic activities—what we colloquially mean by "work"—is dominated by spinning, weaving, needlework, the retail of foodstuffs, and the laundering of clothes. This is the picture, for example, suggested by the Parisian *tailles* of 1292 and 1313 and is reflected again in the English poll taxes of 1379 and 1381. It has been shown that women's workshops where sewing and weaving were undertaken seem to have been long-established in parts of continental Europe. This is suggested *inter alia* by evidence from a miracle narrative of St. Walburgis of Heidelheim dated around 895, Chrétien de Troyes' *Yvain* of 1170s, and of the Emperor Frederick II's provisions in 1239 and 1240 for his several palace workshops in Sicily staffed *inter alia* by slave women.[43] It follows that women's work was largely an extension of the domestic, and for that reason appropriate to women. It was also work that girls might start to learn from childhood in the home rather than be trained in once they had reached puberty, as tended to be true of tasks and skills taught to boys. For both these reasons women's work was less valued economically.

Although ideologically women were associated with the domestic and the home, we should be careful not to assume that social practice simply followed ideology. One recent scholar writing of women's work in early medieval Europe, for which she laments the paucity of sources, suggests that "women stayed mostly at home to work." She suggests that later medieval evidence—by which is meant in fact one particular scholar's interpretation of evidence relating to accidental deaths—supports this "traditional picture."[44] The ideology that associated women with the home does indeed have deep historical roots, but a supposed gender–spatial division of labor based on an analysis of English coroners' records tells only of especially risky work activities. It sits uneasily alongside substantial evidence for the range of field work such as weeding, tending livestock and poultry, milking cows and sheep, dairy work, and work at harvest time that were seen as women's work in peasant society.

Many of these tasks are illustrated in the Luttrell Psalter (c. 1340) and *Les très riches heures du Duc de Berry* (c. 1412–16). It must be acknowledged that early medieval calendar illuminations, such as that in Figure 9.3, are more likely to depict men working in the fields, but saints' lives suggest that women performed like tasks at earlier periods. Men, however, consistently preserved a monopoly over plowing—which took on sexual resonances and so was "naturalized" as a male activity—and the use of the scythe for mowing. It is these male activities that are illustrated in an Anglo-Saxon calendar depicting the labors of the months.[45] According to Odo of Cluny, writing in the early tenth century, Gerald of Aurillac was so aghast at seeing a woman plowing that he sent money that she might employ a man to do the task for her.[46] This is in fact a rare clue that once again social practice might not always accord with ideology.

Although men's and women's work may not have changed profoundly or rapidly within peasant society over time or between regions, some changes may be discerned.

FIGURE 9.3 Labors of the months depicting harvesting in August. English painted roundel, third quarter of fifteenth century. © Victoria and Albert Museum, London.

It has been argued that the proliferation of mills in the High Middle Ages may have come largely to free women from having to mill all grain by hand. Over the same period increased demand for textile production may have substantially increased work for women preparing woollen yarn in terms of carding and spinning.[47] From the same time, peasant women also became much involved in viticulture and, in Italy, sericulture. The rapid expansion of towns in the High Middle Ages created a new range of employment opportunities and sucked in migrant labor from the countryside, though it was textile production that most obviously stimulated growth. In the context of labor shortage in the decades after the Black Death, women workers appear often, though not universally, to have been more in demand. They were certainly more conspicuous at harvest time. The larger differences were between the experiences of women of different social ranks, particularly peasant women and townswomen, and between different cultural regions. The significance or otherwise of these trends have been the subject of much scholarly debate, but there is little to suggest they radically changed gender perceptions.

CONCLUSION

In medieval culture, leisure was the indispensable and necessary counterpart to work. As a thirteenth-century model letter put it, "that which lacks daily rest cannot endure."[48] For it to be truly beneficial, however, moderation in pastime, play, rest, or sleep was imperative. As Trevisa's translation of Bartholomaeus Anglicus explained, excess leisure was the cause of bodily distemper and sickness: "also somtyme reste is to myche, and þanne it brediþ … euel humoures, and bringiþ in corrupcioun." Insufficient leisure could be equally detrimental: "som reste is to lite and is vicious, for it refreisschiþ nouȝt kynde þat is wery, noþir releueth feblenes noþir restorith what þat is iwastid." As so often, health and good order depended on an appropriate balance.[49] Leisure, like work, was productive. People played out their roles in society even through their leisure pursuits. Social status, gender, and age all shaped the nature of leisure as they shaped the nature of work. The superior intellect and self-control ascribed to the aristocracy by virtue of their superior birth, together with their martial ethos, both required and permitted them a range of pastimes—hunting, board games, gambling—that were not necessarily shared by, or at least permitted for, the majority of the working population. Play characterized children who were too young to work. Women might sing to nurse a child or while washing, spinning, or sewing, but the comparative invisibility of the leisure activities of women below the level of the aristocracy mirrors the prevailing sense that women's work was natural to their sex and so did not truly constitute labor.

NOTES

Introduction

1 Stephen A. Epstein, *Wage Labor and Guilds in Medieval Europe* (Chapel Hill: The University of North Carolina Press, 1991), 173–5.
2 William Chester Jordan, *The Great Famine: Northern Europe in the Early Fourteenth Century* (Princeton, NJ: Princeton University Press, 1996), 115–23.
3 Benedict of Nursia, *The Rule of St Benedict*, trans. Anthony C. Meisel and M. L. del Mastro (New York: Doubleday, 1975), chaps. 48, 86.
4 See respectively Janet Burton and Julie Kerr, *The Cistercians in the Middle Ages* (Woodbridge: Boydell Press, 2011), 104–24; Barbara H. Rosenwein, *To be the Neighbor of St. Peter: The Social Meaning of Cluny's Property, 909–1049* (Ithaca, NY: Cornell University Press, 1989), 36–48, 203–5; Felice Lifshitz, *Religious Women in Early Carolingian Francia: A Study of Manuscript Transmission and Monastic Culture* (New York: Fordham University Press, 2014), 193–200.
5 Anne E. Lester, "Cares Beyond the Walls: Cistercian Nuns and the Care of Lepers in Twelfth- and Thirteenth-Century Northern France," in *Religious and Laity in Western Europe 1000–1400: Interaction, Negotiation, and Power*, eds. Emilia Jamroziak and Janet Burton (Turnhout: Brepols, 2006), 197–224.
6 Sara Ritchey, "The Wound's Presence and Bodily Absence: The Experience of God in a Fourteenth-Century Manuscript," in *Sense, Matter, and Medium: New Approaches to Medieval Material and Literary Culture*, eds. Fiona Griffiths and Kathryn Starkey (Berlin: De Gruyter, 2018), forthcoming.
7 Norman Davis, Richard Beadle, and Colin Richmond, eds., *Paston Letters and Papers of the Fifteenth Century*, 3 vols. (Oxford: Oxford University Press, 2004–2005).
8 Richard Britnell, "The Pastons and their Norfolk," *Agricultural History Review* 36 (1988): 132–44.
9 Keith D. Lilley, *Urban Life in the Middle Ages, 1000–1450* (New York: Palgrave, 2002), 234–8.
10 Clive Orton et al., "Medieval Novgorod: Epitome of Early Urban Life in Northern Europe," *Archaeology International* 2 (1998): 31–8; and more generally Mark A. Brisbane et al., eds., *The Archaeology of Medieval Novgorod in Context: A Study of Centre/Periphery Relations* (Oxford: Oxbow Books, 2012).
11 Carl-Ludwig Holtfrerich, *Frankfurt as a Financial Centre: From Medieval Trade Fair to European Banking Centre* (Munich: Verlag C. H. Beck, 1999), 31–69.
12 Kathryn L. Reyerson, *Business, Banking and Finance in Medieval Montpellier* (Toronto: Pontifical Institute of Mediaeval Studies, 1985), ix–x, 127–34. A classic Flemish study is Raymond De Roover, *Money, Banking and Credit in Mediaeval Bruges* (Cambridge, MA: The Mediaeval Academy of America), 1948.
13 Judith M. Bennett, *Ale, Brew, and Brewsters in England: Women's Work in a Changing World, 1300–1600* (Oxford: Oxford University Press, 1996).

14 Maryanne Kowaleski, "Women's Work in a Medieval Town: Exeter in the Late Fourteenth Century," in *Women and Work in Preindustrial Europe*, ed. Barbara A. Hanawalt (Bloomington: University of Indiana Press, 1986), 147–8.
15 *The Trotula: A Medieval Compendium of Women's Medicine*, ed. and trans. Monica H. Green (Philadelphia: University of Pennsylvania Press, 2001), xi, 17–52, quotation on 123–5.
16 Monica H. Green, "Women's Medical Practice and Health Care in Medieval Europe," in *Sisters and Workers in the Middle Ages*, eds. Judith M. Bennett et al. (Chicago, IL: University of Chicago Press, 1989), 44, 62, 73–7.
17 Barbara Hanawalt, *Growing Up in Medieval London: The Experience of Childhood in History* (Oxford: Oxford University Press, 1993), 129–42, 157–63, 173–89; Nicholas Orme, *Medieval Children* (New Haven, CT: Yale University Press, 2001), 98–100, 306–17.
18 David Nicholas, *The Growth of the Medieval City: From Late Antiquity to the Early Fourteenth Century* (London: Longman, 1997), 83–4, 90–1, 102–8.
19 Samuel K. Cohn, Jr., *Popular Protest in Late Medieval Towns* (Cambridge: Cambridge University Press, 2013), 16–17.
20 Richard Britnell, "Specialization of Work in England," *Economic History Review* 54 (2001): 1–16 at 4–14.
21 Monika Obermeier, "'Ancilla.' *Beiträge zur Geschichte der unfreien Frauen im Frühmittelalter* (Pfaffenweiler: Centaurus Verlagsgesellschaft, 1996), 166–232; Helena Graham, "'A Woman's Work...': Labour and Gender in the Late Medieval Countryside," in *Woman is a Worthy Wight: Women in English Society, c.1200–1500*, ed. Peter Jeremy Piers Goldberg (Phoenix Mill: Alan Sutton, 1992), 129–44.
22 Epstein, *Wage Labor and Guilds*, 4.
23 Paul Freedman, "Peasant Anger in the Late Middle Ages," in *Anger's Past: The Social Uses of an Emotion in the Middle Ages*, ed. Barbara H. Rosenwein (Ithaca, NY: Cornell University Press, 1998), 171–88.
24 Epstein, *Wage Labor and Guilds*, 50–101.
25 Lilley, *Urban Life*, 222–3.
26 The plague hit some areas and localities much harder than others, and more fourteenth-century records survive in some places than others, making it difficult to estimate the overall mortality rate. Colin Platt, *King Death: The Black Death and its Aftermath in Late Medieval England* (London: University College London Press, 1996), 1–31.
27 David Nicholas, *The Later Medieval City: 1300–1500* (London: Longman, 1997), 14.
28 Giovanni Boccaccio, *The Decameron*, trans. Guido Waldman (Oxford: Oxford University Press, 1993), 6–14.
29 Rosemary Horrox, trans. and ed., *The Black Death* (Manchester: Manchester University Press), 19.
30 Shona Kelly Wray, *Communities and Crisis: Bologna During the Black Death* (Leiden: Brill, 2009), 99–146, 203–21.
31 Philip Ziegler, *The Black Death* (New York: Harper, 1969), 243–7.
32 Lawrence R. Poos, *A Rural Society After the Black Death* (Cambridge: Cambridge University Press, 1991), 208–27.
33 Nicholas, *The Later Medieval City*, 80–3.
34 Mavis Mate, *Daughters, Wives and Widows After the Black Death: Women in Sussex, 1350–1535* (Woodbridge: Boydell Press, 1998), 193–8.

Chapter One

1. Michael North, *The Expansion of Europe, 1250–1500* (Manchester: Manchester University Press, 2007), 368.
2. Christopher Dyer, *Making a Living in the Middle Ages: The People of Britain 850–1520* (New Haven, CT: Yale University Press, 2002), 13.
3. Mark Bailey, *A Marginal Economy? East Anglian Breckland in the Later Middle Ages* (Cambridge: Cambridge University Press, 1989), 158–99.
4. Adriaan Verhulst, *The Carolingian Economy* (Cambridge: Cambridge University Press, 2002), 72–5.
5. Edward Miller and John Hatcher, *Medieval England: Rural Society and Economic Change, 1086–1348* (London: Longman, 1978), 128–33.
6. Steven A. Epstein, *An Economic and Social History of Later Medieval Europe, 1000–1500* (Cambridge: Cambridge University Press, 2009), 46–7.
7. *Secular Lyrics of the XIVth and XVth Centuries*, ed. Rossell H. Robbins (Oxford: Clarendon Press, 1952), 62.
8. Barbara A. Hanawalt, *The Ties that Bound: Peasant Families in Medieval England* (Oxford: Oxford University Press, 1989), 124–6.
9. Jacques Le Goff, *Time, Work, and Culture in the Middle Ages* (Chicago, IL: University of Chicago Press, 1980), 46–7.
10. Christopher Dyer, "Work Ethics in the Fourteenth Century," in *The Problem of Labour in Fourteenth-Century England*, eds. James Bothwell, Peter Jeremy Piers Goldberg, and W. Mark Ormrod (York: York Medieval Press, 2000), 21–41.
11. Dyer, *Making a Living*, 281.
12. Carlo M. Cipolla, *European Culture and Overseas Expansion* (Harmondsworth: Penguin, 1970), 114–28.
13. Bruce M. S. Campbell, "The Land," in *A Social History of England 1200–1500*, eds. Rosemary Horrox and W. Mark Ormrod (Cambridge: Cambridge University Press, 2006), 221.
14. Hanawalt, *The Ties that Bound*, 145–6.
15. ["Whan Adam dalf and Eve span, Wo was thanne a gentilman?"] Thomas Walsingham, "Historia Anglicana," in *The Peasants' Revolt of 1381*, 2nd ed., ed. Richard Barrie Dobson (London: Macmillan, 1983), 374.
16. George Kane and E. Talbot Donaldson, eds., *Piers Plowman: The B Version* (Berkeley: The University of California Press, 1975), Passus VI.
17. 'Ballad of a Tyrannical Husband', in *The Trials and Joys of Marriage*, ed. Eve Salisbury (Kalamazoo, MI: Medieval Institute Publications, 2002), 85–93.
18. Mavis Mate, *Daughters, Wives, and Widows after the Black Death: Women in Sussex, 1350–1535* (Woodbridge: Boydell Press, 1998), 194.
19. Heather Swanson, *Medieval Artisans: An Urban Class in Late Medieval England* (Oxford: Basil Blackwell, 1989), 35, 42–3, 74; Peter Jeremy Piers Goldberg, *Women, Work, and Life Cycle in a Medieval Economy: Women in York and Yorkshire, c.1300–1520* (Oxford: Clarendon Press, 1992), 118–37; Arnaldo Rui Azevedo De Sousa Melo, "Women and Work in the Household Economy: The Social and Linguistic Evidence from Porto, c.1340–1450," in *The Medieval Household in Christian Europe, c. 850–c. 1550: Managing Power, Wealth and the Body*, eds. Cordelia Beattie, Anna Maslakovic, and Sarah Rees Jones (Turnhout: Brepols, 2003), 249–69.
20. Peter Jeremy Piers Goldberg, ed., *Women in England, c. 1275–1525* (Manchester: Manchester University Press, 1995), 205.

21 Hanawalt, *The Ties that Bound*.
22 Jacques Lefort, "The Rural Economy, Seventh–Twelfth Centuries," in *The Economic History of Byzantium*, 3 vols., eds. Angeliki E. Laiou and Charalampos Bouras (Washington, DC: Dumbarton Oak Studies, 2002), i, 241.
23 Goldberg, *Women*, 158–202; Christiane Klapisch-Zuber, "State and Family in a Renaissance Society: The Florentine Catasto of 1427–30," in *Women, Family, and Ritual in Renaissance Italy*, ed. Christiane Klapisch-Zuber (Chicago, IL: University of Chicago Press, 1985), 1–22.
24 David Farmer, "The *Famuli* in the Later Middle Ages," in *Progress and Problems in Medieval England*, eds. Richard H. Britnell and John Hatcher (Cambridge: Cambridge University Press, 1996), 207–36; Stephen H. Rigby, *English Society in the Later Middle Ages: Class, Status and Gender* (Basingstoke: Macmillan, 1995), 39.
25 Dyer, *Making a Living*, 133.
26 Simon A. C. Penn and Christopher Dyer, "Wages and Earnings in Late Medieval England: Evidence from the Enforcement of the Labour Laws," *Economic History Review* 43 (1990): 356–76.
27 Norman J. G. Pounds, *An Economic History of Medieval Europe* (New York: Longman, 1974), 482; Édouard Perroy, "Wage Labour in France in the Later Middle Ages," *Economic History Review* 8 (1955–6): 232–9.
28 See Chapter Four for Peter Stabel's discussion about how itinerant work influenced workers' identities.
29 Chris Wickham, *Framing the Early Middle Ages: Europe and the Mediterranean, 400–800* (Oxford: Oxford University Press, 2005), 261–3; Lefort, "The Rural Economy," 241–2.
30 Paul H. Freedman, *Images of the Medieval Peasant* (Stanford, CA: Stanford University Press, 1999), 17.
31 Epstein, *An Economic and Social History*, 16; Lefort, "The Rural Economy," 241.
32 *Breve XV de Villanova* (before 829), col. 84, in Verhulst, *The Carolingian Economy*, 38–9.
33 Dyer, *Making a Living*, 38.
34 Campbell, "The Land," 212.
35 Epstein, *An Economic and Social History*, 50, 52–4.
36 Ibid., 52.
37 Angeliki E. Laiou, "The Agrarian Economy: Thirteenth–Fifteenth Centuries," in *Economic History of Byzantium*, eds. Laiou and Bouras, i, 334.
38 David Stone, *Decision-Making in Medieval Agriculture* (Oxford: Oxford University Press, 2005), 231–76.
39 Epstein, *An Economic and Social History*, 60; Laiou, "The Agrarian Economy," 337–8; North, *The Expansion of Europe*, 366–7.
40 *Select Documents of the English Lands of the Abbey of Bec*, ed. Marjorie Chibnall (London: Royal Historical Society, 1951), 164–6.
41 Dyer, *Making a Living*, 293–4.
42 Steven A. Epstein, *Wage Labor and Guilds in Medieval Europe* (Chapel Hill: University of North Carolina Press, 1991), 137–8.
43 David Herlihy, *Opera Muliebria: Women and Work in Medieval Europe* (New York: McGraw-Hill, 1990), 146.
44 Edward Miller and John Hatcher, *Medieval England: Towns, Commerce and Crafts, 1086–1348* (London: Longman, 1995), 324–5.
45 Karl Gunnar Persson, *An Economic History of Europe: Knowledge, Institutions and Growth, 600 to Present* (Cambridge: Cambridge University Press, 2010), 22–5.
46 Dyer, *Making a Living*, 279.

47 See Chapter Eight for Robert Braid's detailed analysis of this labor legislation.
48 Rosemary Horrox, *The Black Death* (Manchester: Manchester University Press, 1994), 319–20; John Aberth, ed., *The Black Death: The Great Mortality of 1348–1350* (Boston, MA: Bedford/St Martin's, 2005), 87–91.
49 Penn and Dyer, "Wages and Earnings."
50 Goldberg, *Women, Work*; Sandy Bardsley, "Women's Work Reconsidered: Gender and Wage Differentiation in Late Medieval England," *Past & Present* 165 (1999): 3–29.
51 Herlihy, *Opera Muliebria*, 154–91.
52 Pounds, *An Economic History*, 482–3.
53 John Hatcher, "Unreal Wages: Long-Run Living Standards and the 'Golden Age' of the Fifteenth Century," in *Commercial Activity, Markets and Entrepreneurs in the Middle Ages: Essays in Honour of Richard Britnell*, eds. Ben Dodds and Christian D. Liddy (Woodbridge: Boydell & Brewer, 2011), 1–24.
54 Dyer, *Making a Living*, 287.

Chapter Two

1 Bruce M. S. Campbell, "The Land," in *A Social History of England, 1200–1500*, eds. Rosemary Horrox and W. Mark Ormrod (Cambridge: Cambridge University Press, 2006), 179–237 at 179.
2 The manuscripts are London, British Library, MS Cotton Julius A. vi and London, British Library, MS Cotton Tiberius B. v Pt. 1. For the historical context and artistic and religious significance of the calendars, see Sianne Lauren Shepherd, "Anglo-Saxon Labours of the Months: Representing May–A Case Study" (M.Phil thesis, The University of Birmingham, 2010).
3 David Hill, "Eleventh Century Labours of the Months in Prose and Pictures," *Landscape History* 20, no. 1 (1998): 29–39 at 38.
4 A copy of this manuscript, made near Salzburg, has an identical miniature (Munich, Bayerische Staatsbibliothek, MS Clm. 210). A scribal inscription dates it to 818.
5 London, British Library, Sloane MS 2435, fol. 44^v.
6 James B. Williams, "Working for Reform: *Acedia*, Benedict of Aniane and the Transformation of Working Culture in Carolingian Monasticism," in *Sin in Medieval and Early Modern Culture: The Tradition of the Seven Deadly Sins*, eds. Richard G. Newhauser and Susan J. Ridyard (York: York Medieval Press, 2012), 19–42 at 24.
7 This version of the letter is recorded in the *Exordium Magnum*. *The Great Beginning of Cîteaux: A Narrative of the Beginning of the Cistercian Order: The Exordium Magnum of Conrad of Eberbach*, trans. Benedicta Ward and Paul Savage, ed. E. Rozanne Elder (Trappist, KY: Cistercian Publications, 2012), 42. For the original letter, which differs in places, see Bernard of Clairvaux, Ep. 1, *Sancti Bernardi Opera*. 8 vols., 7:1–11; Bruno Scott James, trans., *The Letters of Bernard of Clarivaux*, Ep. 1, 1–10.
8 Jonathan J. G. Alexander and Leslie C. Jones, "The Annunciation to the Shepherdess," *Studies in Iconography* 24 (2003): 165–98.
9 Mary Dzon, "Joseph and the Amazing Christ-Child of Late-Medieval Legend," in *Childhood in the Middle Ages and the Renaissance: The Results of a Paradigm Shift in the History of Mentality*, ed. Albrecht Classen (Berlin: Walter de Gruyter, 2005), 135–57 at 142.
10 For negative perceptions of Joseph, see Pamela Sheingorn, "Joseph the Carpenter's Failure at Familial Discipline," in *Insights and Interpretations: Studies in Celebration of the Eighty-Fifth Anniversary of the Index of Christian Art*, ed. Colum Hourihane (Princeton, NJ: Princeton University Press, 2002), 156–67.

11 Rosemary Drage Hale, "Joseph as Mother: Adaptation and Appropriation in the Construction of Male Virtue," in *Medieval Mothering*, eds. John Carmi Parson and Bonnie Wheeler (New York: Garland, 1996), 101–16.
12 Orlanda S. H. Lie et al., *Christine de Pizan in Bruges: "Le livre de la cité des Dames" as "Het Bouc van de Stede der Vrauwen" (London, British Library, Add. 20698)* (Hilversum: Verloren, 2015), 7.
13 Dolly Jorgensen, "Illuminating Ephemeral Medieval Agricultural History through Manuscript Art," *Agricultural History* 89, no. 2 (2015): 186–99.
14 David A. Sprunger, "Parodic Animal Physicians from the Margins of Medieval Manuscripts," in *Animals in the Middle Ages*, ed. Nora C. Flores (New York: Routledge, 2016), 67–81.
15 Giles Constable, *Three Studies in Medieval Religious and Social Thought: The Interpretation of Mary and Martha, the Ideal of the Imitation of Christ, the Orders of Society* (Cambridge: Cambridge University Press, 1998), 289.
16 Georges Duby, *The Three Orders: Feudal Society Imagined*, trans. Arthur Goldhammer (Chicago, IL: University of Chicago Press, 1982), 100.
17 Ibid., 13.
18 Anna Somfai, "The Eleventh-Century Shift in the Reception of Plato's *Timaeus* and Calciduis's *Commentary*," *Journal of the Warburg and Courtauld Institutes* 65 (2002): 1–21. See also, *Plato's Timaeus as Cultural Icon*, ed. Gretchen J. Reydams-Schils (Notre Dame, IN: University of Notre Dame Press, 2003).
19 Dominique Boutet, "Le prince au miroir de la littérature narrative (XIIe–XIIIe siècles)," in *Le Prince au miroir de la littérature politique de l'Antiquité aux Lumières*, eds. Frédérique Lachaud and Lydwine Scordia (Mont-Saint-Aignan: Publications des Universités de Rouen et du Havre, 2007), 143–59 at 149.
20 Oliver H. Prior, ed., *Caxton's Mirrour of the World* (London: Early English Text Society, 1913).
21 Robert Kilwardby, *De ortu scientiarum*, 128–29, quoted in Nicola Masciandaro, *The Voice of the Hammer: The Meaning of Work in Middle English Literature* (Notre Dame, IN: University of Notre Dame Press, 2007), 53.
22 Jonathan J. G. Alexander, "Labeur and Paresse: Ideological Representations of Medieval Peasant Labor," *Art Bulletin* 72, no. 3 (1990): 436–52.
23 Cited in G. R. Owst, *Literature and Pulpit in Medieval England* (New York: Barnes and Noble, 1961), 554.
24 Siegfried Wenzel, *The Sin of Sloth: Acedia in Medieval Thought and Literature* (1960; repr. Chapel Hill: University of North Carolina Press, 1967), 105.
25 George Norman Garmonsway, ed., *Aelfric's Colloquy* (London: Methuen and Co., 1939) and Michael Swanton, ed., *Anglo-Saxon Prose* (London: J. M. Dent, 1993), 169–77.
26 Richard Marks, "Sir Geoffrey Luttrell and Some Companions: Images of Chivalry c. 1320–50," *Wiener Jahrbuch für Kunstgeschichte* 46/47 (1993/4): 343–55 at 353.
27 Michael Camille, *Mirror in Parchment: The Luttrell Psalter and the Making of Medieval England* (London: Reaktion Press, 1998), 82–121.
28 Constable, *Three Studies*, 340.
29 Bruce M. S. Campbell, "The Land," 223.
30 J. P. C. Roach, "The City of Cambridge: Medieval history," in *A History of the County of Cambridge and the Isle of Ely: Volume 3, The City and University of Cambridge*, ed. J. P. C Roach (London: Published for the University of London Institute of Historical Research by the Oxford University Press, 1959), 2–15.
31 Constable, *Three Studies*, 340.

32 The four leaves are Paris, Bibliothèque de l'École nationale supérieure des beaux-arts, Mn. mas 90–93.
33 Timothy Husband and Gloria Gilmore-House, *The Wild Man: Medieval Myth and Symbolism* (New York: Metropolitan Museum of Art, 1980), 129–30.
34 Husband and Gilmore-House, *The Wild Man*, 201–02.
35 Ibid., 201.
36 A carpenter is also shown in the pen-and-ink sketch that accompanies the only surviving copy of the ballad in the fragmentary manuscript, Paris, Bibliothèque nationale de France, MS fr. 2374, fol. 1^v, which was made at roughly the same time as Bourdichon's miniature (c. 1500).
37 Masciandaro, *Voice of the Hammer*, 67.
38 Gen. 3:16–19, trans. Sharon Farmer, "Manual Labour, Begging, and Conflicting Gender Expectations in Thirteenth-Century Paris," in *Gender and Difference in the Middle Ages*, eds. Sharon A. Farmer and Carol Braun Pasternack (Minneapolis: University of Minnesota Press, 2003), 261–87 at 261.
39 For Eve spinning, see Kristin B. Aavitsland, *Imaging the Human Condition in Medieval Rome: The Cistercian Fresco Cycle at Abbazia delle Tre Fontane* (Farnham: Ashgate, 2012), 81–9.
40 Nigel J. Morgan, *Early Gothic Manuscripts 1250–1285 (II). A Survey of Manuscripts Illuminated in the British Isles 4* (London: Harvey Miller, 1988), 88–90, no. 118 and fig. 102.
41 See, for example, the Winchester Psalter (London, British Library, Cotton MS Nero C IV, fol. 2^r) cited by Nigel J. Morgan, "Old Testament Illustration in Thirteenth-Century England," in *The Bible in the Middle Ages: Its Influence on Literature and Art*, Medieval and Renaissance Texts and Studies 89, ed. Bernard S. Levy (Binghampton: State University of New York at Binghampton, 1992), 149–98 at 167, n. 44.
42 Morgan, "Old Testament Illustration," 166–7.
43 For Eve multitasking, see, for example, New York, Morgan Library and Museum, MS M 338, fol. 70^v. Additional examples are noted by Meredith Parsons Lillich, *The Gothic Stained Glass of Reims Cathedral* (University Park: Pennsylvania State University Press, 2011), 119–20.
44 *St Odo of Cluny. Being the Life of St. Odo of Cluny by John of Salerno and the Life of St. Gerard of Aurillac by St. Odo*, trans. and ed. Dom Gerard Sitwell (London: Sheed and Ward, 1958), bk. 1, chaps. 21, 114–15.
45 A bearded man, dressed in a monastic habit, is shown spinning in a Book of Hours made in Liège or Tournai, c. 1310–20 (London, British Library, Stowe MS 17, fol. 113^r), but this image is highly unusual. As illustrated by the story of Sardanapalus, the legendary king of Assyria, a man who took up spinning was reviled. See Deirdre Jackson, *Medieval Women* (London: British Library, 2015), 174–5.
46 Einhard, *Vita Karoli magni*, eds. Georg Heinrich Pertz and Georg Waltz, MGH SRG 25 (Hanover: Hahnsche Buchhandlung, 1911), chaps. 19, 23.
47 Merry E. Wiesner, "Spinsters and Seamstresses: Women in Cloth and Clothing Production," in *Rewriting the Renaissance: The Discourses of Sexual Difference in Early Modern Europe*, eds. Margaret W. Ferguson, Maureen Quilligan, and Nancy J. Vickers (Chicago, IL: University of Chicago Press, 1986), 202.
48 London, British Library, Add. MS 42130, fol. 166^v.

49 For example, woman chasing a fox. The Queen Mary Psalter, England, probably London, c. 1310–20. London, British Library, Royal MS 2 B. VII, fol. 158^r.
50 For example, woman beating a man with a distaff. Luttrell Psalter, England, Lincolnshire, c. 1340. London, British Library, Add. MS 42130, fol. 60^r.
51 Philippa A. Henry, "Who Produced the Textiles? Changing Gender Roles in Late Saxon Textile Production," in *Northern Archaeological Textiles: NESAT VII: Textile Symposium in Edinburgh, 5th–7th May 1999*, eds. Frances Pritchard and John Peter Wild (Oxford: Oxbow Books, 2005), 57.
52 Christine de Pizan, *Avision-Christine*, quoted by Deborah McGrady, "What is a Patron? Benefactors and Authorship in Harley 4431, Christine de Pizan's Collected Works," in *Christine de Pizan and the Categories of Difference*, Medieval Cultures 14, ed. Marilynn Desmond (Minneapolis: University of Minnesota Press, 1998), 195–214 at 199.
53 In Christine's *La mutacion de Fortune,* she describes her metaphorical transformation from a woman to a man after her husband died. Christine De Pizan, *Le livre de la mutacion de Fortune*, ed. Suzanne Solente, 4 vols. (Paris: Picard, 1959–1966; repri. New York, Johnson Reprint, 1965); trans. Renate Blumenfeld-Kosinski and Kevin Brownlee, *The Selected Writings of Christine de Pizan* (New York: Norton, 1997), 88–109. For surviving manuscripts, see James Laidlaw, "Christine and the Manuscript Tradition," *Christine de Pizan: A Casebook*, eds. Barbara K. Altmann and Deborah L. McGrady (New York: Routledge, 2003), 231–49.
54 Kathleen L. Scott, "Representations of Scribal Activity in English Manuscripts c. 1400–c. 1490: A Mirror of the Craft?," in *Pen in Hand: Medieval Scribal Portraits, Colophons and Tools*, ed. Michael Gullick (Walkern: The Red Gull Press, 2006), 115–49 at 120–1.
55 Christopher De Hamel, *The Book: A History of the Bible* (London: Phaidon, 2001), 82.
56 Orderic Vitalis, bk. IV, vol. ii, 360–1, cited by Michael T. Clanchy, *From Memory to Written Record: England 1066–1307*, 2nd ed. (Oxford: Blackwell, 1993), 116.
57 "Penna silens siste, laudes refero tibi Christe, Cesset onus triste, labor et liber explicit iste."
58 *Cassiodori senatoris Institutiones*, 1.30.1, quoted and trans. Bruce M. and Bart D. Ehrman, *The Text of the New Testament: Its Transmission, Corruption, and Restoration*, 4th ed. (Oxford: Oxford University Press, 2005), 29–30.
59 Bénédictines du Bouveret, *Colophons de manuscrits occidentaux des originies au XVIe siècle*, 6 vols. (Fribourg, Switzerland: Éditions universitaires, 1965–82), VI, 153, 237.
60 Melissa Moreton, "Pious Voices: Nun-scribes and the Language of Colophons in Late Medieval and Renaissance Italy," in *Essays in Medieval Studies* 29 (2014): 43–73 at 49.
61 Ibid., 49.
62 Quoted in T. A. Heslop, "Eadwine and his Portrait," in *The Eadwine Psalter: Text, Image, and Monastic Culture in Twelfth-Century Canterbury*, eds. Margaret Gibson, T. A. Heslop, and Richard Pfaff (London: Modern Humanities Research Association, 1992), 180.
63 For a reevaluation of the image, see Katherine S. Baker, "The Appended Images of the Eadwine Psalter: A New Appraisal of their Commemorative, Documentary, and Institutional Functions" (MA diss., Emory University, Atlanta, GA, 2008).
64 Richard Gameson, "The Image of the Illuminator," in *Colour: The Art and Science of Illuminated Manuscripts*, ed. Stella Panayotova with the assistance of Deirdre Jackson and Paola Ricciardi (London: Brepols and Harvey Miller, 2016), 74–82.
65 The image of Hildebertus occurs in a copy of Augustine's *City of God*, c. 1130 (Prague, Library of the Prague Metropolitan Chapter, MS Kap. A.xxi, fol. 153^r); the Bening portrait (P.159-1910) is held by the V&A Museum, London.

Chapter Three

1. Bas van Bavel, *Manors and Markets: Economy and Society in the Low Countries, 500–1600* (Oxford: Oxford University Press, 2010), 51–82, 76; Adriaan Verhulst, *The Carolingian Economy* (Cambridge: Cambridge University Press, 2002), 31–7.
2. University of Leicester, *Carolingian Polyptyques: Capitulare de Villis*. Available online: https://www.le.ac.uk/hi/polyptyques/capitulare/site.html (accessed 2015–2016), from Alfred Boretius, ed. *Monumenta Germaniae Historica* (MGH) Capit. 1 (Hanover: Hahnsche Buchhandlung, 1883), no. 32, 82–91, chaps. 5, 24, 34, and generally.
3. Ibid. For England, Christopher Dyer, *Making a Living in the Middle Ages: The People of Britain, 850–1520* (New Haven, CT: Yale University Press, 2002), 39–42, 64, 58–80; Henry Mayr-Harting, *The Coming of Christianity to Anglo-Saxon England* (University Park: The Pennsylvania State University Press, 1972, repre. 1994), 124–7. Also note gift exchanges in the letters of Boniface, an Anglo-Saxon missionary.
4. University of Leicester, *Carolingian Polyptyques: Wissembourg*. Available online:. Available online: www.le.ac.uk/hi/polyptyques/wissembourg/latin2english.html (accessed 2015–2016).
5. University of Leicester, *Carolingian Polyptyques: Bobbio I*. Available online: www.le.ac.uk/hi/polyptyques/bobbio1/latin2english.html); and University of Leicester, *Carolingian Polyptyques: Bobbio II*. Available online: https://www.le.ac.uk/hi/polyptyques/bobbio2/latin2english.html (accessed 2015–2016).
6. Verhulst, *Carolingian Economy*, 35.
7. *Bobbio I* and *II*.
8. *Bobbio I and II*.
9. Quoted in Gerald Hodgett, *A Social and Economic History of Medieval Europe* (London: Methuen & Co., 1972), 170.
10. See Dyer, *Making a Living*, 271–86, 330–62; Hodgett, *Social and Economic History*, 199–217; David Herlihy, *The Black Death and the Transformation of the West*, ed. Samuel K. Cohn (Cambridge, MA: Harvard University Press, 1997).
11. Steven A. Epstein, *An Economic and Social History of Later Medieval Europe, 1000–1500* (Cambridge: Cambridge University Press, 2009), 45–7; Hodgett, *Social and Economic History*, 21; Georges Duby, *The Early Growth of the European Economy: Warriors and Peasants from the Seventh to the Twelfth Century*, trans. Howard B. Clarke (Ithaca, NY: Cornell University Press, 1974), 17–24.
12. See the daily trading account of Domenico Lenzi in Giuliano Pinto, *Il Libro del biadaiolo: carestie e annona a Firenze dalla metà del '200 al 1348* (Florence: Leo S. Olschki, 1978).
13. Emmanuel LeRoy Ladurie, *Montaillou: Cathars and Catholics in a French Village, 1294–1324*, trans. Barbara Bray (London, Scholar Press, 1978), 3–5.
14. See Epstein, *Later Medieval Europe*, 45–7.
15. Dyer, *Making a Living*, 24; Lynn White, Jr., *Medieval Technology and Social Change* (London: Oxford University Press, 1962, repri. 1973), 39–78.
16. White, *Medieval Technology*, 39–78; Epstein, *Later Medieval Europe*, 45–7.
17. See, for example, *Wissembourg*.
18. Carlo Cipolla, *Before the Industrial Revolution: European Society and Economy, 1000–1700*, 3rd ed. (New York: W. W. Norton & Company, 1994), 140–3.
19. John Muendel, "The Internal Functions of a 14th-Century Florentine Flour Factory," *Technology and Culture* 32 (1991): 498–520.
20. Pamela Nightingale, *A Medieval Mercantile Community: The Grocers' Company and the Politics and Trade of London, 1000–1485* (New Haven, CT: Yale University Press, 1995), 6–22.

21 Peter Sawyer, "Markets and Fairs in Norway and Sweden Between the Eighth and Sixteenth Centuries," in *Markets in Early Medieval Europe: Trading and "Productive" Sites, 650–850*, eds. Tim Pestell and Katharine Ulmschneider (Bollington: Windgather Press, 2003), 168–74.
22 Jessica Dijkman, *Shaping Medieval Markets: The Organisation of Commodity Markets in Holland, c. 1200–c. 1450* (Leiden: Brill, 2011), 1–4.
23 Marc Bloch, *Feudal Society*, vol. 1, trans. L. A. Manyon (Chicago, IL: University of Chicago Press, 1961), 16–7, 15–38.
24 See the Bayeux Tapestry.
25 Charles D. Stanton, *Medieval Maritime Warfare* (Barnsley: Pen & Sword Maritime, 2015), 15, 111–35, 159–84; Frederic Chapin Lane, *Venice: A Maritime Republic* (Baltimore: Johns Hopkins University Press, 1973), 14, 163–4.
26 White, *Medieval Technology and Social Change*, 1–38; R. Allen Brown, *The Normans* (New York: St. Martin's Press, 1984), 33–9 and generally.
27 Brown, *Normans*, 39.
28 David S. Bachrach, "Crossbows for the King: The Crossbow during the Reigns of John and Henry III of England," *Technology and Culture* 45 (2004): 102–19 at 108.
29 Brown, *Normans*, 32–39. For armour, Christopher Allmand, *The Hundred Years' War: England and France at War, c. 1300–c. 1450* (Cambridge: Cambridge University Press, 1988–2001), 61, 66.
30 David S. Bachrach, "The Military Administration of England: The Royal Artillery (1216–1272)," *The Journal of Military History* 68 (2004): 1083–104.
31 For the extensive trading cities and products, see Francesco Balducci Pegolotti, *La pratica della mercatura*, ed. Allan Evans (Cambridge, MA: The Medieval Academy of America, 1936).
32 For changes in late medieval warfare, particularly in England and France, see Allmand, *The Hundred Years' War*, 37–53, 60–7, 73–6, 91–115, 123–50.
33 Adrian R. Bell, Chris Brooks, and Paul Dryburgh, "Advance Contracts for the Sale of Wool in Medieval England: An Undeveloped and Inefficient Market?" *ISMA Centre Discussion Papers in Finance DP2005-01*, February 2005. Available online: http://www.icmacentre.ac.uk/pdf/discussion/DP2005-01.pdf (accessed 2015–2016).
34 Richard W. Clement, "Medieval and Renaissance Book Production," Utah State University, *Library Faculty & Staff Publications*, Paper 10 (1997). Available online: http://digitalcommons.usu.edu/lib_pubs/10 (accessed 2015–2016); Raymond Clemens and Timothy Graham, *Introduction to Manuscript Studies* (Ithaca, NY and London: Cornell University Press, 2007), 3–17, 49–64.
35 Clement, "Book Production"; Clemens and Graham, *Manuscript Studies*, 18–48.
36 Timothy B. Husband, *The Art of Illumination: The Limbourg Brothers and the Belles Heures of Jean de France, Duc de Berry* (New York: The Metropolitan Museum of Art and New Haven, CT: Yale University Press, 2008), 59.
37 Robert S. Lopez, *The Commercial Revolution of the Middle Ages, 950–1350* (Englewood Cliffs, NJ: Prentice-Hall, 1971), 56–84, 85–147.
38 Dijkman, *Medieval Markets*, 4–5.
39 Cornelius Walford, "An Outline History of the Hanseatic League, More Particularly in Its Bearings upon English Commerce," *Transactions of the Royal Historical Society* 9 (1881): 82–136, at 91.
40 Dijkman, *Medieval Markets*, 110.
41 Walford, "Hanseatic League," 98.

42 Mike Burkhardt, "The German Hanse and Bergen—New Perspectives on an Old Subject," *Scandinavian Economic History Review* 58 (2010): 60–79, at 63.
43 Stephen R. Epstein, "Regional Fairs, Institutional Innovation, and Economic Growth in Late Medieval Europe," *The Economic History Review* 47 (1994): 459–82, at 470.
44 Nightingale, *London Grocers*, 35.
45 Ellen Wedemeyer Moore, *The Fairs of Medieval England: An Introductory Study* (Toronto: Pontifical Institute of Mediaeval Studies, 1985), 10–23, chap. 5; Dijkman, *Medieval Markets*, chap. 2.
46 Dijkman, *Medieval Markets*, 48.
47 Moore, *Fairs*, 22–3 and generally.
48 Ibid., Table 13, 47–59, 143–54 and generally.
49 Ibid.,150, 154–7.
50 Ibid., 47, 94, 156–66, chap. 4.
51 Nightingale, *London Grocers*, 66–8, 86–7, 166.
52 Moore, *Fairs*, 96–9.
53 Ibid., 34–5.
54 Nightingale, *London Grocers*, 64–5.
55 Moore, *Fairs*, 24–5.
56 Nightingale, *London Grocers*, 83–8, 136.
57 Moore, *Fairs*, 281–93 and R. D. Face, "Techniques of Business in the Trade between the Fairs of Champagne and the South of Europe in the Twelfth and Thirteenth Centuries," *The Economic History Review*, n.s., 10 (1958): 427–38.
58 Face, "Techniques of Business," 427, n. 2, 428.
59 Moore, *Fairs*, 159, 285, 288.
60 Face claims land transport; Lopez claims sea. Face, "Techniques of Business," 434, and R. D. Face, "The *Vectuarii* in the Overland Commerce between Champagne and Southern Europe," *The Economic History Review*, n.s., 12 (1959): 239–46 at 239.
61 Moore, *Fairs*, 284–8; Face, "Techniques of Business," 429, 438.
62 Face, "Techniques of Business," 430–36; and Face, "*Vectuarii*."
63 Face, "Techniques of Business," 437; Moore, *Fairs*, 288–9.
64 Dijkman, *Medieval Markets*, 55–6, 137, 60.
65 Epstein, "Regional Fairs," 463–4.
66 On consumerism, Susan Mosher Stuard, *Gilding the Market: Luxury and Fashion in Fourteenth-Century Italy* (Philadelphia: University of Pennsylvania Press, 2006), 1–55, 122–45 and generally.
67 Richard Goldthwaite, *The Building of Renaissance Florence: An Economic and Social History* (Baltimore: Johns Hopkins University Press, 1980), 288–301 and generally.
68 Ibid.,124 and generally.
69 Ibid., 171–203.
70 Ibid, 212–37, particularly 214–19, 227.
71 Ibid., 231–6, 240.
72 On Italian market spaces and monuments, Dennis Romano, *Markets and Marketplaces in Medieval Italy, c. 1100 to c. 1440* (New Haven, CT: Yale University Press, 2015), 13–70.
73 The discussion of the Florentine markets is adapted from Marie Ito, "Orsanmichele—The Florentine Grain Market: Trade and Worship in the Later Middle Ages" (PhD diss., The Catholic University of America, 2014). Available online: http://aladinrc.wrlc.org/handle/1961/15313; and Marie Ito, "A Public Presence: The Role of Women in Commerce

74 Antonio Pucci, "Proprietà di Mercato Vecchio," in *The Towns of Italy in the Later Middle Ages*, trans. Trevor Dean (Manchester: Manchester University Press, 2000), 121–4 at 122.
75 Ibid., 123.
76 Giovanni Villani, *Nuova cronica*, ed. Giovanni Porta (Parma: Ugo Guanda Editore, 1991), 12:94. Available online: http://www.classicitaliani.it/villani/cronica_12.htm (accessed 2015–2016), "Entravano del mese di luglio … CCCC some di poponi per dì," versus Carlo Cipolla, *Before the Industrial Revolution: European Society and Economy, 1000–1700*, 3rd edn. (New York: W. W. Norton & Company, 1994), 196.
77 From Domenico Lenzi's account in Pinto, *Biadaiolo*.
78 Pinto, *Biadaiolo*, 75–8. I have converted Pinto's 51,500 *moggia* into retail bushels.
79 John Muendel, "The Internal Functions of a 14th-Century Florentine Flour Factory," *Technology and Culture* 32 (1991): 498–520 at 501–2.
80 Romolo Caggese, ed., *Statuti della Republica fiorentina*, vol. 1: *Statuto del Capitano del Popolo del anni 1322–25*, new ed. with introduction and notes by Giuliano Pinto, Francesco Salvestrini, and Andrea Zorzi (Florence: Leo S. Olschki, 1999), bk. IV, chap. 31; bk. V, chap. 117 ("*Statuto 1322–1325*"); Francesca Morandini, ed., *Statuti delle arti degli oliandoli e pizzicagnoli e dei beccai di Firenze (1318–1346)* (Florence: Leo S. Olschki, 1961), 219, 1346 butchers' statutes, chap. 19.
81 Villani, *Cronica nuova*, 12:94; Cipolla, *Before the Industrial Revolution*, 195–6.
82 James M. Murray, *Bruges: Cradle of Capitalism, 1280–1390* (Cambridge: Cambridge University Press, 2005), 56, 59–61 and generally.
83 Ibid., 63–8, 72–7, 180.
84 Ibid., 111.
85 Jan Dumolyn, "Economic Development, Social Space and Political Power in Bruges, c. 1127–1302," in *Contact and Exchange in Later Medieval Europe: Essays in Honour of Malcolm Vale*, eds. Hannah Skoda et al. (Woodbridge: Boydell Press, 2012), 45, citing Thomas Boogaart.
86 Murray, *Bruges*, 77–80, 119–22, 182, 219, chap. 8; Barbara A. Hanawalt, *The Wealth of Wives: Women, Wealth, and Law in Late Medieval London* (New York: Oxford University Press, 2007), chap. 9.
87 Murray, Bruges, 109–10, 222–3, 304.
88 Maureen Fennell Mazzaoui, *The Italian Cotton Industry in the Later Middle Ages, 1100–1600* (Cambridge: Cambridge University Press, 1981), 36, 7–45.
89 Ibid., 29–33, 45, 102–3.
90 Ibid., 74–9, 87–104.
91 Dumolyn, "Economic Development," 46.
92 Murray, *Bruges*, 308–26.
93 See Gene A. Brucker, *Renaissance Florence* (Berkeley: University of California Press, 1969, 1983), 61–2. The Florentine trader Datini recorded pay differentials, translated in Dean, *The Towns of Italy*, 116–19.
94 See Romolo Caggese, ed., *Statuti della Republica fiorentina*, vol. 2: *Statuto dal Podestà dell'anno 1325*, new ed. with introduction and notes by Giuliano Pinto, Francesco Salvestrini, and Andrea Zorzi (Florence: Leo S. Olschki, 1999), bk. III, chap. 48 ("*Statuto 1325*"). On benches, Yvonne Elet, "Seats of Power: Benches in Early Modern Florence," *Journal of the Society of Architectural Historians*, 61 (2002): 444–69.

95 Robert Davidsohn, *Forschungen zur Geschichte von Florenz*, vol. 3 (Berlin: Ernst Siegfried Mittler and Son, 1901), 221–9; and generally Steven A. Epstein, *Wage Labor and Guilds in Medieval Europe* (Chapel Hill: University of North Carolina Press, 1991).
96 The discussion of Florentine women is adapted from Ito, "A Public Presence"; for Bruges, Murray, *Bruges*, 304–7, 300–26; for London, Hanawalt, *Wealth of Wives*, 3–13, 160–84, 208–16.
97 See Morandini, *Statuti*, "Oliandoli," 7 (1318 text), 87–8 (1345 text, opening clauses); Guido Pampaloni, "Il più antico statuto dell'arte degli oliandoli di Firenze," in *Saggi di Linguistica e Filologia Italiana e Romanza (1946–1976)*, vol. 2, ed. Arrigo Castellani (Rome: Salerno editrice, 1980), 150; Epstein, *Wage Labor and Guilds*, 210–11.
98 Morandini, *Statuti*, 195–259, butchers, for 1346.
99 Richard Marshall, *The Local Merchants of Prato: Small Entrepreneurs in the Late Medieval Economy* (Baltimore: Johns Hopkins University Press, 1999), 40.
100 Merry E. Wiesner, *Working Women in Renaissance Germany* (New Brunswick: Rutgers University Press, 1986), 32–3, 38–9, 55.
101 David Herlihy, *Opera Mulierbria: Women and Work in Medieval Europe* (New York: McGraw-Hill, 1990), 144–5.
102 Wiesner, *Germany*, 27.
103 *Statuto 1322–1325*, bk. I, chap. 17; bk. I, chap. 19; bk. I, chap. 21; bk. I, chap. 22.
104 Ibid., bk. I, chap. 39.
105 Ibid., bk. I, chap. 33; bk. I, chap. 42; *Statuto 1325*, bk. III, chap. 47.
106 Judith Bennett, *Ale, Beer and Brewsters in England: Women's Work in a Changing World, 1300–1600* (Oxford: Oxford University Press, 1996), 10–18, 31, 78–85.
107 Wiesner, *Germany*, 3.

Chapter Four

1 Dominique Cardon, *La draperie au Moyen Âge* (Paris: CNRS Éditions, 1999); Franco Franceschi, *Oltre il tumulto. I lavoratori dell'Arte della Lana fra Tre e Quattrocento* (Florence: Olschki Editore, 1993), 33–66.
2 John H. Munro, "Medieval Woollens: Textiles, Textile Technology and Industrial Organisation," in *The Cambridge History of Western Textiles*, ed. David Jenkins (Cambridge: Cambridge University Press, 2003), 181–227; Peter Stabel, "Les draperies urbaines en Flandre aux XIIIe–XVIe siècles," in *Wool: Products and Markets (13th–20th Century)*, ed. Giovanni Fontana (Padua: CLEUP, 2004), 355–80.
3 Peter Stabel, "The Market-Place and Civic Identity in Late Medieval Flanders," in *Shaping Urban Identity in Late Medieval Europe*, eds. Marc Boone and Peter Stabel (Leuven: Garant, 2000), 43–64.
4 Hugo Soly, "The Political Economy of Guild-Based Textile Industries: Power Relations and Economic Strategies of Merchants and Master Artisans in Medieval and Early Modern Europe," in *The Return of the Guilds*, eds. Jan Lucassen et al. (Cambridge: Cambridge University Press, 2008), 45–71.
5 Georges Espinas, *Les origines du capitalisme, 1. Sire Jehan Boinebroke* (Lille: E. Raoust, 1933); Hans van Werveke, *De Koopman-ondernemer en de ondernemer in de Vlaamsche lakennijverheid van de Middeleeuwen* (Brussels: Royal Academy, 1946).
6 Peter Stabel, "Labour Time, Guild Time? Working Hours in the Cloth Industry of Medieval Flanders and Artois," *Low Countries Journal of Social and Economic History* 11 (2014): 27–53.

7   Catharina Lis and Hugo Soly, *Worthy efforts: Attitudes to Work and Workers in Pre-industrial Europe* (Leiden: Brill, 2012), 342–9.
8   Peter Stabel, "The Move to Quality Cloth: Luxury Textiles, Labour Markets and Middle Class Identity in a Medieval Textile City. Mechelen in the Late Thirteenth and Early Fourteenth Centuries," in *Europe's Rich Fabric: The Consumption, Commercialisation, and Production of Luxury Textiles*, eds. Bart Lambert and Katherine Wilson (Farnham: Routledge, 2016), 159–80.
9   Marc Boone and Jelle Haemers, "The Common Good: Governance, Discipline and Political Culture," in *City and Society in the Low Countries*, eds. Bruno Blondé et al. (Cambridge: Cambridge University Press, forthcoming).
10 The "communal" movement also took root in the countryside. Peter Blickle, *Kommunalismus. Skizzen einer gesellschaftlichen Organisationsform* (Munich: Oldenbourg, 2000).
11 M. S. Kempshall, *The Common Good in Late Medieval Political Thought* (Oxford: Oxford University Press, 1999), 17.
12 Guido Alfani, "Economic Inequality in Northwestern Italy: A Long-Term View (Fourteenth to Eighteenth Centuries)," *Journal of Economic History* 75 (2015): 1058–96; Wouter Ryckbosch, "Economic Inequality and Growth before the Industrial Revolution: the Case of the Low Countries (14th–19th Centuries)," *European Review of Economic History* 20 (2016): 1–22.
13 Catharina Lis and Hugo Soly, "Subcontracting in Guild-Based Export Trades, 13th–18th Centuries," in *Guilds, Innovation, and the European Economy*, ed. Maarten Prak (Cambridge: Cambridge University Press, 2008), 81–113.
14 Peter Stabel, "Social Mobility and Apprenticeship in Late Medieval Flanders," in *Learning on the Shop Floor: Historical Perspectives on Apprenticeship*, eds. Bert De Munck et al. (New York: Berghahn, 2007), 158–78.
15 Peter Stabel, "Working Alone? Single Women and Economic Activity in the Cities of the County of Flanders (Early 13th–Early 15th century)," in *Singles in the Cities of North-West Europe*, eds. Julie De Groot et al. (London: Palgrave Macmillan, 2016), 27–49.
16 Our knowledge of rural work is framed by the best-studied case of medieval England. See John Hatcher and Mark Bailey, *Modelling the Middle Ages: The History and Theory of England's Economic Development* (Oxford: Oxford University Press, 2001).
17 Erik Thoen and Tim Soens, "The Family or the Farm: A Sophie's Choice? The Late Medieval Crisis in the Former County of Flanders," *The Medieval Countryside* 13 (2005): 195–224.
18 Robert Brenner, "Agrarian Class Structure and Economic Development in Pre-Industrial Europe," *Past and Present* 70 (1976): 30–74.
19 Adriaan Verhulst, *The Carolingian Economy* (Cambridge: Cambridge University Press, 2002), 11–22; Chris Wickham, *Framing the Early Middle Ages* (Oxford: Oxford University Press, 2005), 442–518; Jean-Pierre Devroey and Anne Nissen, "Early Middle Ages, 500–1000," in *Struggling with the Environment. Land Use and Productivity*, eds. Erik Thoen and Tim Soens (Turnhout: Brepols, 2015), 11–70.
20 Chris Wickham, *Medieval Europe* (New Haven, CT: Yale University Press, 2016), 104–10.
21 Guy Bois, *Crise du féodalisme. Economie rurale et démographie en Normandie orientale du début du XIVe siècle au milieu du XVIe siècle* (Paris: FNSP, 1976), 137–214.
22 Bruce Campbell et al., *A Medieval Capital and its Grain Supply: Agrarian Production and Distribution in the London Region, c. 1300* (London: Institute of British Geographers, 1993).
23 Richard H. Britnell, *The Commercialisation of English Society, 1000–1500* (Manchester: Manchester University Press, 1996), 79–81, 164–71.

24 Erik Thoen and Tim Soens, "Contextualizing 1500 Years of Agricultural Productivity and Land Use in the North Sea Area: Regionally Divergent Paths Towards the World Top," in *Struggling with the Environment*, eds. Erik Thoen and Tim Soen, 455–99.
25 Christopher Dyer, *Making a Living in the Middle Ages: The People of Britain 850–1520* (London: Penguin, 2002), 183–6, 346–62.
26 John Langdon, *Horses, Oxen and Technological Innovation: The Use of Draught Animals in English Farming from 1086 to 1500* (Cambridge: Cambridge University Press, 1986), 251.
27 Richard Jones, "Understanding Medieval Manure," in *Manure Matters: Historical and Ethnographic Perspectives*, ed. Richard Jones (Farnham: Ashgate, 2012), 145–58.
28 Sheilagh C. Ogilvie and Markus Cerman, eds., *European Proto-Industrialization* (Cambridge: Cambridge University Press, 1996), 140, 156–7.
29 Simon Penn and Christopher Dyer, "Wages and Earnings in Late Medieval England: Evidence from the Enforcement of the Labour Laws," *Economic History Review* 43 (1990): 356–76. See also Chapter Six in this volume.
30 Various contributions in Mireille Mousnier, ed., *L'artisan au village dans l'Europe médiévale et moderne* (Toulouse: Presses universitaires du Mirail, 2000).
31 Philipp Braunstein, *Travail et entreprise* (Brussels: De Boeck, 2003).
32 Verhulst, *Carolingian Economy*, 75–6.
33 Judith Bennett, *Ale, Beer, and Brewsters in England: Women's Work in a Changing World, 1300 to 1600* (Oxford: Oxford University Press, 1996).
34 Rudolf Holbach, *Frühformen von Verlag und Grossbetrieb in der gewerblichen Produktion (13.– 16. Jahrhundert)* (Stuttgart: Steiner, 1994), 47–8.
35 Bas van Bavel, *Manors and Markets: Economy and Society in the Low Countries 500–1600* (Oxford: Oxford University Press, 2010), 242–52.
36 Roland Recht, ed., *Les bâtisseurs des cathédrales gothiques* (Strasbourg: Musées de la ville de Strasbourg, 1989), 61–177.
37 On mobility and work more generally see Marianne O'Doherty and Felicitas Schmieder, eds., *Travels and Mobilities in the Middle Ages from the Atlantic to the Black Sea* (Turnhout: Brepols, 2015).
38 Jeroen Deploige and Peter Stabel, "Textile Entrepreneurs and Textile Workers," in *Golden Times: Wealth and Status in the Middle Ages*, eds. Véronique Lambert and Peter Stabel (Tielt: Lannoo, 2016), 240–81.
39 Lis and Soly, *Worthy Efforts*, 313–23.
40 David Herlihy, *Medieval Households* (Cambridge, MA: Harvard University Press, 1985), 131–56; Tine de Moor and Jan Luiten van Zanden, "Girl Power: The European Marriage Pattern and Labour Markets in the North Sea Region in the Late Medieval and Early Modern Period," *Economic History Review* 63 (2010): 1–33.
41 Stabel, "Working Alone," 38–49.
42 Gervase Rosser, "Crafts, Guilds, and the Negotiation of Work in the Medieval Town," *Past and Present* 154 (1997): 3–31.
43 Bert De Munck, "Fiscalizing Solidarity from Below: Poor Relief in Antwerp Guilds," in *Serving the Urban Community*, ed. Manon van der Heijden (Amsterdam: Aksant, 2009), 168–93.
44 Steven A. Epstein, *Wage Labor and Guilds in Medieval Europe* (Chapel Hill: University of North Carolina Press, 1991), 164–9.
45 Stabel, "Move to Quality Cloth," 159–80.
46 Patrick Lantschner, *The Logic of Political Conflict in Medieval Cities. Italy and the Southern Low Countries, 1370–1440* (Oxford: Oxford University Press, 2015), 44–5.

47 Jan Dumolyn, "Guild Politics and Political Guilds in Fourteenth-Century Flanders," in *The Voices of the People in Late Medieval Europe: Communication and Popular Politics*, eds. Jan Dumolyn et al. (Turnhout: Brepols, 2014), 15–48.
48 Stephan R. Epstein, "Craft Guilds, Apprenticeship and Technological Change in Preindustrial Europe," *Journal of Economic* History 58 (1998): 684–713.
49 Katherine Lynch, *Individuals, Families and Communities in Europe, 1200–1800: the Urban Foundations of Western Society* (Cambridge: Cambridge University Press, 2003).
50 Kim Overlaet, "Replacing the Family? Beguinages in Early Modern Western European Cities: An Analysis of the Family Networks of Beguines Living in Mechelen (1532–1591)," *Continuity and Change* 29 (2014): 325–47.
51 Lis and Soly, *Worthy Efforts*, 451–68.
52 Peter Stabel, "Guilds in Late Medieval Flanders: Myths and Realities of Guild Life in an Export-Oriented Environment," *Journal of Medieval History* 30 (2004): 187–212.
53 See Chapter Five in this volume.
54 For an introduction to the literature: James R. Farr, *Artisans in Europe 1300–1914* (Cambridge: Cambridge University Press 2000) and Lucassen, *Return of the Guilds*.
55 James Davis and Peter Stabel, "Formal and Informal Trade in the Late Middle Ages. The Islamic World and Northwest Europe Compared," in *Il commercio al minuto. Domanda e offerta tra economia formale e informale*, ed. Giampiero Nigro (Florence: Florence University Press), 15–37.
56 For the controversy between guild pessimists and optimists: Stephan R. Epstein, "Craft Guilds in the Premodern Economy: a Comment," *Economic History Review* 61 (2008): 155–74; Sheilagh Ogilvie, "Rehabilitating the Guilds: A Reply," *Economic History Review* 61 (2008): 175–82.
57 Myriam Carlier and Peter Stabel, "Questions de moralité dans les villes de la Flandre au bas moyen âge: sexualité et activité urbaine (bans échevinaux et statuts de métiers)," in *Faire Banz, edictz et statuts: légiférer dans la ville médiévale*, ed. Jean-Marie Cauchies (Brussels: FUSL, 2002), 241–62.
58 Various contributions in De Munck, *Learning on the Shop Floor*.
59 Martha Howell, *Production and Patriarchy in Late Medieval Cities* (Chicago, IL: Chicago University Press, 1986); Claire Crowston, "Women, Gender and Guilds in Early Modern Europe: An Overview of Recent Research," in *Return of the Guilds*, ed. Lucassen, 19–44.
60 Sharon Farmer, *The Silk Industries of Medieval Paris: Artisanal Migration, Technological Innovation, and Gendered Experience* (Philadelphia: University of Pennsylvania Press, 2016), 106–36; Margaret Wensky, "Women's Guilds in Cologne in the Later Middle Ages," *Journal of European Economic History* 11 (1982): 631–50.
61 Stabel, "Working Alone," 27–49.
62 Gervase Rosser, *The Art of Solidarity in the Middle Ages: Guilds in England 1250–1550* (Oxford: Oxford University Press, 2015).
63 Stabel, *Guilds*, 187–212.
64 Peter Arnade and Walter Prevenier, *Honor, Vengeance, and Social Trouble: Pardon Letters in the Burgundian Low Countries* (Ithaca, NY: Cornell University Press, 2015), 2, 49–52; Inneke Baatsen and Anke De Meyer, "Forging or Reflecting Multiple Identities? Analyzing Processes of Identification in a Sample of Fifteenth-Century Letters of Remission from Bruges and Mechelen," *Revue du Nord* 30 (2014): 23–39; Jan Dumolyn, "Let Each Man Carry on with His Trade and Remain Silent: Middle Class Ideology in the Urban Literature of the Late Medieval Low Countries," *Cultural and Social History* 10 (2013): 169–89.

Chapter Five

1. Lynn White, Jr., *Medieval Technology and Social Change* (Oxford: Oxford University Press, 1962). See also his *Medieval Religion and Technology: Collected Essays* (Berkeley: University of California Press, 1978). For a recent historiographical appreciations, see Shana Worthen, "The Influence of Lynn White, Jr.'s *Medieval Technology and Social Change*," *History Compass* 7, no. 4 (2009): 1201–17.
2. Michael Toch, "Agricultural Progress and Technology in Medieval Germany: An Alternative Model," in *Technology and Resource Use in Medieval Europe*, eds. Elizabeth Bradford Smith and Michael Wolfe (Aldershot: Ashgate, 1997), 160.
3. Pamela O. Long, "Invention, Secrecy, and Theft: Meaning and Context in the Study of Late Medieval Technical Transmission," *History and Technology* 16 (2000): 223–41 at 237.
4. See the contributions by Bruce Campbell, Mavis Mate, and John Langdon in *Medieval Farming and Technology: The Impact of Agricultural Change in Northwest Europe*, ed. Grenville Astill and John Langdon (Leiden: Brill, 1997).
5. Adam Robert Lucas, "Industrial Milling in the Ancient and Medieval Worlds: A Survey of the Evidence for an Industrial Revolution in Medieval Europe," *Technology and Culture* 46, no. 1 (2005): 1–30 at 18.
6. Jan Klápště and Petr Sommer, eds., *Arts and Crafts in Medieval Rural Environment*, Ruralia 6 (Turnhout: Brepols, 2007).
7. Janet Snyder, "On the Road Again: Limestone Sculpture in Twelfth-Century France," in *Working with Limestone: The Science, Technology and Art of Medieval Limestone Monuments*, ed. Vibeke Olson (Farnham: Ashgate, 2011), 167–88.
8. Steven R. Epstein, "Craft Guilds, Apprenticeship, and Technological Change in Pre-Industrial Europe," *The Journal of Economic History* 58, no. 3 (1998): 684–713 at 684–5.
9. Long, "Invention, Secrecy, and Theft," 224–5.
10. Michael J. T. Lewis, "The Origins of the Wheelbarrow," *Technology and Culture* 35, no. 3 (1994): 453–75 at 453, 456, 465–70.
11. Andrea L. Matthies, "The Medieval Wheelbarrow," *Technology and Culture* 32, no. 2, Part 1 (1991): 356–64.
12. Eva Anderson, *Tools for Textile Production from Birka and Hedeby* (Stockholm: The Birka Project, 2003), 27–29, 150–1.
13. Ruth Mazo Karras, "'This Skill in a Woman is By No Means to Be Despised': Weaving and the Gender Division of Labor in the Middle Ages," in *Medieval Fabrications: Dress, Textiles, Clothwork, and Other Cultural Imaginings*, ed. E. Jane Burns (New York: Palgrave, 2004), 94–7.
14. Patrice Beck, Philippe Braunstein, and Michel Philippe, "Wood, Iron, and Water in the Othe Forest in the Late Middle Ages: New Findings and Perspectives," in *Technology and Resource Use*, eds. Smith and Wolfe, 173–7.
15. Rudolf Palme, "Alpine Salt Mining in the Middle Ages," *Journal of European Economic History* 19, no. 1 (1990): 117–36 at 117, 121–6, 130, 133–4.
16. Cedric E. Gregory, *A Concise History of Mining (Revised Edition)* (Lisse: A. A. Balkema Publishers, 2001), 108–10; Richard C. Hoffmann, *An Environmental History of Medieval Europe* (Cambridge: Cambridge University Press, 2014), 216–9.
17. Lucas, "Industrial Milling," 22.
18. Gerhard Dohrn-van Rossum, *History of the Hour: Clocks and Temporal Orders*, trans. Thomas Dunlap (Chicago, IL: University of Chicago Press, 1996, c. 1992), 305–7.
19. Most prominently White, *Medieval Technology and Social Change*, 39–41.

20 See Figure 3.1.
21 Georges Comet, "Technology and Agricultural Expansion in the Middle Ages: The Example of France North of the Loire," in *Medieval Farming and Technology*, eds. Astill and Langdon, 22–5; Bjørn Poulsen, "Agricultural Technology in Medieval Denmark," in Ibid., 132–3; and Janken Myrdal, "The Agricultural Transformation of Sweden, 1000–1300," in Ibid., 153–60; Joachim Henning, "Revolution or Relapse? Technology, Agriculture and Early Medieval Archaeology in Germanic Central Europe," in *The Langobards Before the Frankish Conquest: An Ethnographic Perspective*, eds. Giorgio Ausenda et al. (Woodbridge: Boydell Press, 2009), 152–62.
22 Poulsen, "Agricultural Technology," 134.
23 John Langdon, *Horses, Oxen and Technological Innovation: The Use of Draught Animals in English Farming from 1066 to 1500* (Cambridge: Cambridge University Press, 1986), 9–14.
24 Toch, "Agricultural Progress," 161; Georges Raepsaet, "The Development of Farming Implements Between the Seine and the Rhine from the Second to the Twelfth Centuries," in *Medieval Farming and Technology*, eds. Astill and Langdon, 57–8.
25 Poulsen, "Agricultural Technology," 133–4.
26 Comet, "Technology and Agricultural Expansion," 29–30.
27 Erik Thoen, "The Birth of 'the Flemish Husbandry'," in *Medieval Farming and Technology*, eds. Astill and Langdon, 74–85.
28 Peter Hoppenbrouwers, "Agricultural Production and Technology in the Netherlands," in *Medieval Farming and Technology*, eds. Astill and Langdon, 96–101, 106, 109.
29 George C. Maniatis, "The Byzantine Olive Oil Press Industry: Organization, Technology, Pricing Strategies," *Byzantion* 82 (2012): 259–77 at 259–69.
30 Expiracíon García Sánchez, "Agriculture in Muslim Spain," in *The Legacy of Muslim Spain*, ed. Salma Khadra Jayyusi (Leiden: Brill, 1992), 987–99; Comet, "Technology and Agricultural Expansion," 12–13.
31 Lewis Mumford, *Technics and Civilization* (New York: Harcourt, Brace and Company, 1934), 113–18.
32 Marc Bloch, "Avènement et conquêtes du moulin à eau," *Annales d'histoire économique et sociale* 7 (1935): 538–63, later translated to English as "The Advent and Triumph of the Watermill," in *Land and Work in Mediaeval Europe: Selected Papers by Marc Bloch*, trans. J. E. Anderson (Berkeley: University of California Press, 1967), 136–68.
33 For more on ancient and medieval mills, see Adam Lucas, *Wind, Water, Work: Ancient and Medieval Milling Technology* (Leiden: Brill, 2006).
34 Paolo Squatriti, "Water Mills in Italy," in *Technology and Resource Use*, eds. Smith and Wolfe, 130–1.
35 Ibid., 127–36.
36 Colin Rynne, "Waterpower in Medieval Ireland," in *Working With Water in Medieval Europe*, ed. Paolo Squatriti (Leiden: Brill, 2000), 1–50.
37 Philip Rahtz and Robert Meeson, *An Anglo-Saxon Watermill at Tamworth*, CBA Research Report 83 (London: Council for British Archaeology, 1992), 14.
38 Richard Holt, "Mechanization and the Medieval English Economy," in *Technology and Resource Use*, eds. Smith and Wolfe, 139, 145–9.
39 Sophia Germanidou, "Watermills in Byzantine Greece (Fifth to Twelfth Centuries): A Preliminary Approach to the Archaeology of Byzantine Hydraulic Milling Technology," *Byzantion* 84 (2014): 185–201 at 187–8, 195–200.
40 Thomas F. Glick, "Hydraulic Technology in al-Andalus," in *The Legacy of Muslim Spain*, ed. Jayyusi, 974–86.

41 Thomas F. Glick and Helena Kirchner, "Hydraulic Systems and Technologies of Islamic Spain: History and Archaeology," in *Working with Water*, ed. Squatriti, 292–302, 313–15.
42 Paul Benoit and Joséphine Rouillard, "Medieval Hydraulics in France," in *Working with Water*, ed. Squatriti, 194–7; Comet, "Technology and Agricultural Expansion," 31; Lucas, "Industrial Milling," 14–15.
43 Lucas, "Industrial Milling," 15–16.
44 Eleanora Carus-Wilson, "An Industrial Revolution of the Thirteenth Century," *Economic History Review* 11 (1941): 39–60; Holt, "Mechanization and the Medieval English Economy," 150–4; Benoit and Rouillard, "Medieval Hydraulics in France," 193.
45 Dohrn-van Rossum, *History of the Hour*, 35–7, 64.
46 *Royal Frankish Annals*, in *Carolingian Chronicles*, trans. Bernhard Walter Scholz (Ann Arbor: University of Michigan Press, 1970), 87.
47 Among the most influential advocates of this idea is Jacques Le Goff, *Time, Work, and Culture in the Middle Ages*, trans. Arthur Goldhammer (Chicago, IL: University of Chicago Press, 1980), 29–57.
48 Dohrn-van Rossum, *History of the Hour*, 94, 134–52.
49 Ingo Schwab, ed., *Das Prümer Urbar* (Düsseldorf: Droste Verlag, 1983), 166–255.
50 Dohrm-van Rossum, *History of the Hour*, 290–315.
51 Robert Mark, "Technological Innovation in High Gothic Architecture," in *Technology and Resource Use*, eds. Smith and Wolfe, 12–18, 23–5.
52 Dieter Kimpel examined this issue in a number of publications, first in "Le développement de la taille en série dans l'architecture médiévale et son rôle dans l'histoire économique," *Bulletin monumental* 135, no. 3 (1977): 195–222 and more recently in "Les méthodes de production des cathédrales," in *Les bâtisseurs des cathédrales gothiques*, ed. Roland Recht (Strasbourg: Editions des musées de la ville de Strasbourg, 1989), 91–100.
53 Vibeke Olson, "The Whole is the Sum of its Parts: Standardizing Medieval Stone Production," in *Working with Limestone*, ed. Olson, 193–203.
54 Lynn T. Courtenay, "Scale and Scantling: Technological Issues in Large-Scale Timberwork of the High Middle Ages," in *Technology and Resource Use*, eds. Smith and Wolfe, 42–75.
55 Long, "Invention, Secrecy, and Theft," 224, 231–3.
56 Epstein, "Craft Guilds," 687–8.
57 Valerie L. Garver, *Women and Aristocratic Culture in the Carolingian World* (Ithaca, NY: Cornell University Press, 2009), 228–33.
58 Nigel Hiscock, "Discipline and Freedom in the Shaping of Stone: The Interface of Architecture, Structure and Sculpture in the Late Middle Ages," in *Working with Limestone*, ed. Olson, 242–8.
59 Derek Keene, "The Textile Industry," in *Object and Economy in Medieval Winchester*, vol. 1, ed. Derek Keene (Oxford: Clarendon Press, 1990), 203–8.
60 C. Fortina, I. Memmi Turbanti, and F. Grassi, "Glazed Ceramic Manufacturing in Southern Tuscany (Italy): Evidence of Technological Continuity throughout the Medieval Period (10th–14th Centuries)," *Archaeometry* 50, no. 1 (2008): 30–47.
61 W. Patrick McCray, "Creating Networks of Skill: Technology Transfer and the Glass Industry of Venice," *Journal of European Economic History* 28 (1999): 301–33 at 303–10, 313–14.
62 Long, "Invention, Secrecy, and Theft," 228–9.
63 Ibid., 228–9.
64 McCray, "Creating Networks," 309, 313–17.

65 Kelly DeVries and Robert Douglas Smith, *Medieval Military Technology*, 2nd ed. (Toronto: University of Toronto Press, 2012), 36–9.
66 *History and Politics in Late Carolingian and Ottonian Europe: The* Chronicle *of Regino of Prüm and Adalbert of Magdeburg*, trans. Simon MacLean (Manchester: Manchester University Press, 2009), 185.
67 For a key reassessment of this tactic's influence, see Bernard S. Bachrach, "Charles Martel, Mounted Shock Combat, the Stirrup, and Feudalism," *Studies in Medieval and Renaissance History* 7 (1970): 49–75.
68 DeVries and Smith, *Medieval Military Technology*, 38–41.
69 Kelly DeVries, "Catapults are not Atomic Bombs: Towards a Redefinition of 'Effectiveness' in Premodern Military Technology," *War in History* 4 (1997): 454–70 at 464–9.
70 Walter Berry, "Use and Non-Use of Limestone in Romanesque Burgundy: The Example of Autun," in *Working with Limestone*, ed. Olson, 155–6.

Chapter Six

1 The topic for the 2017 Conference of the Australian and New Zealand Association of Medieval and Early Modern Studies, for instance, is "Mobility and Exchange."
2 Geoffrey Chaucer, *The Riverside Chaucer*, ed. Larry Dean Benson (Oxford: Oxford University Press, 2008).
3 Florin Curta, ed., *Neglected Barbarians* (Turnhout: Brepols, 2010).
4 Julia M. H. Smith, *Europe after Rome: A New Cultural History 500–1000* (Oxford: Oxford University Press, 2005), 152–3.
5 Edward A. Wrigley and Roger S. Schofield, *The Population History of England, 1541–1871: A Reconstruction* (London: Edward Arnold, 1981), 15–16.
6 John Hatcher and Mark Bailey, *Modelling the Middle Ages: The History and Theory of England's Economic Development* (Oxford: Oxford University Press, 2001), 7–10.
7 See, for instance, Gregory Clark, "The Long March of History: Farm Wages, Population, and Economic Growth, England 1209–1869," *Economic History Review* 60, no. 1 (2007): 97–135; and a prototype of such work: Ernest H. Phelps-Brown and Sheila Hopkins, "Seven Centuries of the Prices of Consumables, Compared with Builders' Wage Rates," *Economica* 92 (1956): 296–314.
8 Maryanne Kowaleski, *Local Markets and Regional Trade in Medieval Exeter* (Cambridge: Cambridge University Press, 1995), 371. See copies of the documents in Margery M. Rowe, ed., *Tudor Exeter: Tax Assessments 1489–1595, Including the Military Survey 1522* (Exeter: Devon and Cornwall Record Society, 1977).
9 Nicholas Orme, *The Churches of Medieval Exeter* (Exeter: Impress Books, 2014), 2–3.
10 Mark Bailey, *The Decline of Serfdom in Late Medieval England: From Bondage to Freedom* (Woodbridge: Boydell & Brewer, 2014).
11 Stephen R. Epstein, *An Island for Itself: Economic Development and Social Change in Late Medieval Sicily* (Cambridge: Cambridge University Press, 1992), 329–31.
12 Ferran Garcia-Oliver, *The Valley of the Six Mosques: Work and Life in Medieval Valldigna* (Turnhout: Brepols, 2012), 196.
13 Ibn Fadlān, *Ibn Fadlān and the Land of Darkness, Arab Travellers in the Far North*, trans. and eds. Paul Lunde and Caroline Stone (London: Penguin, 2012), 40.
14 Gerald of Wales, *The Journey Through Wales and The Description of Wales*, trans. Lewis Thorpe (London: Penguin, 1978), 24–45.
15 Richard A. McKinley, *The Surnames of Norfolk and Suffolk in the Middle Ages* (London: Phillimore, 1975), 78–9.

16 Marisa Bueno Sánchez, "Power and Rural Communities in the Banū Salīm Area (Eighth–Eleventh Centuries): Peasant and Frontier Landscapes as Social Construction," in *Power and Rural Communities in Al-Andalus: Ideological and Material Representations*, eds. Adela Fábregas and Flocel Sabaté, TMC 15 (Turnhout: Brepols, 2015), 39–41.

17 Christopher Dyer, *An Age of Transition? Economy and Society in England in the Later Middle Ages* (Oxford: Oxford University Press, 2005), 36; Lawrence R. Poos, "Population Turnover in Medieval Essex," in *The World We Have Gained: Histories of Population and Social Structure*, eds. Lloyd Bonfield, Richard M. Smith, and Keith Wrightson (Oxford: Basil Blackwell, 1986), 1–22.

18 Mark Bailey, *Medieval Suffolk: An Economic and Social History, 1200–1500* (Woodbridge: Boydell Press, 2007), 162.

19 Christopher Dyer, *Making a Living in the Middle Ages: The People of Britain 850–1520* (New Haven, CT: Yale University Press, 2002), 62–3, 68.

20 David Nicholas, *The Later Medieval City: 1300–1500* (London: Routledge, 1997), 53–8.

21 Nicholas Dean Brodie, "'The Names of All the Poore People': Corporate and Parish Relief in Exeter, 1560s–1570s," in *Experiences of Poverty in Late Medieval and Early Modern England and France*, ed. Anne M. Scott (Farnham: Ashgate, 2012), 107–31.

22 Corine Maitte, "The Cities of Glass: Privileges and Innovations in Early Modern Europe," in *Innovation and Creativity in Late Medieval and Early Modern European Cities*, eds. Karel Davids and Bert De Munk (London: Routledge, 2014), 35–54.

23 Anu Lahtinen, "'A Knight from Flanders': Noble Migration and Integration in the North in the Late Middle Ages," in *Immigration/Emigration in Historical Perspective*, ed. Ann Katherine Issacs (Pisa: Pisa University Press, 2007), 79–92.

24 Heinrich Härke, "Archaeologists and Migrations: A Problem of Attitude," in *From Roman Provinces to Medieval Kingdoms*, ed. Thomas F. X. Noble (New York: Routledge, 2006), 262–76.

25 Jean W. Sedlar, *East Central Europe in the Middle Ages, 1000–1500* (Seattle: University of Washington Press, 1994), 408.

26 Art Cosgrove, *A New History of Ireland, Volume II: Medieval Ireland 1169–1534* (Oxford: Oxford University Press, 1987), 447–8.

27 Nickiphoros I. Tsougarakis, *The Latin Religious Orders in Medieval Greece, 1204–1500* (Turnhout: Bretpols, 2012), xviii–xxii, 275–310.

28 Robin R. Mundill, *England's Jewish Solution: Experiment and Expulsion, 1262–1290* (Cambridge: Cambridge University Press, 1998), 1–15.

29 Brian A. Catlos, *Muslims of Medieval Latin Christendom, c. 1050–1614* (Cambridge: Cambridge University Press, 2014), 174.

30 Yaron Matras, *The Romani Gypsies* (Cambridge, MA: Belknap Press, 2015).

31 Nicholas Dean Brodie, "Beggary, Vagabondage, and Poor Relief: English Statutes in the Urban Context" (PhD diss., University of Tasmania, 2010).

32 Sidney Webb and Beatrice Webb, *English Local Government: English Poor Law History, Part I, the Old Poor Law* (London: Longmans, 1927), v–xx.

33 David R. Carr, ed., *The First General Entry Book of the City of Salisbury, 1387–1452*, Wiltshire Record Society 54 (Salisbury: Wiltshire Record Society, 2001), 243.

34 Brodie, "Beggary, Vagabondage, and Poor Relief," 75–80.

35 See, for instance, Nancy Edwards, *The Archaeology of Early Medieval Ireland* (New York: Routledge, 1999), 49–67; Günter P. Fehring, *The Archaeology of Medieval Germany: An Introduction*, trans. Ross Samson (London, Routledge, 2015), 171–4.

36 W. G. Hoskins, *The Making of the English Landscape* (Middlesex: Penguin, 1970), 45–136.

37 Francis Prior, *Britain in the Middle Ages: An Archaeological History* (London: Harper Perennial, 2007), 108–43, 223–56.
38 Erik Thoen, "The Birth of 'The Flemish Husbandry': Agricultural Technology in Medieval Flanders," in *Medieval Farming and Technology: The Impact of Agricultural Change in Northwest Europe*, eds. Grenville Astill and John Langdon (Leiden: Brill, 1997), 69–88.
39 Nicholas Dean Brodie, "Reassessing 27 Henry VIII, c. 25 and Tudor Welfare: Changes and Continuities in Context," *Parergon* 31, no. 1 (2014): 111–36.
40 Christopher Dyer, *Standards of Living in the Later Middle Ages: Social Change in England c. 1200–1520*, rev. ed. (Cambridge: Cambridge University Press, 1998), 158–60: citing himself: Christopher Dyer, "Changes in Diet in the Late Middle Ages: the Case of Harvest Workers," *Agricultural History Review* 36 (1988), 21–37.
41 David Stone, *Decision-Making in Medieval Agriculture* (Oxford: Oxford University Press, 2005), 148.
42 Dyer, *Making a Living*, 125.
43 Paul B. Newman, *Growing up in the Middle Ages* (Jefferson: McFarland & Co., 2007), 172.
44 Ian Gordon Summers, *The Moorlands of England and Wales: An Environmental History 8000 BC–AD 2000* (Edinburgh: Edinburgh University Press, 2003), 65.
45 Joseph F. O'Callaghan, *A History of Medieval Spain* (Ithaca, NY: Cornell University Press, 1975), 478.
46 Jenny Kermode, *Medieval Merchants: York, Beverley and Hull in the Later Middle Ages* (Cambridge: Cambridge University Press, 1998), 251; Marco Polo, *The Travels*, trans. and ed. Ronald Latham (London: Penguin, 1958).
47 Mark R. Cohen, *Under Crescent and Cross: The Jews in the Middle Ages* (Princeton, NJ: Princeton University Press, 1994), 79–82.
48 Margaret Labarge, *A Medieval Miscellany* (Ottawa: Carleton University Press, 1997), 204.
49 H. S. Bennett, *The Pastons and their England* (Cambridge: Cambridge University Press, 2003), 120–4.
50 Colum Hourihane, *The Mason and His Mark: Mason's Marks in the Medieval Irish Archbishoprics of Cashel and Dublin* (Oxford: John and Erica Hedges and Archaeopress, 2000).

Chapter Seven

1 Peter Brown, *Through the Eye of a Needle: Wealth, the Fall of Rome, and the Making of Christianity in the West, 350–550 AD* (Princeton, NJ: Princeton University Press, 2012), 68–9.
2 Lester K. Little, *Religious Poverty and the Profit Economy in Medieval Europe* (1978; repr. Ithaca, NY: Cornell University Press, 1983).
3 James William Brodman, *Charity and Welfare: Hospitals and the Poor in Medieval Catalonia* (Philadelphia: University of Pennsylvania Press, 1998), 136–8.
4 Elma Brenner, "The Care of the Sick and Needy in Twelfth- and Thirteenth-Century Rouen," in *Society and Culture in Medieval Rouen, 911–1300*, eds. Leonie V. Hicks and Elma Brenner (Turnhout: Brepols, 2013), 342.
5 Bronislaw Geremek, *Poverty: A History*, trans. Agnieszka Kolokowska (1989; trans. Oxford: Blackwell Publishers, 1994), 16–17.
6 Quotations are from the Douay-Rheims translation of the Vulgate.
7 Geremek, *Poverty*, 16–20; Miri Rubin, *Charity and Community in Medieval Cambridge* (Cambridge: Cambridge University Press, 1987), 4–15; Michel Mollat, *The Poor in the Middle Ages: An Essay in Social History*, trans. Arthur Goldhammer (1978; trans. New

Haven, CT: Yale University Press, 1986). On Carolingian attitudes, Rachel Stone, *Morality and Masculinity in the Carolingian Empire* (Cambridge: Cambridge University Press, 2012), 215 and 235.
8   Rubin, *Charity and Community*, 15. On cycles of shortfall and plenty, see Sharon Farmer, *Surviving Poverty in Medieval Paris: Gender, Ideology, and the Daily Lives of the Poor* (Ithaca, NY: Cornell University Press, 2002), 63.
9   Andrew Brown, *Civic Ceremony and Religion in Medieval Bruges* c. *1300–1520* (Cambridge: Cambridge University Press, 2011), 208.
10 Mollat, *The Poor in the Middle Ages*, 32.
11 Ibid., 105.
12 Geremek, *Poverty*, 54–5.
13 Ibid., 18.
14 Mollat, *The Poor in the Middle Ages*, 70–1.
15 Brian Tierney, *Medieval Poor Law: A Sketch of Canonical Theory and Its Application in England* (Berkeley: University of California Press, 1959), 55; Geremek, *Poverty*, 26.
16 Rubin, *Charity and Community*, 70–1.
17 Tierney, *Medieval Poor Law*, 53–60 and Brian Tierney, "The Decretists and the 'Deserving Poor'," *Comparative Studies in Society and History* 1, no. 4 (1959): 360–73.
18 Geremek, *Poverty*, 70–1.
19 Mollat, *The Poor in the Middle Ages*, 106.
20 On men disguised as beggars, see Mollat, *The Poor in the Middle Ages*, 109–10; and Farmer, *Surviving Poverty in Medieval Paris*, 62–7.
21 Marjorie Keniston McIntosh, *Poor Relief in England, 1350–1600* (Cambridge: Cambridge University Press, 2012), 4–10.
22 James William Brodman, *Charity and Religion in Medieval Europe* (Washington, DC: The Catholic University of America Press, 2009; eBook, 2011); James G. Clark, *The Benedictines in the Middle Ages* (Woodbridge: Boydell Press, 2011), 167–9.
23 Brodman, *Charity and Welfare*, 3.
24 I use the capitalized term "Hospitaller" to refer to the Knights of the Hospital of Saint John in Jerusalem and the lower-case term "hospitaller" to refer to the variety of religious who founded and worked in hospitals while living in community, typically following the religious Rule of Saint Augustine. Brodman, *Charity and Religion*, 9, 93–4.
25 Ibid., 223–6.
26 Mollat, *The Poor in the Middle Ages*, 87, 135–44; Clark, *The Benedictines in the Middle Ages*, 182–3. On captives and the redeeming orders, Jarbel Rodriguez, *Captives and their Saviors in the Medieval Crown of Aragon* (Washington, DC: The Catholic University of America Press, 2007).
27 Mollat, *The Poor in the Middle Ages*, 147. Note that the English translation has "Crusaders," not Croziers, which is the word used in the French (*Croisiers*), and refers to a branch of hospitallers.
28 Clark, *The Benedictines in the Middle Ages*, 184.
29 Anne E. Lester, "Cares Beyond the Walls: Cistercian Nuns and the Care of Lepers in Twelfth- and Thirteenth-Century Northern France," in *Religious and Laity in Western Europe, 1000–1400: Interaction, Negotiation, and Power*, eds. J. Burton and E. Jamroziak (Turnhout: Brepols, 2006), 197–224; Burton and Kerr, *The Cistercians in the Middle Ages*, 194.
30 Clark, *The Benedictines in the Middle Ages*, 186.

31 Brown, *Through the Eye of a Needle*.
32 Brodman, *Charity and Religion*, 50; Mollat, *The Poor in the Middle Ages*, 38.
33 Stone, *Morality and Masculinity*, 241.
34 Brodman, *Charity and Religion*, 50–1.
35 Nicholas Orme and Margaret Webster, *The English Hospital, 1070–1570* (New Haven, CT: Yale University Press, 1995), specifically 1 and 58, and *passim*.
36 Mollat, *The Poor in the Middle Ages*, 147.
37 Rubin, *Charity and Community*, 100–1.
38 Ibid., 111–13, 119.
39 Ibid., 104.
40 Brodman, *Charity and Welfare*, 73.
41 Rubin, *Charity and Community*, 150–1.
42 Brodman, *Charity and Welfare*, 31–2.
43 Ibid., 111.
44 Mollat, *The Poor in the Middle Ages*, 141; Brodman, *Charity and Welfare*, 18–19.
45 Brodman, *Charity and Welfare*, 26–7.
46 Stone, *Morality and Masculinity*, 239–40.
47 Adam J. Davis, "The Social and Religious Meanings of Charity in Medieval Europe," *History Compass* 12, no. 12 (2014): 935–50, at 937.
48 Mollat, *The Poor in the Middle Ages*, 99 and 142–3; Brodman, *Charity and Religion*, 191. In general on guilds in medieval society, see Steven A. Epstein, *Wage Labor and Guilds in Medieval Europe* (Chapel Hill: University of North Carolina Press, 1991).
49 Epstein, *Wage Labor and Guilds*, 167–8.
50 On charity in Florence, see John Henderson, *Piety and Charity in Late Medieval Florence* (Chicago, IL: University of Chicago Press, 1994); Brodman, *Charity and Religion*, 199–201; James R. Banker, *The Culture of San Sepolchro during the Youth of Piero della Francesca* (Ann Arbor: University of Michigan Press, 2003), 38.
51 Augustine Thompson, *Cities of God: The Religion of the Italian Communes, 1125–1325* (University Park: Pennsylvania State University Press, 2005), 86–8, 94–5.
52 Thompson, *Cities of God*, 193–6; André Vauchez, *The Laity in the Middle Ages: Religious Beliefs and Devotional Practices*, trans. Margery J. Schneider (1987; trans. 1993; repr. Notre Dame, IN: University of Notre Dame Press, 2002), 53–60.
53 Brodman, *Charity and Religion*, 184–5; Mollat, *The Poor in the Middle Ages*, 143.
54 Frances Andrews, *The Early Humiliati* (Cambridge: Cambridge University Press, 2007).
55 Walter Simons, *Cities of Ladies: Beguine Communities in the Medieval Low Countries, 1200–1265* (Philadelphia: University of Pennsylvania Press, 2001), esp. 54–5. On the largest beguinages from the mid-thirteenth century through the first half of the sixteenth century: "Surrounded by walls and sometimes even by moats, these courts often constituted a city within the city—a 'city of beguines' (*civitas beghinarum*)."
56 Brodman, *Charity and Religion*, 185–6; Simons, *Cities of Ladies*, 36, 77–8.
57 Simons, *Cities of Ladies*, 80–1, 97.
58 On beguines in Paris, see Tanya Stabler Miller, *The Beguines of Medieval Paris: Gender, Patronage, and Spiritual Authority* (Philadelphia: University of Pennsylvania Press, 2014).
59 Brodman, *Charity and Welfare*, 136–8.
60 Brown, *Civic Ceremony and Religion*, 220–1.
61 Brodman, *Charity and Welfare*, 55, 68–9.
62 Ibid., 103, 111.
63 Ibid., 117.

64 Philip Gavitt, *Gender, Honor, and Charity in Late Renaissance Florence* (Cambridge: Cambridge University Press, 2011), 9.
65 Brodman, *Charity and Welfare*, 123.

Chapter Eight

1 Robert C. Palmer, *English Law in the Age of the Black Death 1348–1381: A Transformation of Governance and Law* (Chapel Hill: University of North Carolina Press, 1993), 1–6; Bertha Haven Putnam, *The Enforcement of the Statutes of Labourers During the First Decade after the Black Death 1349–1359* (New York: Columbia University Press, 1908; Lawrence R. Poos, "The Social Context of Statute of Labourers Enforcement," *Law and History Review* 1 (1983): 27–52; Nora Kenyon (Ritchie), "Labour Conditions in Essex in the Reign of Richard II," *Economic History Review*, 2nd ser., 4 (1934): 429–451; Elaine Clark, "Medieval Labor Law and the English Local Courts," *American Journal of Legal History* 27 (1983): 330–53; Judith Bennett, "Compulsory Service in Late Medieval England," *Past and Present* 209 (2010): 7–51.

2 Robert Braid, "'*Et non ultra*': Politiques royales du travail en Europe occidentale au XIVe siècle," *La Bibliothèque de l'École des chartes* 161 (2003): 437–91; Samuel K. Cohn, "After the Black Death: Labour Legislation and Attitudes Towards Labour in Late-Medieval Western Europe," *Economic History Review*, 2nd ser., 60 (2007): 457–85.

3 Gen. 3:17, 19; Job 5:7; Ps. 127:2. Jacques Le Goff, "Pour une étude du travail dans les idéologies et les mentalités du Moyen Âge," in *Lavorare nel medioevo. Rappresentazioni ed esempi dall'Italie dei secc. X–XVI* (Todi: L'Accademia Tudertina, 1983), 9–33; and "Travail, techniques et artisans dans les systèmes de valeurs du haut Moyen Âge (Vème–Xème siècle)," in *Un autre Moyen Âge* (Paris: Gallimard, 1999), 105–26.

4 Ambrose of Milan, *De officiis ministrorum*, III.6, *Patrologiae Latinae* 16, ed. J. P. Migne, cols. 156–8.

5 Siegfried Wenzel, *The Sin of Sloth:* Acedia *in Medieval Thought and Literature* (Chapel Hill: University of North Carolina Press, 1960), 29, 175, 179.

6 *The Irish Penitentials*, ed. Ludwig Bieler, *Scriptores Latini Hiberniae* 5 (Dublin: Dublin Institute for Advanced Studies, 1963), 121.

7 Francis of Assisi, *Opuscula Sancti Patris Francisci Assisiensis, Bibliotheca Franciscana ascetica mediiaevi*, XII, Quaracchi (Rome: Editiones Collegii S. Bonaventurae ad Claras Aquas, 1978), 311.

8 Lev. 19:3, 19:30.

9 *Ancient Laws and Institutes of England*, ed. Benjamin Thorpe (London: Commissioners of the Public Records of the Kingdom, 1840), chaps. 43, 20–44. There are over a dozen other royal statutes in England regulating the work days prior to the thirteenth century.

10 *Cortes de los antiguos reinos de León y Castilla*, 5 vols. (Madrid: Real Academia de la Historia, 1861–1903), I, 23, art. 6.

11 *Cortes*, I, 24, art. 11.

12 *Decretum magistri Gratiani*, ed. Aemilius Friedberg, *Corpus iuris canonici*, I (Leipzig: B. Tauchnitz, 1879), "Tempora ferandi," III, 3, c. I.

13 Lev. 19:13, Deut. 24:14–15, Jer. 22:13.

14 Mal. 3:5.

15 Ws. 10:17. The Latin term *merce* can refer to a wage or some other kind of reward, but the reference to work (*laboure*) makes the association with a labor contract relatively clear.

16 Mt. 10:10; Lk. 10:7.

17 1 Cor. 3:8. See also Steven A. Epstein, "The Theory and Practice of the Just Wage," *Journal of Medieval History* 17, no. 1 (1991): 53–69.
18 Mt. 20.1–16.
19 John W. Baldwin, *Medieval Theories of the Just Price: Romanists, Canonists and Theologians in the Twelfth and Thirteenth Centuries*, Transactions of the American Philosophical Society, new series, vol. 49, part 4 (Philadelphia, PA: American Philosophical Society, 1959), 18, 21, 29–31, 54–7, 67–8; Odd Langholm, "The Medieval Schoolmen (1200–1400)," in *Ancient and Medieval Economic Ideas and Concepts of Social Justice*, eds. S. Todd Lowry and Barry Gordon (New York: Brill, 1998), 439–501, 464–5.
20 *Institutes*, in *Corpus iuris civilis*, I, ed. Paul Krueger (Berlin: Weidmann, 1886), Lib. III, Tit. 25 ("*De location et conduction*"), *Digeste*, in *Corps de droit civil romain*, I–VI, eds. Henri Hulot, Jean-François Berthelot et al., 17 vols. (Metz–Paris: Chez Rondonneau, 1803–1810), Livre XIX, Tit. II, para. 38, ("*De operis non praetitis*") and para. 51, art. 1 ("*Locavi opus faciendum*"), *Codex*, in *Corpus iuriscivilis*, II, ed. Paul Krueger (Berlin: Weidmann, 1877), Lib. IV, Tit. LXV ("*De locato et conducto*").
21 Epstein, "The Theory and Practice of the Just Wage," 53–69.
22 *Capitularia regum francorum*, in *Monumenta Germaniae Historica Leges, Capit.* 1, ed. Alfred Boretius (Hanover: Hahnsche Buchhandlung, 1883), 73–8, chaps. 4 and 5.
23 *Cortes*, I, 1–11, in particular 8, art. 29.
24 *Cortes*, I, 109–10.
25 *Cortes*, I, 54–63, 64–85.
26 Maestro Jacobo De La Leys, "De criadoset de los servientes, (c. 1250–1255)," in *Memorial Histórico Español. Colección de documentos, opúsculos y antigüedades*, II (Madrid, 1851), Tit. VII, 198–9.
27 *Ordonnances des roys de France de la troisième race*, ed. Eusèbe de Laurière, 21 vols. (Paris: Imprimerie royale, 1723–1849), I, 427–8, 431.
28 *Sources d'histoire médiévale: IXème–milieu du XIVème siècle*, eds. Ghislain Brunel and Elisabeth Lalou (Paris: Larousse, 1992), 489–91.
29 *Ordonnances des roys de France*, II, 43–5, 49–50.
30 Archives nationales de France, JJ, 66, fol. 364^v, no. 888, *Ordonnances des roys de France*, XII, 521–2.
31 *Ordonnances des roys de France*, II, 270–8.
32 James Davis, "Baking for the Common Good: A Reassessment of the Assize of Bread in Medieval England," *Economic History Review*, 2nd ser., 57 (2004): 465–502; Judith Bennett, *Ale, Beer, and Brewsters in England: Women's Work in a Changing World, 1300–1600* (Oxford: Oxford University Press, 1996), 99.
33 *Calendar of the Fine Rolls preserved in the Public Record Office*, eds. H. C. Maxwell Lyte, et. al., 20 vols. (London, 1911–49), t. III, 128 (May 10, 1322); *Rotuli Parliamentorum ut et petitiones et placita in parliamento*, ed. John Strachey, 6 vols. (London, 1767–77), I, 295.
34 *Court Rolls of Ramsey, Bury and Hepmangrove, 1268–1600*, ed. and trans. Edwin B. DeWindt (Toronto: Pontifical Institute of Mediaeval Studies, 1990), 1287:57, 1295:92, 93, 96, 114, 1297:[2]:4, 1306, 32–41; *Court Rolls of the Abbey of Ramsey and of the Honor of Clare*, ed. Warren Ortman Ault (New Haven, CT: Yale University Press, 1928) and W. O. Ault, "Open-field Husbandry and the Village Community: A Study of Agrarian By-laws in Medieval England," *Transactions of the American Philosophical Society*, vol. 55, pt. 7 (Philadelphia, PA: American Philosophical Society, 1965): 15, no. 34; *The Court Baron: Being Precedents for Use in Seignorial and other Local Courts*, ed. Frederic W. Maitland, Selden Society, IV (London: B. Quaritch, 1891), 129, 143, 146.

35 Ault "Open-field Husbandry," no. 22, 36, 48; Lev. 19:9–10.
36 *The Court Rolls of the Abbey of Ramsey*, 216; *Court Rolls of Ramsey*, 1308:18; *The Court Baron*, 132.
37 Anthony Musson, "New Labour Laws, New Remedies? Legal Reaction to the Black Death Crisis," in *Fourteenth-Century England I*, ed. Nigel Saul (Woodbridge: Boydell Press, 2000), 75–7, 86–8; and "Reconstructing English Labour Laws: A Medieval Perspective," in *The Middle Ages at Work: Practicing Labour in Late Medieval England*, eds. Kellie Robertson and Michael Uebel (New York: Palgrave Macmillan, 2004), 113–14.
38 *Munimenta Gildhallae Londoniensis: Liber Albus, Liber Custumarum et Liber Horn*, ed. Henry T. Riley, 3 vols., Rolls Series (1859–1862), II, 86–8; Thomas Hudson Turner, *Some Account of Domestic Architecture in England from the Conquest to the End of the Thirteenth Century*, 4 vols. (Oxford: J. H. Parker, 1852), I, 281–3. See also William Cunningham, *The Growth of English Industry and Commerce During the Early and Middle Ages* (Cambridge: Cambridge University Press, 1890), 501–2; Mary Bateson, "A London Municipal Collection of the Reign of John," *English History Review* 17 (1902): 480–511, 707–30, at 711.
39 *Munimenta, Liber Custumarum*, II, 99–100, 541–3.
40 *Munimenta, Liber Albus*, I, 334.
41 *Calendar of Early Mayor's Court Rolls, 1298–1307*, ed. Arthur H. Thomas (Cambridge: Cambridge University Press, 1924), 53–5, 102–3, 157.
42 George Unwin, *The Gilds and Companies of London* (London: Methuen, 1908, repr. 1963); Gary Richardson, "Guilds, Laws, and Markets for Manufactured Merchandise in Late-Medieval England," *Explorations in Economic History* 41 (2004): 1–25.
43 Robert Braid, "Behind the Ordinance: Economic Regulation and Market Control in London Before the Black Death," *The Journal of Legal History* 34, no. 1 (2013): 3–30.
44 Caroline M. Barron, *London in the Later Middle Ages. Government and People 1200–1500* (Oxford: Oxford University Press, 2004), 2, 206–7.
45 *Statuts d'Arles*, in Charles Giraud, *Essai sur l'histoire du droit français au Moyen Âge*, 2 vols. (Paris: Videcoq, 1846), II, 185–245, art. 154; *Statuts de Tarascon*, in Édouard Bondurand, *Mémoires de l'Académie de Nîmes*, 7ème série, 14 (1891), 27–160, art. 91.
46 *Statuts d'Avignon*, in *Coutumes et règlements de la République d'Avignon au XIIIe siècle*, ed. René De Maulde-la-Clavière (Paris: L. Larose, 1879), art. 145.
47 *Statuts de Marseille*, in Louis Mery and F. Guindon, *Histoire analytique et chronologique des actes et des délibérations du corps et du conseil de la municipalité de Marseille*, 7 vols. (Marseille: Feissat et Demonchy, 1841–73), IV, chaps. 15–18, V, chaps. 2–3.
48 *Statuts de Marseille*, V, chap. 7; Archives Municipales de Marseille, BB 11, 212–13 (January 1310).
49 *Statuts d'Avignon*, art. 35; *Statuts de Salon*, in Louis Gimon, *Chroniques de la ville de Salon depuis son origine jusqu'en 1792* (Aix: Remondet-Aubin, 1882), art. 83; *Statuts de Tarascon*, art. 20.
50 *Statuts d'Arles*, art. 146, *Statuts d'Avignon*, art. 125, *Statuts de Marseille*, V, 8; *Statuts de Tarascon*, art. 148. A measure also adopted by Charles II, Count of Provence, in 1290. (Bibliothèque nationale de France, MS lat. 4767, fol. 35).
51 Archives communales d'Aix, BB 28, fol. 17.
52 *Statuts d'Avignon*, art. 35, 145.
53 *Statuts de Marseille*, II, chap. 34.
54 *Statuts de Provence*, Bibliothèque nationale de France, MS lat. 4767, fol. 7–14; *Statuts d'Arles*, art. 65, 66, 76, 77, 121, 138; *Statuts de Marseille*, I, art. 20, 29 68; *Archives communales de Marseille*, BB 14, fol. 6; *Statuts d'Avignon*, art. 23, 24, 123; *Statuts de Salon*, art. 85.

55 Catherine Lis and Hugo Soly, "Labour Laws in Western Europe, 13th–16th centuries," in *Working on Labour: Essays in Honor of Jan Lucassen*, eds. Mercal van der Linden and Leo Lucassen (Leiden: Brill, 2012), 304.
56 Marc Boone, "Social Conflicts in the Cloth Industry at Ypres (late 13th–early 14th century): The Cockerulle Reconsidered," in *Ypres and the Medieval Cloth Industry in Flanders: Archeological and Historical Contributions*, eds. Marc Dewilde, Anton Ervynck, and Alexis Wielemans (Zelik: Instituut voor het Archeologisch Patrimonium, 1998), 147–55, cited in Lis and Soly, "Labour Laws."
57 Albert the Great, *Commentarii in IV Sententiarum Petri Lombardi*, in *Opera Omnia* (Borgnet), t. 29, IV, xvi, 46, p. 638; Thomas Aquinas, *Summa Theologica*, in *Opera Omnia* (Léonine), t. 4–12 (Rome, 1888–1906), II–II, 77, 2–3; Henry of Ghent, *Quodlibet* I, 40 in *Opera Omnia*, t. 5, p. 230.
58 Thomas Aquinas, *Summa Contra Gentiles*, in *Opera Omnia* (Léonine), t. 13–15 (Rome, 1918–1930), III, 134, 2, Robert Mannyng, *HandlyngSynne*, I, 166–7.
59 Palmer, *Transformation of English Law*, 1–6.
60 Samuel K. Cohn, *The Black Death Transformed: Disease and Culture in Early Renaissance Europe* (London: Arnold and Oxford University Press, 2002); Ole J. Benedictow, *The Black Death, 1346–1353, The Complete History* (Woodbridge: Boydell Press, 2004). Although these two scholars strongly disagree about the precise nature of the disease, they agree on the devastating effects it had on the population.
61 Robert Braid, "Economic Behavior, Markets and Crises: the English Economy in the Wake of Plague and Famine in the 14th century," in *Economic and Biological Interactions in Pre-Industrial Europe from the 13th to the 18th Century*, ed. Simonetta Cavaciocchi (Florence: Firenze University Press, 2010), 339–40.
62 Braid, "Behind the Ordinance," 23–5.
63 *Calendar of the Patent Rolls* (London, 1891–1982), (1348–50), 458, 526; (1350–4), 26–8; Putnam, *Enforcement*, Appendix, 27.
64 Archives communales de Brignoles, AA 504.
65 Archives communales de Marseille, BB 20 fols. 36^r, 39^v, 61^r, 63^v, 153^r.
66 Archives communales de Brignoles, AA 504.
67 Archives communales de Sisteron, BB 10, BB 81, Livre Vert, fols. 47.
68 *Ordonnances des roys de France*, II, 350–5, 489–90.
69 *Ordonnances des roys de France*, II, 438, 563–6, III, 32.
70 *Ordonnances des roys de France*, V., 193–4, VIII, 493–4.
71 "Ordenamientos de menestrales y posturas (1351)," *Cortes de los antiguos reinos de León y de Castilla*, Real Academia de la Historia, 5 vols. (Madrid: Est. tip. de los sucesores de Rivadeneyra, 1861–1903), II, 75–123.
72 "Ordenamientos de las Cortes de Toro (1369)," *Cortes de los antiguosreinos de León y de Castilla*, II, 164–84.
73 Amada Lopez de Menese, "Documentos acerca de la Peste Negra en los dominios de la Corona de Aragon," in *Estudios de Edad Media de la Corona de Aragon*, t. VI (Saragosa, 1956), 357–63, no. 78 and 79.
74 Gunnar Tilander, "Fueros aragoneses desconocidos, promulgados a consecuencia de la gran peste de 1348," *Revista de filologia española* 22 (1935): 1–33 and 113–52.
75 Pascual Savall y Dronda and Santiago Penén y Debesa, *Fueros, observancias y actos de Corte del Reino de Aragón* (Saragosa: Consejo Superior de Investigaciones Científicas, Escuela de Estudios Medievales, 1866), II, 177.
76 Lis and Soly, "Labour Laws," 307, 310.

77 Elisabeth Carpentier, *Une ville devant la peste, Orvieto et la peste noire de 1348* (Paris: École Pratique des Hautes Études, 1962), 242.
78 Cohn, "After the Black Death," 466, 468.
79 Carpentier, *Une ville devant la peste*, 149–52; William M. Bowsky, "The Impact of the Black Death Upon Sienese Government and Society," *Speculum* 39, no. 1 (1964): 1–34, at 26; Cohn, "After the Black Death," 472, 472.
80 Lis and Soly, "Labour Laws."
81 John Gower, *Mirour de l'omne*, ed. G. C. Macaulay, in *The Complete Works of John Gower*, I (Oxford: Clarendon Press, 1889), I, 293; William Langland, *The Vision of William Concerning Piers the Plowman*, ed. Walter W. Skeat, 2 vols. (Oxford: Clarendon Press, 1866), version C, passus IX, I, 223, lines 327–35.
82 Odd Langholm, *The Legacy of Scholasticism in Economic Thought: Antecedents of Choice and Power* (Cambridge: Cambridge University Press, 1998), 132–4.
83 George O' Brien, *An Essay on Medieval Economic Teaching* (New York: B. Franklin, 1920), 106–7; Raymond de Roover, *La pensée économique des scolastiques. Doctrines et méthodes* (Paris: Institut d'études médiévales, 1971), 62–3.
84 Edmund B. Fryde, "Peasant Rebellions and Peasant Discontents," in *The Agrarian History of England and Wales*, ed. Joan Thirsk, vol. 3: 1348–1500, ed. Edward Miller (Cambridge: Cambridge University Press, 1991), 760, 780.
85 Cited in Nigel Saul, *Richard II* (New Haven, CT: Yale University Press, 1997), 74.

Chapter Nine

1 Gen. 3:16–19.
2 R. H. Hilton, *English and French Towns in Feudal Society: A Comparative Study* (Cambridge: University of Cambridge Press, 1992), 109.
3 Gen. 2:2–3.
4 Dorothy Whitelock, ed., *English Historical Documents, 500–1097*, 2nd ed. (London: Eyre and Spottiswood, 1979), no. 31.
5 *Lex Frisionum*, ed. Karl Von Richthofen (Leeuwarden: G. T. N. Suringar, 1866), 18.
6 *Las Siete Partidas*, ed. Robert I. Burns, trans. Samuel Parsons Scott, 5 vols. (Philadelphia: University of Pennsylvania Press, 2000–2001), I, 257 (Pt. I, Tit. XXIII, Law II).
7 Piotr Górecki, *Economy, Society, and Lordship in Medieval Poland, 1100–1250* (New York: Holmes and Meier, 1992), 109.
8 Whitelock, ed., *English Historical Documents, 500–1097*, no. 33.
9 4 Henry, IV, 1402, c. 14, *Statutes of the Realm*, vol. 2 (London, 1816), 137.
10 *Concilia Scotiae*, Bannantyne Club, 116, 2 vols. (Edinburgh: T. Constable, 1866), vol. 2, 38, 40.
11 G. R. Owst, *Literature and Pulpit in Medieval England: A Neglected Chapter in the History of English Letters and of the English People* (Oxford: Oxford University Press, 1961), 394.
12 Richard Morris, ed., *Dan Michel's Ayenbite of Inwyt*, Early English Text Society, Original Series 23 (London: N Trübner and Co., 1866), 207, 213–14.
13 Frederick James Furnivall, ed., *Political, Religious, and Love Poems. Some by Lydgate, Sir Richard Ros, Henry Baradoun, Wm. Huchen, etc.*, Early English Text Society, Original Series, 15 (New York: K. Paul, Trench, Trübner and Co., 1903), 38, lines 540–1.
14 H. N. MacCracken, "Lydgatiana," *Archiv für das Studium der neueren Sprachen und Literaturen* 131 (1913): 54, lines 36–8.

15 M. A. Manzalaoui, ed., Secretum Secretorum: *Nine English Versions*, vol. 1, Early English Text Society, Original Series 276 (Oxford: Oxford University Press, 1977), 223.
16 "Therefore al þat is ordeyned to reste by kynde is acountid more nobil and more worthi whanne it is fynalliche in reste þan it is whanne it is in meuynge, as þe ende is more worthi þan þinges þat beeþ oredeyned for þe ende": M. C. Seymour et al., eds., *On the Properties of Things: John Trevisa's Translation of Bartholomaeus Anglicus* De Proprietatibus Rerum, 2 vols. (Oxford: Oxford University Press, 1975), I, 340.
17 Geoffrey Chaucer, "Parsons Tale," in *The Riverside Chaucer*, ed. Larry Dean Benson, 3rd ed. (Oxford: Oxford University Press, 1987), 773.
18 "How the Wise Man Taught his Son," in Frederick J. Furnivall, ed., *The Babees Book*, Early English Text Society, Original Series 32 (London: N. Trübner and Co.,1868), 49.
19 William Langland, *Piers Plowman: The B Version*, eds. George Kane and E. Talbot Donaldson (London: Athlone Press, 1975), 327, line 341; 329, lines 359–60.
20 Chaucer, "The Cook's Tale," in *The Riverside Chaucer*, ed. Benson, 85, lines 4376, 4385–7.
21 Rosemary Horrox, ed. and trans., *The Black Death* (Manchester: Manchester University Press, 1994), 312–13.
22 *Ordonnances des roys de France de la troisième race*, vol. 2 (Paris: L'Imprimerie Royale, 1729), 564.
23 G. Persson, "Consumption, Labour and Leisure in the Late Middle Ages," in *Manger et boire au Moyen Âge: Actes du colloque de Nice (October, 15–17 1982)* (Nice: Les Belles Lettres, 1984), 211–23.
24 Christopher Dyer, *Standards of Living in the Later Middle Ages: Social Change in England c. 1200–1520* (Cambridge: Cambridge University Press, 1998), 224; Richard C. Allen and Jacob Weisdorf, "Was There an Industrious Revolution Before the Industrial Revolution? An Empirical Exercise for England, c. 1300–1830," *Economic History Review*, 2nd ser. 64, no. 3 (2011): 715–29, at 722.
25 Chaucer, "The Pardoner's Tale," in *The Riverside Chaucer*, ed. Benson, 198, lines 627–8.
26 W. A. Baillie-Grohman and F. Baillie-Grohman, eds., *The Master of Game by Edward, Second Duke of York: The Oldest English Book on Hunting* (London: Chatto and Windus, 1909), 4–8.
27 Scott, trans., *Las Siete Partidas*, II, 296 (Pt. II, Tit. VI, Law XX).
28 Langland, *Piers Plowman: The B Version*, 349–50, lines 29–32.
29 J. A. Giles, ed. and trans., *William of Malmesbury's Chronicle of the Kings of England* (London: Henry G. Bohn, 1847), 300.
30 Alfred Heales, *The Records of Merton Priory* (London: H. Frowde, 1898), 268–9.
31 Seymour et al., eds., *On the Properties of Things*, 340.
32 Scott, trans., *Las Siete Partidas*, II, 297 (Pt. II, Tit. VI, Law XXI).
33 Albrecht Classen, "Chess in Medieval German Literature: a Mirror of Social-Historical and Cultural, Religious, Ethical and Moral Conditions," in *Chess in the Middle Ages and the Early Modern Age: A Fundamental Thought Paradigm of the Premodern World*, ed. Daniel E. Sullivan (Berlin: De Gruyter, 2012), 20.
34 Malcolm Vale, *The Princely Court: Medieval Courts and Culture in North-West Europe, 1270–1380* (Oxford: Oxford University Press, 2001), 172–8.
35 Edith Rickert, trans., *Chaucer's World*, eds. Clair C. Olson and Martin M. Crow (New York: Columbia University Press, 1948), 130.
36 "Tous geux de Dez, de Tables, de Palmes, de Quilles, de Palet, de Soules, de Billes, et tous autres telz geux": *Ordonnances des roys de France de la troisième race*, vol. 5 (Paris: L'Imprimerie Royale, 1736), 172.

37 The English legislation goes back to 1365. The Scottish acts of 1424 and 1457 forbade golf as well as football.
38 Edith Rickert, trans., *The Babees Book: Medieval Manners for the Young* (London: Chatto and Windus, 1908), 35.
39 Vale, *The Princely Court*, 177–8.
40 Nicola McDondald, "Games Medieval Women Play," in *The Legend of Good Women: Context and Reception*, ed. Carolyn P. Collette (Cambridge: D. S. Brewer, 2006), 176–98.
41 Scott, trans., *Las Siete Partidas*, IV, 973 (Pt. IV, Tit. XIX, Law III).
42 Theodore Evergates, "Aristocratic Women in the County of Champaign," in *Aristocratic Women in Medieval France*, ed., Theodore Evergates. (Philadelphia: University of Pennsylvania Press, 2010), 87.
43 David Herlihy, *Opera Muliebria: Women and Work in Medieval Europe* (New York: McGraw-Hill, 1990), 80–1, 85.
44 Lisa M. Bitel, *Women in Early Medieval Europe, 400–1100* (Cambridge: Cambridge University Press, 2002), 204, 212.
45 See London, British Library, Cotton MS Julius A. vi dating from the eleventh century.
46 Bitel, *Women in Early Medieval Europe, 400–1100*, 208.
47 Constance Hoffman Berman, "Women's Work in Family, Village, and Town after 1000 CE: Contributions to Economic Growth?," *Journal of Women's History* 19, no. 3 (2007): 10–32.
48 Martha Carlin and David Crouch, trans. and eds., *Lost Letters of Medieval Life: English Society, 1200–1250* (Philadelphia: University of Pennsylvania Press, 2013), 275.
49 Seymour et al., eds., *On the Properties of Things*, 341.

FURTHER READINGS

Alexander, Jonathan J. G. "*Labeur* and *Paresse*: Ideological Representations of Medieval Peasant Labor." *Art Bulletin* 72, no. 3 (1990): 436–52.
Astill, Grenville, and John Langdon, eds. *Medieval Farming and Technology: The Impact of Agricultural Change in Northwest Europe*. Leiden: Brill, 1997.
Bailey, Mark. *The Decline of Serfdom in Late Medieval England: From Bondage to Freedom*. Woodbridge: Boydell & Brewer, 2014.
Bennett, Judith. *Ale, Beer and Brewsters in England: Women's Work in a Changing World, 1300–1600*. Oxford: Oxford University Press, 1996.
Bennett, Judith, et al., eds. *Sisters and Workers in the Middle Ages*. Chicago, IL: University of Chicago Press, 1989.
Braid, Robert. "'*Et non ultra*': Politiques royales du travail en Europe occidentale au XIVe siècle." *La Bibliothèque de l'École des chartes* 161 (2003): 437–91.
Brenner, Elma. "The Care of the Sick and Needy in Twelfth- and Thirteenth-Century Rouen." In *Society and Culture in Medieval Rouen, 911–1300*, edited by Leonie V. Hicks and Elma Brenner. Turnhout: Brepols, 2013.
Brodman, James William. *Charity and Welfare: Hospitals and the Poor in Medieval Catalonia*. Philadelphia: University of Pennsylvania Press, 1998.
Brodman, James William. *Charity and Religion in Medieval Europe*. Washington, DC: The Catholic University of America Press, 2009.
Brown, Andrew. *Civic Ceremony and Religion in Medieval Bruges c. 1300–1520*. Cambridge: Cambridge University Press, 2011.
Brundage, James A. "Legal Aid for the Poor and the Professionalization of the Law in the Middle Ages." *Journal of Legal History* 169 (1988): 169–79.
Burton, Janet, and Julie Kerr. *The Cistercians in the Middle Ages*. Woodbridge: Boydell Press, 2011.
Camille, Michael. *Mirror in Parchment: The Luttrell Psalter and the Making of Medieval England*. London: Reaktion Press, 1998.
Cipolla, Carlo. *Before the Industrial Revolution: European Society and Economy, 1000–1700*. 3rd ed. New York: W. W. Norton and Company, 1994.
Clark, James G. *The Benedictines in the Middle Ages*. Woodbridge: Boydell Press, 2011.
Cohn, Samuel K. "After the Black Death: Labour Legislation and Attitudes Towards Labour in Late-Medieval Western Europe," *Economic History Review*, 2nd ser., 60 (2007): 457–85.
Constable, Giles. *Three Studies in Medieval Religious and Social Thought: The Interpretation of Mary and Martha, the Ideal of the Imitation of Christ, the Orders of Society*. Cambridge: Cambridge University Press, 1998.
Davis, Adam J. "The Social and Religious Meanings of Charity in Medieval Europe." *History Compass* 12, no. 12 (2014): 935–50.
Dijkman, Jessica. *Shaping Medieval Markets: The Organisation of Commodity Markets in Holland, c.1200–c.1450*. Leiden: Brill, 2011.

Dohrn-van Rossum, Gerhard. *History of the Hour: Clocks and Temporal Orders*, translated by Thomas Dunlap. Chicago, IL: University of Chicago Press, 1996, c. 1992.

Duby, Georges. *The Three Orders: Feudal Society Imagined*, translated by Arthur Goldhammer. Chicago, IL: University of Chicago Press, 1980.

Dumolyn, Jan. "Economic Development, Social Space and Political Power in Bruges, c. 1127–1302." In *Contact and Exchange in Later Medieval Europe: Essays in Honour of Malcolm Vale*, edited by Hannah Skoda, Patrick Lantschner, and R. L. J. Shaw, 33–57. Woodbridge: Boydell Press, 2012.

Dyer, Christopher. *Standards of Living in the Later Middle Ages: Social Change in England c. 1200–1520*. Cambridge: Cambridge University Press, 1998.

Dyer, Christopher. *Making a Living in the Middle Ages: The People of Britain 850–1520*. New Haven, CT: Yale University Press, 2002.

Epstein, Steven A. *Wage Labor and Guilds in Medieval Europe*. Chapel Hill: University of North Carolina Press, 1991.

Epstein, Steven A. *An Economic and Social History of Later Medieval Europe, 1000–1500*. Cambridge: Cambridge University Press, 2009.

Epstein, Stephen R. "Regional Fairs, Institutional Innovation, and Economic Growth in Late Medieval Europe." *The Economic History Review* 47 (1994): 459–82.

Epstein, Stephen R. "Craft Guilds, Apprenticeship, and Technological Change in Pre-Industrial Europe," *The Journal of Economic History* 58, no. 3 (1998): 684–713.

Farmer, Sharon. *Surviving Poverty in Medieval Paris: Gender, Ideology, and the Daily Lives of the Poor*. Ithaca, NY: Cornell University Press, 2002.

Gameson, Richard. "The Image of the Illuminator." In *Colour: The Art and Science of Illuminated Manuscripts*, edited by Stella Panayotova with Deirdre Jackson and Paola Ricciardi, 74–82. Turnhout: Brepols, 2016.

Gavitt, Philip. *Gender, Honor, and Charity in Late Renaissance Florence*. Cambridge: Cambridge University Press, 2011.

Geremek, Bronislaw. *Poverty: A History*, translated by Agnieszka Kolokowska. Oxford: Blackwell Publishers, 1994.

Goldberg, Peter Jeremy Piers. *Women, Work, and Life Cycle in a Medieval Economy: Women in York and Yorkshire, c.1300–1520*. Oxford: Clarendon Press, 1992.

Hanawalt, Barbara A., ed. *Women and Work in Preindustrial Europe*. Bloomington: University of Indiana Press, 1986.

Hanawalt, Barbara A. *The Ties that Bound: Peasant Families in Medieval England*. Oxford: Oxford University Press, 1989.

Hanawalt, Barbara A. *The Wealth of Wives: Women, Wealth, and Law in Late Medieval London*. Oxford: Oxford University Press, 2007.

Hatcher, John, and Mark Bailey. *Modelling the Middle Ages: The History and Theory of England's Economic Development*. Oxford: Oxford University Press, 2001.

Henderson, John. *Piety and Charity in Late Medieval Florence*. Chicago, IL: University of Chicago Press, 1994.

Herlihy, David. *Opera Muliebria: Women and Work in Medieval Europe*. New York: McGraw-Hill, 1990.

Jorgensen, Dolly. "Illuminating Ephemeral Medieval Agricultural History through Manuscript Art." *Agricultural History* 89, no. 2 (2015): 186–99.

Laiou, Angeliki E., and Charalampos Bouras, eds. *The Economic History of Byzantium*, 3 vols. Washington, DC: Dumbarton Oak Studies, 2002.

Langdon, John. *Horses, Oxen and Technological Innovation: The Use of Draught Animals in English Farming from 1066 to 1500*. Cambridge: Cambridge University Press, 1986.

Le Goff, Jacques. *Time, Work, and Culture in the Middle Ages*, translated by Arthur Goldhammer. Chicago, IL: University of Chicago Press, 1980.

Lis, Catharina, and Hugo Soly. "Labour Laws in Western Europe, 13th–16th centuries." In *Working on Labour: Essays in Honor of Jan Lucassen*, edited by Mercal Van Der Linden and Leo Lucassen, 299–321. Leiden: Brill, 2012.

Little, Lester K. *Religious Poverty and the Profit Economy in Medieval Europe*. Ithaca, NY: Cornell University Press, 1983 [1978].

Long, Pamela O. "Invention, Secrecy, and Theft: Meaning and Context in the Study of Late Medieval Technical Transmission," *History and Technology* 16 (2000): 223–41.

Lucas, Adam. *Wind, Water, Work: Ancient and Medieval Milling Technology*. Leiden: Brill, 2006.

McCray, W. Patrick. "Creating Networks of Skill: Technology Transfer and the Glass Industry of Venice." *Journal of European Economic History* 28 (1999): 301–33.

McIntosh, Marjorie Keniston. *Poor Relief in England, 1350–1600*. Cambridge: Cambridge University Press, 2012.

Mollat, Michel. *The Poor in the Middle Ages: An Essay in Social History*, translated by Arthur Goldhammer. New Haven, CT: Yale University Press, 1986.

Moreton, Melissa. "Pious Voices: Nun-scribes and the Language of Colophons in Late Medieval and Renaissance Italy." *Essays in Medieval Studies* 29 (2014): 43–73.

Murray, James M. *Bruges: Cradle of Capitalism, 1280–1390*. Cambridge: Cambridge University Press, 2005.

Nightingale, Pamela. *A Medieval Mercantile Community: The Grocers' Company and the Politics and Trade of London, 1000–1485*. New Haven, CT: Yale University Press, 1995.

Smith, Elizabeth Bradford, and Michael Wolfe, eds. *Technology and Resource Use in Medieval Europe*. Aldershot: Ashgate, 1997.

Thompson, Augustine. *Cities of God: The Religion of the Italian Communes, 1125–1325*. University Park: Pennsylvania State University Press, 2005.

Tierney, Brian. 'The Decretists and the "Deserving Poor," *Comparative Studies in Society and History* 1, no. 4 (1959): 360–73.

Tierney, Brian. *Medieval Poor Law: A Sketch of Canonical Theory and Its Application in England*. Berkeley: University of California Press, 1959.

Van Bavel, Bas. *Manors and Markets: Economy and Society in the Low Countries, 500–1600*. Oxford: Oxford University Press, 2010.

Van Engen, John. *Sisters and Brothers of the Common Life: The* Devotio Moderna *and the World of the Later Middle Ages*. Philadelphia: University of Pennsylvania Press, 2008.

Vauchez, André. *The Laity in the Middle Ages: Religious Beliefs and Devotional Practices*, translated by Margery J. Schneider. Notre Dame, IN: University of Notre Dame Press, 2002.

Verhulst, Adriaan. *The Carolingian Economy*. Cambridge: Cambridge University Press, 2002.

Wenzel, Siegfried. *The Sin of Sloth: Acedia in Medieval Thought and Literature*. Chapel Hill: University of North Carolina Press, 1967 [1960].

White, Lynn. *Medieval Technology and Social Change*. Oxford: Clarendon Press, 1962.

Wiesner, Merry E. "Spinsters and Seamstresses: Women in Cloth and Clothing Production." In *Rewriting the Renaissance: The Discourses of Sexual Difference in Early Modern Europe*, edited by Margaret W. Ferguson, Maureen Quilligan, and Nancy J. Vickers, 191–205. Chicago, IL: University of Chicago Press, 1986.

INDEX

Adam and Eve 10, 20, 50–6, 165–7
Ælfric of Eynsham (c. 955–c. 1010) 24, 46, 118, 166
agriculture
 archaeological remains 5, 102, 125
 environmental conditions 14, 68, 89
 field or crop rotation 69, 87, 104, 125–6
 mobility of workers 125–7
 occupation 1–2, 31, 66–8
 seasonality 15–17, 24, 89, 125
 tools 33, 39–40, 53, 89, 100, 102–6, 166–7
almsgiving 79, 132, 135–40, 142–6, 159
apprentices 7–8, 21–2, 26, 81, 111, 143. *See also* guilds; masters
Aragon 28, 142, 147–8, 160, 171
aristocracy
 leisure 165, 170–2, 179
 relationship with workers 9, 15, 48–9, 132
artisans 4, 9–10, 26, 67, 107, 166

baking 6, 8–9, 80, 155
Barcelona 71, 73, 141–2, 147–8
beguines 94, 132, 145–6
Benedictines 34, 131, 133, 137–9, 146. *See also* monks; nuns
Bening, Simon 34, 43, 63
Bible
 charity 133, 138
 conceptions of work 50–6, 146, 152–3, 165–6, 177
 manuscripts 59, 166
bishops. *See* clerics
Black Death 11–12
 effects on labor market 6, 13, 23, 27–8, 68, 121, 171
 effects on labor ordinances 4, 151, 158–62
 effects on leisure 165, 170–1
 effects on mobility 115, 119, 124, 160–2
 effects on political culture 163
Boccaccio, Giovanni 11, 53, 55, 171

books of hours 32, 34, 37–40, 43, 56
brewing 5–6, 19, 82, 87, 90, 155
Bruges 71, 73–4, 76, 78–80, 145
 manuscripts 37, 40–1
butchers
 in cities 8, 26
 on estates 16
 images 33–4, 38
 slaughterhouses 3
 women 6
by-occupations 4, 9, 14, 17
Byzantine Empire 22, 25, 69, 71, 106–8

calendars 15, 31–4, 41, 177–8
Canterbury Tales (Geoffrey Chaucer) 116, 170, 172
Carolingian Empire
 agriculture 15, 102
 charity 140, 143
 currency 154
 estates 66–7, 69, 87–8
 hunting 172
 mills 106
 monasticism 35–6
 textile production 14, 90
 warfare 112
carts 68, 77, 104, 128. *See also* wagons
Castile
 charitable institutions 142, 148
 labor ordinances 4, 28, 152, 154–5, 160–1, 168, 171, 176
 leisure 172–3
 livestock 14
Catalonia 24, 28, 134, 141–2, 160, 171
 servile labor 88
charity 10, 79, 133–8
 guilds 9, 93, 143
 rural 125
 urban 146–7
Charlemagne 57, 108, 153
chess 173–5. *See also* games; pastimes
children. *See also* education
 childrearing 3, 18, 36, 40, 57, 176–7
 nursing 148, 176

orphans and foundlings 142–3, 147–8
play 174–6, 179
poverty 135, 137
at work 6–8, 22, 28, 36, 69, 76, 78, 127
Cistercians 2, 36, 138–9. *See also* lepers;
    monks; nuns
cities 8, 14, 73–7, 102, 120–1, 132–3
clerics 34–5, 132, 135, 139–42, 171–3
clocks 17, 96, 102, 108, 113. *See also* time
    reckoning
Cluniacs 2, 36, 138–9. *See also* monks
collective action 9, 90, 92, 96, 159
Cologne 74, 97, 140, 143
common good 10, 46, 86, 133, 139–45, 162
confraternities 9, 132, 142–5
construction 23, 76, 90, 109–10, 129–30,
    156–7. *See also* stonework;
    timberwork
Crusades 71–2, 107, 115

dairying 5, 18, 21, 177
de Pizan, Christine 37–41, 58, 60
Decretum (Gratian) 136, 153, 167
Denmark 82, 102, 104
division of labor
    by gender 5–9, 11, 20–2, 56–9, 87, 90, 97,
        100–1, 106, 165–6, 176–8
    three orders 4, 42–5, 118–19, 129, 132, 166
Domesday Book 22, 107, 120

education 43, 46, 58, 109, 139, 177
England
    agriculture 8–9, 14, 31, 66, 88, 99
    Black Death 11, 13, 27
    brewing 6, 155
    charity 139, 144
    children 7
    cities 8
    education 46
    horses as work animals 104
    hospitals 140–1
    Jews 122
    labor ordinances 4, 28, 151–2, 155, 157,
        159, 166, 168, 171
    leisure 165–6, 168–76
    manuscripts 48–9, 53, 61
    mills 102, 106–7
    mining 14
    mobility 120, 159
    occupations 26
    servile labor 25, 119, 168
    shepherding 127
    technological change 100, 112–13

trade 69, 71, 73–5
vagrancy 124
wage labor 23, 29
warfare 70
entertainers 1, 10, 91
estates
    church estates 24
    demesnes 13, 22, 87
    manors 15, 24–5, 65, 117, 119–20
    monastic estates 24, 67–8, 108
    royal estates 66–7
    workers 23–26, 88

fairs 4, 17, 71–5, 79, 101
family. *See* household
feast days 17, 25, 69, 73, 137–9, 145. *See also*
    holidays
finance
    banking 4, 74–5, 77, 79, 166
    credit 14, 75, 142
    currency 69, 132–3, 154–5, 163
fishing 17–18, 22, 69, 90, 128
Flanders. *See* Low Countries
Florence 76–82
    Black Death 11
    catasto (tax assessment) 22
    confraternities 143–4
    hospitals 141, 143, 147
    labor ordinances 160–1, 171
    population 8
food occupations 1, 17, 46, 137, 177
France
    agriculture 68–9
    construction 113, 130
    hospitals 147
    ironworking 101
    labor ordinances 4, 28, 155, 160, 171
    leisure 175
    manuscripts 37, 38, 44–5, 47, 50, 52,
        160
    mills 102, 106
    orphanages 147
    servile labor 25
    technology 100
    wage labor 23, 29
Francia/Frankish Empire 8, 24. *See also*
    Carolingian Empire

games 165, 168, 170, 173, 175. *See also*
    chess; pastimes
German Empire
    confraternities 143–4
    construction 113

finance 4
horses as work animals 104
hospitals 141
labor ordinances 162, 171
manuscripts 54, 156
metal working 14
mills 102
mining 101
trade 69
wage labor 29
women 81
guilds. *See also* apprentices; masters
   dispute settlement 156
   exclusion of Jews 4
   migration 112, 121
   organization 9, 92–8, 168–9
   regulation 10, 86, 96–7, 108, 112, 168
   technology 100
   women 21, 97

Hanse (Hanseatic League) 73, 85
harrow 32, 103–4, 127
harvesting 15, 18–19, 67, 125–6, 178
holidays (holy days) 17, 77, 142, 152–3, 163, 167–8. *See also* feast days
Holy Roman Empire. *See* German Empire
horses 70, 89, 101, 103–4, 128–9
Hospitallers (including Hospitallers or Knights of the Hospital of St. John in Jerusalem) 132, 138–9
hospitals 2, 81, 135, 138–41, 144–5
household 5–8, 17–23, 29, 53, 87–90, 143
Humiliati 132, 145
hunting 14, 66, 165, 172–3, 175. *See also* fishing; pastimes

Iberia. *See also* Aragon; Castile; Catalonia; Valencia
   al-Andalus 106–7
   charity 139, 143
   hospitals 140–1
   migration 120, 122–3
   Portugal 171
   shepherding 13, 127
idleness 2, 155, 160, 170–1. *See also* sloth
immigration 79, 120–1. *See also* migration
Ireland 107, 122, 173
Italy
   banking 4
   confraternities 143–4
   construction 113
   fairs 75
   labor ordinances 160–1, 171
   manuscripts 36, 59
   mills 102, 106–7
   peasants 25
   technology 99
   textile production 15, 71
   urbanization 14
   work conditions 88

Jews 4, 122, 128–9, 138, 157
journeymen 17, 21, 26, 86. *See also* guilds

leatherwork 26, 107, 127–8
leisure 1, 11–12, 165–79
León. *See* Castile
lepers 2, 133, 139–40, 145
livestock
   cattle 27, 89, 177
   goats 14, 67
   oxen 15, 104, 128
   pigs 16, 18, 67
   raising 8, 11, 66, 127
   sheep 13–14, 27, 55, 56, 67, 89, 177
   shepherding 37, 45, 127
London 71–4, 88, 120, 157
Low Countries
   agriculture 25, 88, 104, 125
   Black Death 171
   city growth 8, 14, 76
   hospitals 141
   labor ordinances 158, 162
   land reclamation 69, 104
   textile production 14, 74, 79, 85–6, 92, 94
   trade 73–5
   work cultures 85–6, 92–3, 97–8
Luttrell Psalter (London, British Library, Add. MS 42130) 48, 58, 175, 177

manors. *See* estates
manuals 100, 106, 109, 112
manuscripts 2, 31, 59–63, 71–2
markets 6, 71–3, 77–8, 104
Marseilles 71, 73, 79, 157, 159
medicine 6, 34–5, 138
Mediterranean Sea 115
   cultural region 16, 68–9, 100, 105
   migration 122
   mills 106
   slavery 10
   viticulture 14
mendicant orders 135–6. *See also* monks; nuns

Dominicans 46–7, 133, 169, 175
Franciscans 133, 136, 144, 152
merchants 10, 26, 71, 74–5, 121, 128–9
messengers 2, 74, 129
metalworking 1, 3, 8, 26, 103, 107
migration 14, 115, 117–18, 120, 122–3. *See also* immigration
Milan 8, 132, 140, 147, 171
mills 2, 8, 78, 101–2, 104–7, 178
mining 14, 90, 101–2
monks 2
   charity 137–9
   devotional labor 34–6, 46, 61
   manuscript production 59, 71–2
morality
   guild 23, 97–8
   leisure 168–71, 174
   work ethic 10, 29, 46–8, 159
Muslims 107, 112, 120, 122, 138

Naples 8, 71, 73, 160
Norway 69, 73, 102, 157, 161, 173
nuns 2, 46, 61, 137, 139

oil production 105–7
On the Properties of Things (Bartholomaeus Anglicus) 34–5, 169–70, 173, 179

Paris
   charitable institutions 141, 143, 147
   construction 130
   labor ordinances 17
   manuscripts 50, 52, 55, 59, 60, 72
   occupations 26
   population 8, 132
   trade 71
   women's work 81, 97, 177
pastimes 168–75. *See also* chess; games; hunting
peasants 1, 25, 89–91, 107, 118–19, 132–7. *See also* agriculture; servile labor
Peasants' Revolt of 1381 (England) 9, 48, 162, 166
Piers Plowman (William Langland) 21, 29, 162, 170, 172
plowing
   depictions 32, 66
   men's work 20–1, 56, 87, 168, 177
   occupation 15, 46–8, 127
   technological changes 2, 69, 102, 104
Poland 139, 171
polyptychs 24, 67–8, 108
population 14, 27, 102, 116–18, 120

pottery 5, 18, 26, 111, 120
poultry 5, 18, 21–2, 58, 177
poverty 2, 10, 23–6, 117–18, 131–7
priests. *See* clerics
prostitution 6, 79, 97, 170, 176
Provence 11, 138, 143, 157–61, 163, 171
psalters 48–9, 53, 59–61, 166–7

rents 14, 18, 24–5, 88
rest 1, 165–6, 169–70, 179
Rouen 73, 133, 140, 173
Rule of St Benedict 2, 34, 137
Russia 3–4, 120

Sabbath 1, 17, 65, 152, 157, 168–9
schools. *See* education
secular clergy. *See* clerics
serfs. *See* servile labor
servants 8, 21–3, 48, 129, 148
servile labor 24–5, 66, 87, 119, 136
ships and shipping 69–70, 72, 90, 128
Sicily 71, 79, 120, 177
sin 2, 135, 158, 171
slavery 10, 15, 24, 88, 106, 136
sloth 46–7, 152, 170. *See also* idleness
smiths 14, 18, 90, 101
social welfare 131–3, 142, 148
Spain. *See* Aragon; Castile; Catalonia; Iberia; Valencia
specialization of labor 8, 26, 88
spinning. *See also* textile production; wool, production
   by-occupation 18–21, 127
   wheel 41, 79, 107
   women 6, 52, 55–8, 80, 90, 101, 166–7, 176–8
stonework. *See also* construction
   buildings 109, 113–14
   occupations 1, 76, 90, 111
   technology 100
Sweden 69, 100, 102, 105
Swiss Confederation 81, 143

Tacuinum sanitatis 38, 78, 80, 82
tanning. *See* leatherwork
textile production. *See also* spinning; weaving; wool, production
   archaeological remains 3, 5, 176–7
   in cities 8, 26, 58, 79–128
   mills 107
   occupation 1
   women 5–6, 14, 19–21, 67, 90, 97, 108, 111, 176–8

theft 100, 109, 112
theology 152, 158, 162
timberwork 37–8, 101, 107, 109. *See also* construction
time reckoning 17, 85, 108–9, 157
transmission of knowledge and skills 90, 94, 96, 100, 111–12. *See also* apprentices; education

vagrants 115, 123–4
Valencia 120, 123, 142, 147
Venice 8, 69, 79, 111–12, 121, 166, 171
Vikings 69, 100–1, 112, 115
viticulture 13–14, 89, 178

wage labor 23–6, 89, 157
wages
    documentation 13, 88
    rates 23, 28–9, 126
    regulation of 9, 27, 108, 152–3, 155, 156–61
wagons 70, 103–4. *See also* carts
warfare 70–1, 112–13, 129

wealth 2, 13, 48, 131–3, 135–6, 140
weaving. *See also* textile production; wool, production
    archaeological evidence 26
    by-occupation 18
    looms 85, 100–1, 111
    women 6, 58, 87, 176–7
women. *See also* brewing; spinning; textile production; weaving; wool, production
    agriculture 8
    care for the sick at home 6
    conceptions of their labor 3, 18, 176
    leisure 168, 172
    occupations 5–7, 77, 81–3
    wages 28–9
    writers 38–41
woodworking 1, 3, 14, 18, 48–50, 52
wool
    production 18, 80, 85–6, 101, 107, 128
    trade 71, 73–4, 79
    women's work 21, 178
work hours. *See* clocks; time reckoning